TORCHY!

The Biography and Reminiscences of
Roscoe C. Torrance

•

With Bob Karolevitz

•

Featuring an Introduction by
Bob Hope

© 1988 by Roscoe C. Torrance and Robert F. Karolevitz

Library of Congress Catalogue No. 88-071530
ISBN: 0-940161-06-0

Published in the United States by
Dakota Homestead Publishers
Mission Hill, South Dakota
57046

First Printing 1988

Cover and title page portrait
by Stu Moldrem for the
1973 Charles E. Sullivan Award
Puget Sound Sportswriters and Sportscasters

Table of Contents

Torchy Torrance, the printing executive and concessions operator, was, in effect, the alter ego of the man who was everlastingly involved in athletic pursuits, charitable endeavors and civic promotions. No wonder friends in Seattle called him "Mr. Everything." (Special Collections Division, University of Washington Libraries)

Dedication

To
Ruth and Madge
and to
Shirley, Bill and John

Torchy's cherished friendship with Bob and Dolores Hope dates back to the 1930s. He has always had unbounded admiration for Bob's continuing dedication under any conditions as a morale-builder for American servicemen and women, and that admiration is extended to Dolores's support and sharing of her husband's unselfish work for the benefit of others.

Our Friend Torchy!

An Introduction by Bob Hope

When Dolores finished reading this book, she handed it to me and said, "you're not going to believe this. I always knew that Torchy was very special, but wait until you read how very special he is. He's everything a man was supposed to be and more."

And so, squeezing a few chapters in here and there, between my crazy schedule, I've finally finished reading one of the most interesting and compelling life stories. I'm amazed at the action Torchy packed into one life. It just doesn't seem possible. We've known Torchy for about fifty years, but until I read the book,

1

I never realized the excitement of his endeavors . . . all the places that Torchy visited and made more exciting for everybody.

Torchy is a doer . . . an innovator . . . the kind of fellow you want around when you're putting a project together. This all happens because of his unique personality.

There's an honesty about Torchy that we learned to admire. However, I never noticed it on the first tee when we were negotiating a deal!!! Dolores said she had the same trouble, except of course when they were teamed up together. There was never a golf partner like Torchy!

Whoever worked with Torchy wanted to do it again. He's touched so many people with his activities and generosity, and he wins everyone over with that great personality. Dolores keeps reminding me that Torchy was all the gals' favorite, but mostly hers. Maybe I should have looked into this!?! She said that Torchy had such an appeal and all the girls thought he was "Very Torchy." Good things come in small packages and he certainly packed a wallop. I never noticed . . . I was only after his golf money.

I was the grand marshal of the Seafair parade a few years ago and Torchy rode in the car with me, and I couldn't figure out how so many people recognized Torchy. Then I thought again about the many nice things he's done for that area in bringing them all the great baseball and football and business successes . . . his record in the Marine Corps. You'll learn as you read this book that he's touched so many people in a good way. He is unforgettable and that will be forever with Dolores and me. Our life and fun in Palm Springs just wouldn't be the same without the delight of Torchy's presence.

So Torchy, dear friend, until the next time, we're sending all our thoughts and wishes for many more years of your real and worthwhile dedication to life.

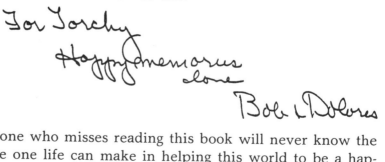

For Torchy
Happy memories
love
Bob & Dolores

P.S. Anyone who misses reading this book will never know the difference one life can make in helping this world to be a happier experience.

2

Before You Read On

Torchy Torrance was already in his eighties when he started to dictate his recollections of years gone by. They all flowed from a phenomenal memory—without notes or diary—as he recalled endless names, dates, places and events. However, he recorded them, not in chronological order, but in segments as they came to mind.

These bits and pieces have been reassembled in this book so that Torchy's inimitable life story can be traced in proper sequence. For identification purposes, the *italics* are his. The collaborator's transitions and embellishments are in roman type.

Prologue

In 1845 the Great Migration to the Oregon Country was at its peak. That year William Sinclair Torrance, a native of Enfield, Massachusetts, was visiting a brother in Cook County, Illinois, where he heard a tempting lecture on the wonderful opportunities available in the far western land.

That had far greater appeal to the 21-year-old son of Jeduthun and Eunice (Gibbs) Torrance than the boot and shoe trade for which he was apparently destined. At the same time, Lot Whitcomb, a Vermonter who had moved west and who then represented Cook County in the Illinois legislature, was contemplating a change of climate – presumably for his wife's health – and he, too, was influenced by the lure of Oregon.

In March of 1847 young Torrance joined an immigrant train of some 147 wagons, captained by Whitcomb, for the long, tedious journey westward from Illinois. It took more than seven months for the party to travel by way of St. Joseph, Missouri, over the Oregon Trail to Fort Hall and eventually to Oregon City. Along the way the large train was harassed but never attacked by Indians, and Will Torrance was among those assigned to ride ahead beyond the Cascade Mountains to secure horses to replace those which were stolen or otherwise worn out by the arduous journey.

Whitcomb had wisely included tools and a set of sawmill irons in his personal gear. He established a claim between Oregon City and Portland at the head of navigation on the Willamette

(Opposite page) Torchy Torrance's grandfather rode westward over the Oregon Trail and eventually became a pioneer of Washington's Palouse country. A saddle was not unfamiliar to his grandson because Torchy himself had had a brief experience as an Idaho cowboy. (Special Collections Division, University of Washington Libraries)

Torchy's grandparents were William Sinclair Torrance and Mary Jane Whitcomb. She was the daughter of Lot Whitcomb, a Milwaukie, Oregon, pioneer and entrepreneur. (Emily Wilson collection)

River, and during the spring and summer of 1848 erected the sawmill which was to become the source of his fortune.

Will Torrance became closely allied with the older man. He took a claim across the river from Whitcomb, worked in the mill and in April of 1849 he married Lot's daughter, Mary Jane. The Whitcomb-Torrance enterprise was an extremely profitable success, largely because of the California gold rush. Their mill – along with others on the Willamette – shipped to San Francisco all the lumber they could produce for use as mining timbers and sluice boxes by the '49ers.

Will joined his father-in-law and Joseph Kellogg, a ship-builder, in the platting of Milwaukie, Oregon, in 1849; the building of a grist mill in conjunction with their lumber operation; and in the most ambitious enterprise of all, the construction of a 160-foot sternwheeler steamboat, the *Lot Whitcomb*, which was launched with great celebration on Christmas day, 1850.

If Will Torrance had any regrets about his close ties to his wife's father, it might have been because he relinquished an earlier donation claim at Portland to join Lot Whitcomb in Milwaukie. The land stretched for a mile along the east side of the Willamette River and extended back from the stream an additional mile. Will and another man stepped it off and blazed the trees. Later he paid fifty cents to record the claim, but when Congress passed a law requiring personal occupancy of the land, he abandoned it to pursue the multiple enterprises with his father-in-law. (He would have been worth millions had he held the claim which eventually became the eastern portion of Portland.)

Meanwhile, Will and Mary Jane had begun to raise a family which, in time, was to include thirteen children, one of whom died at birth. On September 27, 1862, their eighth child – William Grant – was born. The father had switched from Democrat to Republican over the slavery issue and had named his son for Ulysses S. Grant, then coming to prominence as a Union general in the Civil War.

By this time Will Torrance had left the mill business and was involved in farming. Then, whether because of restlessness or other reasons, he sold his claim for $4,000 in 1864 and spent part of two years in pursuit of gold in the mines near Boise, Idaho. In 1872 he moved his family to Whitman County, Washington Territory, where he took up land along the Palouse River at a place later known as Torrance Bridge. His older son, Edgar, had preceded him to the region where wheat farming was then in its early pioneering stage.

The Torrance children grew up in the rolling hills of Whitman County and began to establish families of their own. Eunice Irene, the oldest daughter, married Quinland Diamond (also known

William Grant Torrance and Margaret A. Kirby were married on December 5, 1891. They made their home at Diamond, Washington, where their five children – only three of whom survived to adulthood – were born. Maggie (as Margaret was always known) died on August 25, 1903, at the age of 37. (Special Collections Division, University of Washington Libraries)

Roscoe Conkling Torrance was born on September 2, 1899, at Diamond, Washington, the second son of William Grant and Margaret Kirby Torrance. He was named after Senator Roscoe Conkling of New York, a 19th century politican much admired by William Torrance.

as Dimond), who platted a town named after himself on the railroad between Colfax and Endicott. William Grant, the second son, married Margaret A. Kirby of Dayton on December 5, 1891; and the young couple established their home in Diamond where Will tended a large garden, did occasional carpentry and was employed at the grain elevator.

Maggie (as Margaret was always known) had her first child — Kirby Earl — on January 7, 1893. Her second — Jessie Echo — was born that same year on December 10. Another daughter — Marie Marguerite — joined the family on April 8, 1898, and then — on September 2, 1899 — a second son arrived.

William Grant Torrance — like his father, William Sinclair — was a dedicated Republican and ardent reader of *FRA Magazine* and other politically oriented publications of the day. He had been an especially avid fan of Senator Roscoe Conkling of New York, a dissident Republican who, by his support of a third term for President Grant, had once split the party he had helped establish. The senator himself had been considered for the presidency in 1876, and although his bid was unsuccessful, he continued as a political force until his death in 1888.

Far away in the hinterlands at Diamond, Washington, Will Torrance was so loyal to his Republican idol that when his wife Maggie bore their second son, he promptly named him in memory of the late senator: Roscoe Conkling Torrance, the subject of this book.

Chapter 1

Redhead from the Palouse Country

It was especially appropriate that the town where Roscoe Conkling Torrance was born should be named Diamond. In a different context, it was to be another diamond—a baseball diamond—which would become the stepping stone to a wide-ranging career for the feisty little redhead from the Palouse Country.

At the turn of the century, the village of Diamond consisted of a blacksmith shop, a general store, a grain elevator, a feed mill and a public school, all clustered alongside the Ayer-Spokane branch of the Union Pacific Railroad.

Young Roscoe's memories of his birthplace were limited. On August 25, 1903—when he was not quite four years old—his mother died at age 37, apparently from complications in the birth of her third son, William Haldane, who also did not survive. Only hazy recollections of the arrival of the horse-drawn hearse from Colfax stayed with him. He had no memories at all of the earlier death of his sister, Marie Marguerite, on Christmas day, 1901, or that of his grandfather—William Sinclair Torrance—on November 5, 1902.

To care for his three remaining children, Will hired a housekeeper (remembered only as Mrs. Stark). Roscoe was left alone with her all day while his older brother and sister were in school, and the relationship was a combative one.

In later years he recalled:

It seemed I couldn't do anything that Mrs. Stark liked, and I was forever in the dog house. Either I was getting paddled on the behind, or I was sent upstairs without food.

9

The children of Will and Maggie Torrance were photographed shortly after the turn of the century while the family still lived at Diamond, Washington. The Torrance youngsters were (left to right): Kirby, Sr., Jessie Echo, Roscoe Conkling and Marie Marguerite, who died on Christmas Day, 1901. (Kirby Torrance, Jr., collection)

A reprieve finally came when Will moved his family to Spokane where they lived in a small guest house behind the residence of Will's older brother, Edgar. Roscoe's life brightened considerably when their new housekeeper, Sophie Voight, proved far less cantankerous than Mrs. Stark—and she was a good cook, too. When he trudged off to begin his formal education at Longfellow School, Sophie also gave him the help and encouragement he needed.

Going to school was a lot of fun for me, and I enjoyed the mile and a half walk each morning and evening. I guess I was a pretty good student because my report cards seemed to indicate that.

To help with the family finances, I got my first job, earning fifty cents a day delivering groceries after school and on Saturdays for a neighborhood store. If I worked long hours on Saturdays, sometimes I got seventy-five cents. For a little extra money I also sold the Sunday Spokesman-Review.

He and his friend Roy Sandburg also operated a sidewalk lemonade stand one summer.

We felt very successful when at the end of the day we had sold about 40 nickel glasses. It was then that I learned my first accounting lesson. Roy took the liberty of dividing our receipts: one nickel to me, one to him; another nickel to me, two to him; one to me and three to him, etc. I soon discovered the discrepancy in his method of distribution and the fight was on. Our neighbors finally pulled us apart and eventually we got matters straightened out and we became even better friends.

It wasn't all work and no play for young Roscoe, however. He found out there was one advantage to being a redhead in Spokane: you got in free at the Clemmer Theater because Jim Clemmer was a carrot-top, too. During the summer he and Roy Sandburg would carry on for hours, pitching, batting and fielding an old ball as they imitated famous major leaguers in their im-

This was the Spokane Torchy knew in the early 1900s, first as an elementary student at Longfellow School and later in his junior and senior years at Lewis and Clark High School. On Sundays he sold the Spokesman-Review. *At Natatorium Park he played baseball and enjoyed the carnival-like atmosphere. For a time he lived near Manito Park where he skated in the wintertime and visited the zoo in the summer. (Spokane Public Library)*

aginary baseball games. He also joined the other lads in some of the typical devilment of the day.

They mixed sulphur and potash together and put the explosive mixture on streetcar tracks. It didn't do any serious damage, but when the car wheels detonated the charge, it frightened the passengers, angered the conductor and delighted the Tom Sawyers who perpetrated the dastardly deed.

On Halloween they tipped over as many as twenty outhouses in a single excursion up and down the alleys of Spokane. They called the outhouses "chic sales" then because an actor-comedian of the era—Charles Partlow Sale whose nickname was "Chic"—had become famous for his skit about outdoor plumbing.

Another escapade might have gotten them into lots of trouble had they been caught. Here's how Roscoe remembered it:

One Sunday several of us wandered out to the local pickle factory about two miles from home. Being naturally curious about the workings of the plant, we scrambled over the fence for a little exploring. In the course of our adventure, one of us pulled a drain plug out of a large pickle vat and gallons of brine gushed out around us.

Horrified, we tried to replace the plug but with no luck. Escape was our next choice, so we crawled back over the fence and ran for home. For a long time we lived in dreadful fear of being caught, but the authorities never did track us down. We learned a good lesson, though.

It was years later before I found out that the bookkeeper of the factory was Harry Lowe Crosby, whose son Bing was to become a good friend of mine.

Young Roscoe added to his moral education on another occasion when he developed a case of puppy love for a pretty little girl in Longfellow School.

When I discovered that her birthday was coming up, I wanted to give her a present. I found a five-and-ten-cent store open on Sunday after I finished selling papers on the corner of Riverside and Lincoln Streets, so I went in to look for a gift. There were some jewelry items on display which looked rather expensive. They cost sixty-five cents each, but my total bankroll was just forty cents, including the nickel I needed to get back home on the streetcar.

What I did next was something which resulted in one of the best lessons of my life. I decided to pick up one of the rings and walk out the door with it. As I did, the assistant manager stopped me and said: "Young man, you have something in your pocket that doesn't belong to you. Just give it back, and in the meantime I'm going to call the police.

I was scared to death, of course, and I talked a blue streak for fifteen or twenty minutes until I convinced him that I realized my error and would NEVER do anything like that again. More than eighty years later the incident was still fresh in my memory.

In January of 1911 – when Kirby and Jessie were old enough to go off to school by themselves – Will Torrance and his younger son moved to American Falls, Idaho, where Will's brother Charles was deputy sheriff. They sat up all the way on the two-and-a-half-day trip by train, arriving at 4 a.m. and then struggling through the snow to the less-than-luxurious accommodations of the Oliver House. Will had invested in a small wheat-and-alfalfa ranch some twelve miles from town, but it was two days before the snow let up and they could arrange horse-and-buggy transportation to their new home.

Will Torrance soon developed a reputation as a good farmer. In time he was able to boast that he won first premium at the Power County Fair for the best exhibits of flax and irrigated alfalfa. He also showed the best irrigated farm display.

The *American Falls Press* recognized him for innovative agricultural practices, too:

> Last spring W. G. Torrance had a few loads of manure which he did not know what to do with, so he hauled it out on his field and scattered it thinly on a long and narrow strip. After plowing it under, he planted potatoes and corn across this strip.
>
> When he dug his potatoes recently, he was surprised to find that the yield was twice as great on the manured strip as on the land not manured. The corn on this strip was a foot higher and more vigorous in every way than the rest of the corn planted at the same time and treated in the same way.

While Will Torrance was establishing his small ranch, he enrolled Roscoe in a nearby one-room school, a building about 30 by 40 feet with 25 desks, one teacher and nine grades. The lad learned quickly that the male teacher didn't go for any foolishness. When one of the older boys continued to harass the other youngsters after he had been warned to desist, the teacher just grabbed him by the collar and the seat of his pants and threw him out an open window which was three or four feet off the ground. After that there was no more trouble in the classroom.

One of Roscoe's schoolmates was a neighbor, Earl Sands, who had moved to Idaho with his family from Groton, South Dakota. The two boys became close friends, sharing their dreams for the future. Earl wanted to become a world famous jockey, and Roscoe had his sights on a career as a major league shortstop. (You'll read more about Earl Sande, as his name was eventually modified by Damon Runyon, later in this book.) Meanwhile, though, there was some growing up to do and plenty of ranch work to fill their spare time.

One of the jobs that Roscoe especially remembered was hauling grain to the town elevator with oxen or mules, choking his way through the blinding dust to and from American Falls and developing, in the process, a lifelong hayfever affliction. But during the summer, whenever he wasn't choring, he practiced for hours, throwing a ragged ball against a barn wall and then fielding it like his idol, Roger Peckinpaugh, who had made it to the major leagues as a shortstop for the Cleveland Indians at the age of 19.

To provide his son greater educational opportunities, Will Torrance permitted Roscoe to move into American Falls where he stayed in a boarding house known as the Boys' Parsonage. Most of the other dozen or so roomers were in their twenties, out of school and working. Because of his small size (he was still in grade school), the older fellows adopted him as their mascot.

The cost for room and board was fifteen dollars a month,

Young Roscoe Torrance accompanied his father to American Falls, Idaho, where he completed his elementary education and the first two years of high school in this building. (American Falls Public Library)

14

so Roscoe got a part-time job at the M. A. Ellsbury Clothing Store, the largest in town. It was a good arrangement because Mr. Ellsbury permitted him to take on his own little sideline:

Many Nez Perce and other Indians lived near American Falls, and on Saturdays some of the men would come to town, get drunk and get thrown in the hoosegow until they sobered up and were turned loose on Monday morning. The Indians called me "Inkypomp," meaning red hair, and for some reason or other, they started leaving some of their money with me on Saturday so that they'd have something to go home with when they got out of jail.

This grew into quite a good business for me because each one gave me a dollar; and they also brought me presents of mocassins, gloves, scarves, beaded bags and arrow heads. After five or six months I had a good inventory of Indian-made goods so I opened up my own establishment on Sunday afternoons when the Union Pacific train came through. It stopped for fifteen minutes to take on water, and that gave the passengers plenty of time to come to my stand to buy souvenirs. I did pretty well, well enough so that I could buy me a slide trombone to play in the town band.

Roscoe's sister Jessie had moved to American Falls and was serving as the deputy auditor of Power County. She and their Uncle Charley, the deputy sheriff, helped the boy get a second job: feeding supper to the jail inmates.

At first this was rather scary because we had two or three murderers there—and the other prisoners weren't very attractive either. But after the first evening things went pretty well, and I kept the job for some time.

(Some years later—on March 17, 1921—Uncle Charles was shot to death by W. H. Ball, described by the American Falls Press *as a "maniac rancher from Pauline." The newspaper reported further that Deputy Sheriff Torrance and a posse were attempting to arrest Ball after the rancher had shot another man. After two shotgun blasts, each of which struck the deputy, the assailant escaped. Torrance died later after surgery failed to save him. Ball was taken into custody when he was brought to St. Anthony's Hospital in Pocatello suffering from wounds which cost him one of his arms. Three months later a jury acquitted him after a four-day trial. Ball, the only witness in his own behalf, testified that he didn't know Torrance was an*

15

officer, and he thought the posse was a mob come to lynch him. He was freed on a plea of self defense.)

Roscoe entered American Falls High School in the fall of 1914, doing reasonably well as a student and especially enjoying the dances, sleigh rides and ice skating parties during the winter months. For him, though, the highlight of the school year came in the spring when the baseball season began. Despite his small stature, he made the starting nine at shortstop, and in his sophomore year he helped lead the team to the finals of the state tournament at Twin Falls.

It would have been nice to report that he was instrumental in winning the title—but it didn't work out that way.

The score was still nothing to nothing in the eighth inning when Twin Falls High School got a man on second base with two out. The next batter hit a pop fly behind third base, and

As a youngster Torchy had one ambition: to become a major league shortstop like his idol, Roger Pekinpaugh of the Cleveland Indians. He was the acknowledged star of the American Falls High School nine as a freshman and sophomore; and, as a 14-year-old, he also played on the town team with his brother Kirby. (Special Collections Division, University of Washington Libraries)

Roscoe raced for the ball, normally an easy chance for him.

Unfortunately, the groundskeeper had left a pail of lime sitting out in left field after he had finished marking the foul line, and the little shortstop stepped in it and fell head over heels just as he was about to make the catch. The runner scored from second, and American Falls lost 1-0. Besides his embarrassment, Roscoe ended up with lime burns on his hands and face.

That didn't end his baseball career in Idaho, however. Even before he had started playing for American Falls High School, he was a fourteen-year-old shortstop and outfielder for the town team on which his brother Kirby also played. Later, when he worked for a state highway surveying crew, Roscoe was invited to join the Twin Falls team for Sunday games. Two of his recollections had nothing to do with baseball, however.

First, I learned about queers, as we called gays in those days. A homosexual ball player came in from the middle west and tried to take liberties with me because I was the smallest member of the team. When I complained, the management ran him out of town.

The second event was more serious because it was to affect me all my life. After a Sunday game we went to a local restaurant where several of us ordered breaded veal cutlets. Well, in those days before refrigeration, some restaurants used formalin [a formaldehyde solution] to keep meat from spoiling. They were supposed to wash it off before they cooked the meat, but in this case they didn't do a very good job.

Four or five of us got sick—and I got it really bad! The sickness affected my eyes. Consequently, the state sent me up beyond New Meadows on the Salmon River as a flagman for the survey crew of the north-south highway, figuring that the mountain air would help me recover from the poisoning. (Eventually I lost the sight of one eye, which may or may not have been caused by that incident.)

And, speaking of poisoning, I got a dose of a different kind when I worked on that survey crew. One night we made camp at a bend in the river. We were all pretty tired, so we pitched our tent, threw our bedding down and hit the sack. About fifteen minutes later I felt something crawling all over me. They were yellow jackets, and they began to sting. There wasn't much else I could do, so I ran to the river and jumped in. It was ice cold, but I got rid of the hornets, although I swelled up and it took me about three weeks to get over the attack.

17

In some ways Roscoe was a little bit of a tough luck kid. When he joined the Boy Scouts and went on his first hike, he slipped on a hill and grabbed a rusty barbed wire which left a lifelong scar on a finger of his throwing hand. When he was a freshman in high school, a clowning classmate pushed his head down on a drinking fountain, breaking off one tooth and seriously damaging another. He suffered the embarrassment of a half-tooth smile until he went off to college—and the second tooth bothered him for years.

Then there was the time he and Glenn Barnard rode their horses down to the bottoms of the Snake River where they occasionally went to rope calves and to try a little cow riding.

This one particular day we had gone down fairly early in the morning and decided to cross a corduroy bridge made of willow branches. The water was high, and when Glenn and I got about half way across, our horses fell through where the willows had been washed away.

Glenn grabbed his horse's tail and was pulled safely out of the water, but when I came up, I was about ten feet from my horse which swam to the shore without me. Weighted down with chaps and sheepskin coat and not being able to swim, I let out a couple whoops and so did Glenn. Then I started to go down the second time and it looked like the end for me.

To my good fortune, Ed Cronkite and Paul Bullfinch were hunting ducks in a canoe not far away, and when they saw me go into the water, they started paddling towards us. They got to me just in time and pulled me out of the river. Once on shore they beat me for a while to get all the water out of me, and then they started a fire to dry our clothes. We were mighty fortunate to be able to ride home.

It was a long time after that before I learned to take a few dog paddles and sidestrokes, enough to get me across an ordinary swimming pool.

Like lots of young boys just feeling their oats, Roscoe decided that he had enough school and wanted to be a cowboy. Surprisingly, his father agreed (probably knowing that the experience would teach him a thing or two).

I went with the L. L. Evans Ranch, herding cattle out of the hills before winter. They put me on night herd which is fine when the weather is beautiful, but when it is stormy and the rains come, the cattle go with the storm and it's pretty nearly impossible to change their minds.

That's what happened to me in my third week as a cowpuncher. I was unable to head them off, and I decided that school was a pretty good place after all. I quit my job and went back to the classroom, much to the pleasure of my dad who, I think, was instrumental in getting me on the night herd to teach me a lesson.

Life in the relatively quiet town of American Falls was pleasant and with few complications, although there were still opportunities to get into mischief. Roscoe learned to dance the waltz and the two-step, and on Saturday nights he joined his friends and neighbors who tripped the light fantastic at Odion Hall. There was one experience he would never forget.

My father told me time after time to stay away from cigarettes, liquor and easy women because all three would cause nothing but problems. That advice came in mighty handy one Saturday night when I was dancing with a girl from out of town who invited me outside. I went, but her intentions were entirely different from mine. Fortunately I was able to avoid any close association with her, because it later developed that she had passed on one of the social diseases to about four of my friends.

For a while Roscoe lived with his brother Kirby, who had come to American Falls to edit the *Power County Press.* He learned to hand-set type for the newspaper, not knowing at the time that it would be another step in the preparation for his future business career. He and Kirby did their own cooking, and Roscoe's specialty was sago pudding [made from the starch of a palm tree, somewhat like tapioca]. He liked it so much that he made big bowlsful which he kept cool under the porch because they had no icebox.

Their house was next door to that of Reverend O. P. Skaggs, a Methodist minister who got the idea for a grocery store on wheels, selling all kinds of food items at discount prices to the people in the town. The humble beginning developed into the huge Skaggs chain which was eventually sold to Safeway; and if Roscoe would have remained in American Falls, he might have become a grocery store manager as so many of the local young men did.

But by January of 1916 it began to look like the United States would be dragged into the war in Europe. Jessie Torrance left American Falls to work for the intelligence service in Washington, D.C., and Roscoe decided he wanted to return to Spokane to finish high school.

That summer he worked on the survey crew again, and when the season ended, he started out from Pollock with a pack on his back to walk the fifty miles or so to the end of the railroad line at Grangeville.

On the second day a car came along, one of the few that ever traveled over such a bad road in that neck of the woods. There was a driver in the front seat and a woman and child in the back. They could only go about fifteen miles an hour as they passed me by. Then I guess they felt sorry for me and waited until I caught up with them. They offered me a ride, and it was a good thing for both of us. I helped repair four blowouts on their Model T before we got to Grangeville, but for me it was still better than walking.

During his two years in American Falls High School, Roscoe developed a crush on a pretty girl named Grace Cronkite. Before he left for Spokane, he wrote her a long letter, telling her how much he loved her and that he hoped they would get together again when they were old enough for marriage. (Some sixty years later Grace returned the letter and teasingly announced that she wasn't going to hold him to his promise. She had married Glenn Bernard, Roscoe's calf-roping buddy.)

In Idaho Kirby E. Torrance, Sr., edited the American Falls Press *which became the* Power County Press. *Torchy learned to hand-set type in his brother's plant, not realizing that he would eventually spend most of his own career in the printing business. (American Falls Public Library)*

Chapter 2

Torchy, Torchy, Torchy!

Roscoe arrived at Lewis and Clark High School in the fall of 1916 two days before classes were to begin. Ed Kuhn, a new-found friend, told him about football and although he had never played the game before and only weighed about 135 pounds, he decided to turn out for the team with 25 or 30 other fellows.

Most of the equipment had already been issued, so I got a suit about twice my size and two shoes that didn't match—one 6½, the other 8½. The headgear was just a small, thin piece of leather and so were the shoulder pads.

It wasn't long before I got into my first scrimmage as a defensive end. I got knocked on my back the first two or three plays, but Coach Emil Hinderman must have thought I had some possibilities because he took me aside after practice and showed me some of the finer points of the game. Later he discovered I had a good throwing arm and he made a quarterback out of me.

In those days the football was almost round so you couldn't grip it. Instead you had to lay it in your hand to throw it, a technique I practiced for an hour or two every day. I got to be a pretty good drop-kicker, too—up to 35 yards. I also played safety on defense. I guess that's where the expression "weak safety" came from.

Football was not to be his big interest or achievement, however. He got his left shoulder banged up in a practice scrimmage against Gonzaga College, and in his senior year his 25-yard drop-kick defeated the sophomores in an interclass game. Most of all, he had a knack for inspiring others, and that became evident during his days at Lewis and Clark.

The Lewis and Clark Journal reported an obvious example

of that leadership trait:

> Roscoe Torrance, baseball captain, Kappa Beta and Senior A, is the official yell leader for Lewis and Clark High School. Students of the school, casting their votes in the *Journal* contest, decided emphatically, giving Torrance a majority of 1,341 over two competitors . . . nearly twice as many as the other two combined.
>
> The contest was the most exciting ever conducted . . . 10 votes were awarded for each new *Journal* subscription and 3 votes for every coupon clipped from the magazine . . . From the *Journal's* standpoint, the contest was a rousing success, resulting in 118 new subscriptions . . .
>
> "The result naturally pleases me greatly," said the new yell leader. "I owe it to the loyal support of my friends and club associates and desire to thank them heartily. I will pledge myself to do my durndest."

Roscoe had proved that he was a logical choice because when he had led cheers before an all-school convocation, the response from the student body was more than he ever expected. Of most lasting importance, however, was when Carolyn Rosenthal, sitting in the front row, shouted out to the little redhead with the broken-tooth grin: "Come on, Torchy, give us another yell!"

From that moment on, Roscoe Conkling Torrance had a new name. "Torchy, Torchy, Torchy" became a familiar cry at Lewis and Clark High School, and though it was just a spontaneous outburst on Carolyn's part, she had invented a monicker which would last a lifetime.

In Spokane Torchy lived first on the south side of town

Torchy received his life-long nickname while he was a student at Lewis and Clark High School in Spokane where he was captain of the baseball team, Yell King and heavily involved in other extra-curricular activities. (Spokane Public Library)

near Manito Park with his father's sister Hettie Stilson, then a widow. To help pay his way, he got a job as a noon-time cashier in the school cafeteria for which he got his meal and fifty cents a day. His only problem came when some of his football teammates tried to sneak through the line with four or five food items instead of the three they were entitled to for their dime. With his cafeteria job and the money he had saved from his work in Idaho, he managed quite well—with one possible exception.

Shortly after I entered Lewis and Clark, I was enamored by a pretty young girl with long curly hair. After about a month I got up enough nerve to ask her for a date. We got permission from her parents to go to a movie, and that's where I thought we were going. But when we got on the streetcar, she said: "Let's go to the Davenport Hotel and dance."

Unfortunately I only had $2.50 in my pocket because I had planned for just a show and maybe a dish of ice cream afterwards. When she insisted on going to the hotel, I had to act like a big shot, so we ended up eating in the restaurant and dancing to the music of Mr. Brill, the violinist. Of course I was terribly nervous all night, and when the bill came, it was for something like seven dollars and some odd cents.

All I could do was to try to explain my predicament to the cashier and hope for the best. She turned out to be quite sympathetic and let me borrow a blank check which I made out for our meals and a tip, planning, as I did, to rush to the bank next morning to borrow enough to cover it.

When I got home, I explained the situation to Aunt Hettie, who gave me the money to get me off the hook with the bank. And, believe me, that was the last date I had with that particular girl!

Being an affable, gregarious sort, Torchy had no trouble making friends and becoming deeply involved in extra-curricular activities. Besides being Yell King, he played trombone in the newly formed school band under Rudolph Meyer; participated in football, basketball, track and baseball; wrote a sports column for *The Lewis and Clark Journal* titled "Diamond Dope"; and first demonstrated the avid patriotism which was to become a hall mark of his life.

On April 6, 1917, the United States declared war on Ger-

When he was still in American Falls, Torchy saved enough money from his Indian souvenir business to buy a trombone. He later played in the Lewis and Clark High School band where he was pictured second from the left in the top row. Drummer Bob Stewart (fifth from the left, front row) was the student leader of the band. (Dr. Robert Stewart collection)

many, and within four days committees from all the large boys' organizations in Spokane met at the Y.M.C.A. to organize a Junior Loyalty League. As a representative of Lewis and Clark's Kappa Beta Club, Torchy was elected to the group's executive board. A *Journal* article reported:

> The league was organized for the purpose of preparing boys for other than military duties. Many boys between the ages of fifteen and twenty who cannot yet enlist waste a lot of time in poolrooms and similar places when they might be doing a service for their country: for example, some boys drive automobiles, some ride bicycles, others can do carpentering, gardening, etc.

Torchy really wasn't interested in carpentering, gardening or riding bicycles for the war effort. He wanted to volunteer for the Tank Corps, but because he was only seventeen, he needed his father's permission. Will Torrance wisely insisted that his younger son stay in school. He himself went into defense work in California, while his other son, Kirby, joined the Army Air Corps and eventually was assigned as an instructor at Kelly Field in San Antonio, Texas.

There was nothing for Torchy to do except finish the school year and then go back to Idaho to work with the survey crew on the new cross-country Lincoln Highway. He had taken the precaution of telling Henry M. Hart, the school principal, that he might have to leave early in the spring to keep his job, and the principal gave his assent. As expected, he got word from the highway department that he was to report on May 15, about two weeks before school was out.

I went to Mr. Hart and reminded him of our conversation, asking if I should take my exams early or take incompletes until I returned in the fall. He denied making any promise to me and told me I wouldn't get any credits if I left and that there would be no makeups when I got back.

Fortunately I had made my earlier request in the presence of one of our teachers, Jerry Dunn. I went out and got him and he stood by me, just about calling the principal a liar. That didn't set well with the administration, but I did get the permission I needed, making up my grades when I returned after the summer with the crew in Idaho.

25

As a high school senior Torchy (third from the left) was recruited to play for the Upstairs Price clothing store nine in Spokane when the team lost its regular shortstop. For his exceptional play he was given a new overcoat by W. W. Price, who got his nickname—"Upstairs"—because of his second-story haberdashery. (Special Collections Division, University of Washington Libraries)

A highlight of his senior year was when he was elected captain of the baseball team, but one of his most memorable games wasn't in a high school uniform. He had returned from his work in Idaho in time to be recruited by the Upstairs Price Clothiers team which had lost its regular shortstop and was in desperate need for a replacement. A newspaper account noted Torchy's heroics in the season's finale:

> Roscoe Torrance, a Lewis and Clark high school boy, was the bright star of the City League double-header yesterday at Natatorium Park . . . It was his timely hit when two were out in the last inning that won for the Clothiers. The score was 2-1.
> Not only did Torrance come through with the hit that won the game, but his fielding was about the best seen in Natatorium Park this year. He started two lightning fast double plays besides handling three other difficult chances, two of which looked to be sure hits.
> Torrance will receive a new overcoat from W. W. Price, backer of the Prices, for delivering the hit that won the game.

Torchy also got $100 in addition to the fur-collared coat which "Upstairs" Price had made for his partner, Jack Gamble. However, Gamble had gone into the service and probably would be away for three or four years, so the young shortstop was the lucky beneficiary. Incidentally, Upstairs Price got his name from his second-story clothing store.

[It's getting ahead of the story, but when Torchy outgrew the coat, he gave it to a friend, Bud Stuht, who wore it in high school and through college. Afterwards he returned it to Torchy, then married, and his wife Ruth remodeled the durable hand-me-down for their daughter Shirley.]

In Torchy's senior year Hettie Stilson moved to a smaller house in another part of the city, so his room was no longer available. He then moved in with the family of George Swartwood, a traveling salesman.

My job was to babysit their young daughter, do the dishes, keep up the yard and, in general, be the man-about-the-house while Mr. Swartwood was gone . . . For that I got a nice room, all my meals and occasionally a five dollar bill when Mr. Swartwood felt the occasion warranted it.

27

Unfortunately, about half way through the school year the family left town, so I had to find a new location. Through his daughter Bernice, I got acquainted with Dr. Albert E. Stuht, then the state health director, who also had two sons, Al and Bud. Doctor Stuht thought it would be a good idea if I would move in and help take care of the boys, which I did. I spent the rest of my senior year with them and, of course, became very close to the family. Sad to say, Al lost his life shortly after that in a tragic car accident on the way to a Washington State football game; and it was Bud who got the overcoat which Upstairs Price gave me.

Torchy's high school career came to a climax when the Lewis and Clark baseball team played North Central for the city championship in a best-of-five series. With Captain Torrance playing shortstop and batting in the leadoff position, the south-siders easily won the first game on April 30, 1918. In the second matchup — which Lewis and Clark also won, 6-3 — he got two hits, and the *Spokesman-Review* reported:

> Torrance made a fine stop of Leslie's grounder over second and caught the North Central third-sacker by a good throw to first in the fifth inning.

After losing the third game on May 10, Lewis and Clark came back four days later to capture the title 7-6 — but hard-luck Torchy missed the thrill of the victory as the *Spokesman-Review* noted: "Roscoe Torrance, the star shortstop of the South Siders was out of the game with a sprained ankle."

Three weeks later he also missed another noteworthy event as 163 members of the class of 1918 received their diplomas at Lewis and Clark High School's 48th commencement. He might have enjoyed Ross Clark Fisher's oration on "The Battle of the Marne," but he was back in Idaho, trying to make a few dollars so he could go on to college in the fall.

Scholastically, he had squeaked by in algebra, physics and history while getting his best grades in English and public speaking. However, in popularity and adeptness with his baseball glove and bat, he rated an unofficial A-plus! His two-year sojourn at Lewis and Clark resulted in numerous lasting and a few career-shaping friendships.

In football, to name a few, I remember playing with "Buck"

Torchy missed his graduation exercises at Lewis and Clark High School in 1918 because he had to return to his highway job in Idaho. Scholastically his grades were fair, but he rated an unofficial A-plus in extra-curricular activities. It was at Lewis and Clark that he met his future wife, Ruth Doris Inkster. (Shirley Torrance Lincoln collection)

Weaver, Art Walther, Ray Davis, Frank Meicho, Oliver Humes, Earl Tilton and Harry Morrison. In baseball there were, among others, Ed Kuhn, Frank Setzer, Dave Cohn, Clarence Fenstermacker, Ray Dean and Boots McNabb. In the band I played trombone with Wallace Gill and Alvin Denny, and our student leader was Bob Stewart on drums. Because I couldn't do the job while I was playing ball, I gave up my Yell King duties to Miller Cowling, who also was manager of our football team.

Of most importance, however, it was at Lewis Clark that Torchy met someone with whom he was to share almost half a century of his life.

One Friday night I went to a dance in a part of town known as Brown's Addition, and a young lady in a red dress caught my eye. I finally worked my way over to where she was sitting and got up enough nerve to ask her for a dance. We hit it off real well, and before long we were going steady. I don't think her family was too sure about me, though, because after our first date, she reported that she had been out with "Torchy," and when her mother asked for my last name, she didn't know it. Of course her mother then thought I was some sort of bum who dropped in at the dance hall and picked up her daughter—and I guess it took three or four years to convince her otherwise.

The young lady's name was Ruth Doris Inkster, a native of Davenport, Washington, who eventually was to play a leading role in this story.

Because his baseball prowess was well known in eastern Washington, Torchy was invited to attend Washington State College and offered a job "picking up towels" in the gym. However, because his brother Kirby had preceded him at the University of Washington in Seattle, he decided to travel across the state to test himself in a new environment. He also was pledged to Kirby's fraternity, Sigma Alpha Epsilon.

Early in September of 1918 American forces under General John J. Pershing had won their first independent victory in the Battle of St. Mihiel. Later that month more than a million doughboys were committed against the Germans in the Meuse-

When Torchy arrived at the University of Washington campus in the fall of 1918, it was a spacious, uncluttered complex on some 530 acres. He was one of less than six thousand students in the school which was to grow into one of the major universities in the U. S. (Special Collections Division, University of Washington Libraries)

Argonne sector. Back home on October 1 the Student Army Training Corps was established on more than 500 college campuses across the U.S., and at the University of Washington freshman Torchy Torrance was one of the first volunteers.

The commander of his S.A.T.C. company was Lt. Jerry Barnett, who was very helpful in preparing him for a possible assignment to an officers' candidate school. Torchy repaid the favor by introducing the lieutenant to a girl the young officer wanted to meet. It turned out to be a lucky move.

I had a date one night and the curfew hour was ten o'clock. I had just said good night to the girl at the sorority house and had about five minutes to get across campus to the barracks. I ran around a corner just as Lieutenant Barnett was coming in the other direction, and I knocked him flat as a pancake. He could have caused me a lot of trouble but he was a good egg, and because I had introduced him to Dorothy Black, he didn't.

The lieutenant recommended Torchy for the Artillery School at Fort Sill, Oklahoma, but just before his orders came through, the Armistic was declared on November 11. To commemorate the end of the war, Professor Edmond S. Meany conducted an impressive ceremony at the University, climaxed by the planting of sixty trees in memory of young Washingtonians who had given their lives for their country. Relieved of his patriotic responsibilities at that point, Torchy was then free to pursue a peacetime college career.

Too small for the Sun Dodger football squad, Torchy played four years of baseball for the University of Washington and then became the freshman coach. Years later Pete Martin, then associate editor of The Saturday Evening Post, *wrote to him: "All I have to do is close my eyes and I can still see you scooping up those hot grounders and pegging them to first base. Even at that age I figured you had personality to burn." (R. C. Torrance collection)*

Chapter 3

Bow Down to Washington

"The University of Washington has never had a more loyal, devoted alumnus than Torchy Torrance."

That assessment by a friend could well be echoed by hundreds of others who witnessed his dedication expressed in countless ways throughout more than seven decades.

Torchy's love affair with his alma mater began as soon as he walked onto the 530-acre campus in Seattle with more than five thousand other students in the fall of 1918. During the first two months, however, it seemed that his college career would be of short duration because of his desire to get into military service. That changed quickly with the signing of the Armistice.

He went through the initiation rites at the Sigma Alpha Epsilon house, got paddled a lot and, at meal times, was commanded to sing such contemporary songs as "'Where Is My Wandering Boy Tonight?" and "Dardanelle." He also was sent on a night-time mission to find a pill box in a cemetery. There the older fraternity brothers, dressed in white sheets, scared the wits out of him when they jumped out from behind the gravestones screaming like banshees.

To earn his room and board at the SAE house, he peeled potatoes in the early morning and helped wash dishes after the evening meal. Such chores were no problem for him because he had been well imbued with the work-ethic in earlier years at Spokane and in Idaho.

Torchy also went out for football, but at 135 pounds or less, he was a mite small to be trading blows with the other Sun Dodgers (as Washington's athletic teams were then known).

Ben Tidball and Sandy Wick coached the University's 1920 freshman football squad pictured here. The Babes, as they were called, lost to Enoch Bagshaw's Everett High School state champs 20-0. Baggy inherited the frosh team the following season as he began his nine-year tenure as coach of the Purple and Gold. Torchy was considered too small for the football team in his freshman year, so he ended up as an equipment manager. (Special Collections Division, University of Washington Libraries)

The only thing I could do real well was drop-kick, but I don't think Gus Henderson, the freshman coach, was too impressed. I had cracked my shoulder in my last year at Lewis and Clark, and because there wasn't any X-ray equipment to amount to anything in those days, all you could do was just try to get well. If you did, you played. If not, you either dropped out or played hurt—which I did most of my last year. At the University, though, the boys were a lot bigger and tougher than in high school, so I decided that it just wasn't the place for me. And the coach agreed.

When the war ended, Darwin Meisnest, who had been in the Naval S.A.T.C. program, was appointed graduate manager of the Associated Students of the University of Washington. The A.S.U.W. had been incorporated in 1902, and—through its board of control consisting of undergraduate officers, alumni and faculty members—was responsible for all student activities, including athletics, publications, dramatics and social events. The graduate manager's position was obviously one of considerable importance.

Meisnest hired Torchy as athletic property manager, and his introduction to the job was a messy one. The football season had just ended on a wet day, and the players had thrown all their soggy, mud-soaked gear into a big pile on the floor of the property room. His formidable task was to sort out all the helmets, shin guards, pants, shirts and shoulder pads, get them cleaned and put away for the winter. He finally accomplished his mission, but there was an unexpected complication.

One of the players had a case of boils and infected two or three others. I wound up getting them from their jerseys. It was a bad situation which persisted through the winter and into the baseball season. Others had the same problem, but it was particularly rough on me.

I moved out of the SAE house and into a private home with Jim and Vic Hurley and their parents. No matter what the doctors or Mrs. Hurley tried, the boils kept popping up between my legs, under my arms and on the back of my neck. Then one day I was at a barbershop on University Avenue which was a hangout for athletes when Guy Noble, a neighborhood cigar store operator, told me he knew how to solve my problem.

"Go to the hardware store," he said, "and buy a pound of lead shot. Put the lead and a pint of milk in a double boiler, boil it

To help pay his way through school, Torchy (third from the left) worked as a student athletic manager and trainer. He was pictured in 1922 with other athletic department aides. (Special Collections Division, University of Washington Libraries)

for an hour and then drain the milk off the shot and drink it."

When the Hurleys were away, I did just what Guy said, and the stuff tasted a lot like oyster stew. Anyway, it was about ten days before the boils cleared up, and I never had one after that. But then I made the mistake of telling the doctors at the University, and one of them said: "You crazy kid! You could have gotten lead poisoning and killed yourself!"

Fortunately it didn't turn out that way, so I guess Guy Noble did me a big favor.

The "star shortstop" from Lewis and Clark High School was an unrecruited walk-on candidate for the freshman baseball squad. Unlike football, his talent and not his size was what counted on the diamond. Coach William H. "Dode" Brinker—who had spent a season with the Philadelphia Phillies in 1912—liked what he saw, and Torchy made the team. It was the beginning of a four-year collegiate career which, it appeared, was leading him toward his youthful dream of a trip to the major leagues.

As a sophomore he decided to run for the class position on the A.S.U.W. board of control. His opponent was Charles F. Frankland, a member of Beta Theta Phi fraternity and a high jumper on the track team. Frankland, a graduate of Seattle's

A new stadium to replace the old Denny Field was inaugurated on November 27, 1920. Puget Sound Bridge and Drydock Company was the contractor for the job which had a total cost of $323,576.58. The Dartmouth Indians defeated the Sun Dodgers 28-7 in the first game played on the field. (University of Washington Athletic Department)

Lincoln High School, was well known by many local students on the campus, so Torchy, from eastern Washington, was an obvious long shot. As it turned out, the redhead from Spokane won the election to his opponent's keen disappointment; but in later years he and Frankland—a prominent Seattle banker—became close friends and worked together on numerous occasions in behalf of the University.

The position on the board of control gave Torchy an insider's view of A.S.U.W. responsibilities and a closer relationship with Dar Meisnest, the graduate manager. It was during his tenure on the board that Meisnest spearheaded a campaign to replace the old Denny Field with a new football stadium. Torchy voted enthusiastically in favor of the project and then helped raise money to construct the 30,000-seat facility, the first of its size to be built on the West Coast.

In his position on the A.S.U.W. board of control, Torchy voted to build the new stadium and then helped in the successful fund-raising campaign which followed. This was one of the promotion gimmicks used to sell the engraved bronze plaques entitling buyers to choice-seat season tickets. (University of Washington Archives)

With decided mixed emotions Torchy served as guest trainer for the Dartmouth football team which inaugurated the new University stadium by defeating the Sun Dodgers 28-7. Coach Doc Spears gave Torchy a Dartmouth blanket for his service. Third from left in the back row was All-American Gus Sonnenberg who later became a professional wrestling champion and "inventor" of the flying tackle maneuver in the ring. The University of Washington's All-American, George Wilson, also gave the wrestling circuit a try, accompanying Sonnenberg on a tour of Australia. (Special Collections Division, University of Washington Libraries)

Puget Sound Bridge and Drydock Company was awarded the contract for the job and ground was broken on May 17, 1920. Meanwhile, about 500 student-salesmen—Torchy among them—began selling small bronze plaques engraved with the name of individual buyers who, for $50, got choice-seat season tickets for two years, and, for $100, a five-year guarantee. About 3,500 plaques were sold, raising a major share of the $323,576.58 which the stadium eventually cost.

The dedication was planned for November 27, 1920, and to focus national attention on the event, the Dartmouth football team was invited to play Coach Leonard "Stub" Allison's Purple and Gold eleven. Transcontinental athletic trips were extremely rare at the time, and to cut down on the expenses of the long railroad trip from Hanover, New Hampshire, Coach Clarence W. "Doc" Spears brought only a limited number of players and no trainer.

Along with his other duties as property manager, Torchy had been appointed assistant trainer for Clarence S. "Hec" Edmundson, the University's basketball and track coach. As such, he was loaned to Doc Spears and the Dartmouth team which worked out for four days at the old Rainier Valley baseball park at Rainier Avenue and McClellan. Torchy had to rush back and forth between there and the campus where he also was involved in plans for the dedication ceremonies.

Work on the stadium was completed just twelve hours before game time. The Purple and Gold team—which the previous year had won five of its six games, including a 120-0 whitewashing of Whitman College—was just one-and-four going into the season's finale. Dartmouth, led by its All-American tackle and future wrestling champion Gus Sonnenberg, was a heavy favorite, but in the early minutes of the game the 28,000 fans were brought to their feet by a spectacular play and the first points scored on the new field.

After the opening kickoff, Dartmouth, as expected, had marched down the field to about the Washington 15-yard line. When the drive was stalled, a field goal was attempted. Sun Dodger tackles Bob Ingram and Newman H. "Zeke" Clark rushed in to block the kick and the ball was deflected into the hands of Bob Abel, an end, who ran the length of the field for a touchdown.

Unfortunately, that was all the offense the Purple and Gold

could muster. The strength of the Dartmouth team, plus the fact that the Washington punter twice kicked the ball off the side of his foot parallel to the line of scrimmage, resulted in a 28-7 win for the visitors from the Ivy League.

It was with mixed emotions that Torchy accepted a gift for his contribution to the victors.

Doc Spears and the team gave me a Dartmouth blanket which meant an awful lot to me at the time. It must have meant a lot to someone else, too, because it was stolen from me a few years later and I never did find out who the culprit was.

Because he was personable and out-going, Torchy soon became a popular figure on the campus. He and Virginia Rush were a smash hit with their dance act in the Junior Girls' Vodvil in Meany Hall, and afterwards he was named Boy Dancer of the Year. As a senior, he was president of the W Club, the Quad Club and a small, prestigious honorary society, the Fir

Members of the well-dressed 1920 Sun Dodger baseball squad posed before leaving on a road trip. Torchy was fourth from the left in the top row; Coach Stub Allison was third from the right in the front. Torchy learned about racial prejudice when Johnnie Prim (front, left) was not permitted to stay in the same hotel with the rest of the team. (Special Collections Division, University of Washington Libraries)

Tree. There was no time left to play his trombone, so he sold it "to keep the creditors off my back." Not everything worked out the way he wanted it to, however.

At that time it was fashionable for a boy to take a girl out for a canoe ride on Lake Washington early in the morning, so I invited Helen Duck, a beautiful young lady from Portland, Oregon, to be my companion one day. We got into the canoe and I paddled out—not too far because I couldn't swim very well and I didn't know if she could either. We had a good time and everything was going along fine until we were almost ready to dock. That's when Helen stood up too quickly, the canoe overturned and we both ended up in waist-high water. There was nothing to do but wade ashore, pulling the canoe after us. Then we had to walk across the campus dripping wet to our respective houses. We were quite a sight for the other students on their way to class. I'll never forget Helen Duck because her name was certainly appropriate that morning.

During those days we fellows occasionally went downtown to a dime-a-dance hall at 5th and Seneca where Ed Leader, the crew coach, was the bouncer. A regular member of our group was Elwood H. "Shorty" Wiles, who was over 21 but looked like a boy of 15. Once when we were there Shorty selected a girl who looked good to him, went up to her with his dime and asked for a dance. She gave him the once-over and said: "I don't dance with a child." And Shorty replied: "Oh, I'm sorry. If I'd have known your condition, I never would have asked you."

As a senior Torchy and Zeke Clark were each prevailed upon to run for the A.S.U.W. presidency, representing the sororities and fraternities against Herbert S. Little, a law student and candidate of the campus independents. Neither of them were particularly enthusiastic about the nomination, so they flipped a coin and Torchy lost and became the candidate.

With the baseball season as a greater priority, he had little time for politicking. His fraternity brothers, led by "Gook" Bevis, got together a quartet and sang songs under the balconies of the various houses in his behalf, but that was about all. In the meantime, Jim Bailey, Little's manager, launched a no-holds-barred campaign of independents and foreign students against the "Greeks" which left a few hard feelings in its wake. As a result, Bailey was hung in effigy after winning the election. Although he never

During his years at the University Torchy played shortstop for several teams during the summer season. This one was sponsored by the B. R. Lewis lumber company of Clear Lake, Washington. When his team won the league championship, Lewis arranged for a big banquet and dance in the town hall to celebrate the victory. Torchy was seated behind the bat boy. (Special Collections Division, University of Washington Libraries)

liked to lose in any endeavor, Torchy took the defeat in stride and went on with his multiple campus activities.

In the spring of 1921 the Sun Dodger baseball team, then coached by Stub Allison, lost the conference championship to Washington State by half a game.

During that summer and others—while I was in college and after—I picked up a little extra money by playing on town teams and in the old Northwest League. At various times I played for Sedro Woolley, Clear Lake, the Bloedel Donovan Lumber Company nine of Bellingham, Stanwood, Wenatchee and Enumclaw. The players on these teams were usually older professionals on the way down or youngsters on the way up, so the competition was pretty tough. Thinking about it brings back lots of memories, although they may not be in the proper chronology.

At Stanwood I remember the time when Heinie Menth was pitching for us, and about the middle of the game he threw a curve ball and his arm broke right above the elbow. You could hear it pop all over the field. We all knew something bad had happened, but we couldn't believe you could break your arm just throwing a ball. He did, though, and it ruined Heinie's career as a player. And he had potential, too.

When I played for Enumclaw against Black Diamond, I really experienced intense rivalry. About the seventh inning the umpire made a call that the folks didn't like, and the fight started. People from both sides swarmed onto the field, and I decided that the wisest thing to do was get out of there. I practically hurdled over the centerfield fence where they had a stile to get in and out of the park. I went to the barn where we changed our clothes, dressed and headed back to Seattle. They never did finish the game, and I guess some of the players and spectators got pretty badly beaten up.

When I played for Wenatchee, our chief rival was Cashmere. Once, on the way over from Seattle, three of us stayed overnight in Waterville where Dewey Webb had invited us to supper on Saturday. He asked us back next morning for breakfast, and in his basement he had some homemade hard cider which he was quite proud of. I had a couple glasses and didn't eat much, so when we got to the ball park where it was about 95 in the shade, I began to get real dizzy. So did Spike Maloney and Elbert Harper who were with me.

We could barely see the ball for two or three innings, and I remember that we stalled for time any way we could, even throwing the ball out of the park until the effects of the cider wore off. The Wenatchee fans couldn't figure out what was wrong. I finally went to the umpire and told him I was terribly sick, so he held up the game for about fifteen minutes while I went to the restroom for a little elimination. I played the rest of the game, but not very well. I learned another good lesson, though: never trust a friend who dispenses hard cider!

At Clear Lake we worked in B. R. Lewis's sawmill when we weren't playing. He was our team sponsor, and when we won the league championship for him, he put on a big banquet and dance in the town hall for all the surrounding territory. It was a big social event, and everybody had a good time. I especially remember B. R. because I became acquainted with one of his daughters and one night I took her to a picture show at the Coliseum Theater in Seattle. They didn't have reservations or private boxes, so you had to line up on the sidewalk—sometimes half way around the block—waiting to get in. That's when B. R. drove up in his big Pierce-Arrow and saw us there. In a voice you could hear all over the place, he shouted:

When the University of Washington baseball team traveled to Japan in 1921, Torchy (shown here with Richard Welts and hosts) told of his experiences in a letter to his father: "At present we are staying in a typical Japanese hotel . . . We sleep on the floor and have bags of rice for pillows . . . The food here is terrible and nearly all of the fellows have colds because of the damp weather and the fact that we have to go around the hotel without shoes." (Special Collections Division, University of Washington Libraries)

"You cheap skate! Why don't you take my daughter to a show where you can buy a reserved seat?" I was embarrassed and so was she, and it was the last time we ever went out together.

In the fall of 1921 the Washington baseball team was scheduled for a four-month tour of Japan. Stub Allison had a personal decision to make, and he chose to give up the football coaching job in favor of the trip to the Orient. For Torchy it meant delaying his graduation, but the opportunity was too good to pass up.

The ocean voyage was an experience in itself. We traveled on the Fushima Maru, *and one of the things I remember was batting practice on the deck, using a big net. Coach Allison figured if we could hit the ball with the ship bobbing up and down, we ought to do okay in Japan.*

We were royally entertained wherever we appeared. The game of baseball fascinated the Japanese people and they turned out in great numbers to see us play. We were a curiosity, I guess.

The Purple and Gold team played 35 games, winning 23 of them, including victories over the very capable Waseda and Keio Universities. After each contest, members of the competing squads paired off by position so that the Japanese could learn the finer points of the game from their visitors.

Of interesting note was the fact that Crown Prince Hirohito, two years younger than Torchy, was then vice-minister of foreign affairs in charge of the tour.

We played in some towns where they had never seen a baseball game before. In northern Japan it got so cold that we wore extra sweaters and had little hibachi fires on the bench to warm our hands before we went to the plate or out in the field. To complicate matters, we all had dysentery at one time or another so dispositions weren't always too good, and that created a problem when we played in Wakayama.

They had built a baseball field in a swampy area virtually over-night, so we didn't have the best playing conditions. There was a big crowd, and the umpire standing behind the pitcher's mound was in a military uniform and wearing white gloves. Everything was going along fine until George Merriott, our third baseman, hit a line drive which the Japanese right fielder picked up on the second or third hop and threw to first base. Merriott had reached the bag by at least two steps, but the umpire called him out.

Well, George headed for him with fire in his eye, and the crowd— not knowing the ways of an American baseball beef—moved in to protect the umpire from what they thought was going to be bodily harm. We didn't know what was going to happen, so we worked our way behind the backstop with bats in our hands, and order wasn't restored until Stub Allison got up on a bleacher seat to talk to the people and to apologize through his interpreter. After that everybody settled down, and a serious incident was avoided. One thing, though: George Merriott was a pretty good boy for the rest of the tour.

Torchy did his share of sightseeing in Kobe, Kyoto and other cities. He was impressed by Mt. Fuji and fascinated by the rice fields and mulberry orchards. However, despite the interesting experience, he wrote to his father: "Believe me, I will really

45

As he had been at Lewis and Clark High School, Torchy (far left in the second row)
was extremely active in extra-curricular activities at the University. This picture of an
unremembered event was taken in 1919. Torchy eventually served as president of the
W Club, the Quad Club and the Fir Tree. (Special Collections Division, University of
Washington Libraries)

be able to appreciate the United States after being [here]." A
proposed trip to China and Manchuria was cancelled because
of the weather, and the team returned home aboard another
Japanese ship, the *Kushima Maru.*

In the following spring Torchy was again at shortstop for
the Sun Dodgers – until the fourth inning of the final game against
Oregon Agricultural College. That's when one of the Oregon
players tipped off his coach that he had seen Torchy play a
game for Ogden, Utah, in the defunct Union Association back
when he was a high school student at American Falls. He was
immediately declared a professional and sent to the bench. R.
L. "Matty" Matthews, who had succeeded Stub Allison as the
Washington coach, argued the decision, but to no avail.

On the basis of their summer-time involvement in various
semi-pro leagues, there were other players on the field who had
played for cash. It was a common practice at the time, and
Torchy could have squealed on at least two members of the
Oregon team who were professionals as much as he was. He
didn't, however, and his college career came to an abrupt end.
Then he had another decision to make.

Charlie Barrett, a scout for the Detroit Tigers, signed me to
a contract, and I was supposed to report to their farm team in
the Three-Eye League (Illinois, Indiana and Iowa) in July. That's
when the University offered me $250 a month to coach freshman
baseball and to be assistant graduate manager under Darwin Meisnest.

That was quite a handsome salary at the time. Since baseball only offered me $125 a month for three months of the summer league, I joined the staff of the University on a permanent basis.

Because of his trip to Japan, he still didn't have his degree. He had started out with the intention of becoming a mining engineer, but after two years Dean Milnor Roberts of the College of Mining called him in and said: "Torchy, I haven't had a request for a mining engineer for a long time, so if I were you, I'd try something else." He then switched and eventually graduated with a major in business administration, officially getting his sheepskin on June 18, 1923.

At twenty-three years of age – with college classes behind him and a steady job ahead – he was truly in his element. Even though he was no longer going to follow in the cleated footsteps of his idol, Roger Peckinpaugh, being paid to be involved in athletics in general and baseball in particular was at least a secondary dream come true.

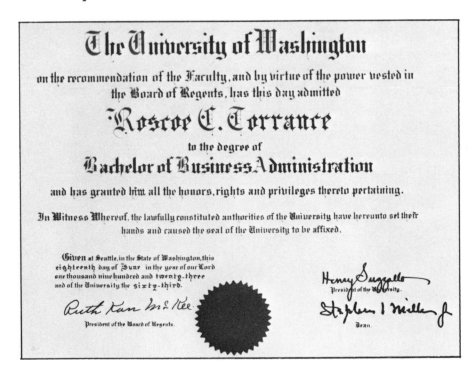

Torchy received his degree in business administration from the University of Washington on June 18, 1923. He had originally intended to major in mining engineering but switched when he was advised that job opportunities were scarce in that particular field.

As a student, a staff member and later as an alumnus, Torchy always maintained a close relationship with the coaches and other athletic department personnel at the University of Washington. When he was assistant graduate manager, he posed (from left to right) with Ray Eckmann, captain of the 1921 Sun Dodger football team and later athletic director; Hec Edmundson, basketball coach; Tubby Graves, football and baseball coach; Leslie J. Ayer, faculty athletic representative; Coach Enoch Bagshaw; Darwin Meisnest, graduate manager; and George McCush, team manager. (Special Collections Division, University of Washington Libraries)

Chapter 4

Cantankerous Coaches and Other Characters

Because of his jobs, his A.S.U.W. activities and four years as a baseball player, Torchy spent considerable time with the University of Washington coaches of the post-World War I era and got to know most of them quite intimately.

The phenomenal Gilmour "Gil" Dobie—whose Sun Dodger football teams went through 61 games without defeat from 1908 through 1916—was gone by the time Torchy arrived on the Seattle campus. His replacement was Claude J. "Jump" Hunt who came from Carleton College in Minnesota. Because of the war, Hunt's teams played only four games in 1917 and two in 1918, winning two, losing three and tying one. Needless to say, students and downtown fans were eager for a return to the Dobie tradition in the first peacetime season which followed.

I was the assistant trainer and property manager for the 1919 team. Coach Jump Hunt had a tough time because most of the players were returning from military service—many of them had been overseas—so they were out of shape and not too easy to discipline.

I used to go to lunch with him every day before practice at Rogers' candy shop cafe on University Avenue. I've never seen anybody eat like Coach Hunt.

He weighed about 240 pounds, had a rather large stomach and always wore a vest. He would spill half of his food, and after two or three weeks his vest would get pretty shiny. When we got back to his office, he would hang it up, put on a sweatshirt and go to work.

He used to tickle himself with his own jokes which didn't always go over too well with the players. On one occasion Ted Faulk, an ex-serviceman and quite bald, had missed a couple of tackles and

Jump hollered: "Faulk, when you lost your hair, your brains must have gone with it."

Then he just laughed and laughed—but the team members didn't think it was funny at all. It was two or three days before he could get them back together again. In the end we had a good season, winning five games—including the 120-0 drubbing of Whitman—and losing only to Oregon 24-13.

Stub Allison succeeded Hunt in 1920. He and Torchy batched together with Bob Ingram and Brick Loher, getting their room as caretakers of Lander and Terry Halls during the football season. It was as good a way as any to get well acquainted.

Stub was a tough coach and a real disciplinarian. He was also a fine football player in his day. Loren Solon was his assistant, and they didn't always have a friendly relationship.

Sometimes to show the players what they wanted them to do, Stub would take over at fullback on the offense and Solon would play center on defense. Then they would bang into each other, and it got to be a real show watching them battle it out in their demonstrations.

Once when Stub went down to scout California, Solon changed the whole offensive program. Allison was gone for almost a week— because it took that long by train—so by the time he returned, he didn't know what was going on. That started a real argument, and the two of them were at odds for the rest of the season. Maybe that's one of the reasons why we won only one game and lost five.

Stub would bet on every game he thought we had a chance of winning, not an unusual thing for coaches—or even players—to do in those days. That year the bookmakers had us a six-point favorite over Montana, so Stub had me go down to Green's cigar store and bet $300 on Washington.

The game was played in a driving rain, but that didn't stop Montana. As I recall, the margin was decided just seconds before halftime. We had punted, and then Referee George Varnell shot his pistol to end the period. The play had already started, but some of our players thought it was time to go to the locker room. Harry Adams caught the ball and ran 60 yards for the score. Montana eventually won 18-14, and Stub lost his $300 and his disposition.

Allison chose to go to Japan with the baseball team in the fall of 1921, so Washington was in the market for a new coach, the third since Gil Dobie. Enoch W. Bagshaw, who had captained the 1907 University team, was then compiling an amazing record at Everett High School just north of Seattle. His 1913 team annihilated Bellingham High 174-0, and in five meetings of the two schools the cumulative score was Everett 369, Bellingham 0.

In 1920 "Baggy"—as the little Welshman was always known—came up with his finest eleven. Featuring a running back named George Wilson, the Everett team literally crushed its Washington state opponents; mangled The Dalles, Oregon, 90-7; walloped East High of Salt Lake City 67-0; and finally out-lasted East Technical High of Cleveland, Ohio, 16-7 for the national championship.

With a record like that, Baggy was a logical choice to restore

The University of Washington athletic staff in the mid-1920s included (front row, left to right): Darwin Meisnest, graduate manager; Bob Butler, crew; Torchy Torrance, assistant graduate manager and freshman baseball coach; Enoch Bagshaw, football; Jim Arbuthnot, physical education and wrestling. (Back row): Bart Spellman, football line coach; Rusty Callow, crew; Wayne Sutton, football end coach; Tubby Graves, football and baseball; Hec Edmundson, basketball and track. (University of Washington Athletic Department)

Washington's winning tradition, so Dar Meisnest hired him for the 1921 season. Fortunately, most of his Everett team came with him; but while they were playing freshman ball, Bagshaw had to struggle to a 3-4-1 record with the varsity, including a humiliating 72-3 loss to California. In 1922, however, Wilson and other members of his high school champions rejoined him and he began a string of winning seasons which was to earn him a place of honor in the annals of his alma mater.

In his new role as assistant graduate manager and freshman baseball coach, Torchy had a continuing involvement with Bagshaw whom he called "a great coach and a fine disciplinarian but the worst public relations person you can imagine." California writers were particularly hard on Baggy, and Mark Kelly of the *Los Angeles Examiner* called his team "beautiful but dumb." The "dumb" label haunted him throughout his stay at Washington. He got his share of revenge, however.

In 1923 we played the University of Southern California for the first time. The odds-makers had USC favored by fifteen points, but they didn't realize what we had in George Wilson and the other players from Everett, not to mention Elmer Tesreau, another fine back.

Now is a good time to bring into this story a school friend of mine from Lewis and Clark High School, Harvey Cassill. He and I borrowed and practically begged money from all our friends until we got a hundred dollars which we bet on Washington at 15 to 1. After the opening kickoff our team held USC on downs to force a punt. On the center snap the ball sailed over the kicker's head and we recovered. After that George Wilson scored, and Washington was on its way to a 22-0 victory. We won fifteen hundred dollars!

With a record of ten wins and one loss to California, Baggy's team was invited to play Navy in the Rose Bowl. In his role as assistant graduate manager, Torchy was involved in ticket sales for the game.

In those days there were about 60,000 seats in the Rose Bowl and each of the participating schools was alloted 20,000 tickets. Captain Byron McCandless, the athletic director for the Naval Academy, set up a program so that sailors at San Diego and San Pedro could buy up to four tickets each, with the money being taken out of their next paycheck.

Well, about four days before the game the fleet was ordered out to sea on maneuvers, and McCandless came rushing up to Pasadena with about 16,000 unsold tickets in two suitcases. We had sold all of our share, so we opened the ticket offices again in Los Angeles and Pasadena and advertised in the papers as best we could. We were still selling on New Year's Day, but even though the stadium wasn't full, we had a very interesting game.

The Navy completed 16 of 20 passes, including their first 14 in a row, to lead us 14-7 with about four minutes to go in the game. Baggy and his assistant coaches—Tubby Graves and Bart Spellman (whose son John later became governor of Washington)— had worked out a guard-eligible pass play and they figured this was a good time to use it. They had talked it over with George Varnell, the referee, so he knew it was coming and wouldn't call it back—if it worked. Well, it did, and Fred Abel passed to guard Jimmy Bryan for the score. Lester Sherman, wearing a size 12 shoe on his kicking foot instead of the usual size 8 because of a broken toe, made the extra point and the game ended 14-14.

There was a sequel which should be noted. Before the game several of us—including Baggy—were invited to a cocktail party at the Huntington Hotel. In the lobby afterwards Mark Kelly of the Examiner *made a very distasteful remark in front of Mrs. Bagshaw. Baggy controlled himself then, but after the game, when Marty Burke, a sportswriter from Kelly's paper, came into the dressing room, the coach grabbed him by the collar and seat of the pants and threw him out the door. Burke, a pleasant fellow unlike his boss, was completely innocent, but anybody with a connection to Kelly really got Baggy's dander up.*

Between football seasons Torchy went on recruiting trips with Coach Bagshaw throughout the state of Washington in a Model T Ford with Torchy at the wheel because Baggy couldn't drive.

We'd go to Ellensburg, Yakima, Sunnyside or wherever their might be a good prospect. We'd give speeches in the assemblies and later answer the kids' questions about the University. The recruiting rivalry with Washington State was intense, and often the high school teachers would get involved—some would support the University and others WSC. We came close to getting into fist fights at some of the places. We never thought about going down into Oregon or California to recruit.

On one trip Baggy decided he wanted to learn to drive. I picked a good spot between Olympia and Shelton for him to take his first lesson. Next thing we knew we were roaring downhill at about 65 miles an hour, the Ford's side flaps flapping like wings and with Baggy clutching the wheel for all he was worth. I was mighty scared, so I reached over and put on the brakes until we finally got the car stopped. I told Baggy to move over and I drove from then on. He never asked to try again.

In 1925 Bagshaw's Huskies (the Sun Dodger name had been dropped) ended the regular season with ten wins and a 6-6 tie with Nebraska in Lincoln, the first trip for the Purple and Gold that far east. Washington was invited back to the Rose Bowl for the second time in two years.

At first the players voted against going. The older ones had been there before, and some didn't want to spend Christmas that far from home. Dar Meisnest kept putting on the pressure, though, and in the end the decision was made to accept the offer. Dartmouth, Princeton and Colgate had all turned down the invitation to come to Pasadena, so the Rose Bowl committee decided to take a chance on a southern school for the first time. Alabama — led by Pooley Hubert and Johnny Mack Brown (who later became a movie star) — was eventually selected to play the Huskies in the final game for George Wilson and Elmer Tesreau.

In those days the Rose Bowl committee handled the parade and the civic celebration while the host team was responsible for all the details of the game — publicity, ticket sales, parking, ushers, hiring of officials and all the other problems which might arise. Dar Meisnest sent me down as manager. I worked with Les Henry, chairman of the Tournament of Roses committee, and Monty Flint, president of the Pacific Savings and Trust Bank, where I had my office.

Mark Kelly of the Examiner *was up to his old tricks and wouldn't give the Huskies or Alabama any space in his paper. To overcome the problem in Los Angeles, I got Bill Leiser of the* San Francisco Chronicle *to come down and handle publicity. Because they had experience from the previous year, I also hired Ed Loder and Andy Anderson of Stanford to help me. Despite the difficulties, we managed to get the job done.*

After the game one of the officials — Walter Ekersall, the great All-American from the University of Chicago — handed me a bill for

$1,500. It was way out of line, and I finally got him to settle for about $500, plus expenses.

(Several years later, after the stock market crashed, Les Henry was sent to prison for mishandling the investments of the actress, Mary Miles Minter; and Monty Flint committed suicide, presumably because of financial losses.)

As Torchy recalled, the game itself was a classic, one of the most exciting in Rose Bowl history. At halftime Washington had what appeared to be a comfortable 12-0 lead, but then Coach Wade Wallace's team roared back, scoring 20 points in just seven minutes of the third quarter while George Wilson was on the bench nursing a first-half injury.

Wilson, by then a recognized All-American, returned in time

All-American George Wilson (left) and his outstanding but less recognized running mate, Elmer Tesreau, posed with Rose Bowl Queen Fay Lamphier. Despite a sterling performance by Wilson, the Huskies lost to Alabama 20-19 on New Year's Day, 1926. (Special Collections Division, University of Washington Libraries)

to throw a touchdown pass to George Guttormsen (one of the Everett boys), but it was too little too late as the Huskies lost 20-19. As an indication of Wilson's importance to the game, when he was in the lineup, the Purple and Gold gained 300 yards and scored 19 points; when he was out for 20 minutes, the Huskies managed only 17 yards while Alabama put its entire total on the board.

Before the game Torchy had been involved in a little problem because of Wilson.

A promoter named Charles C. "Cash-and-Carry" Pyle was barnstorming across the country with a team featuring Harold E. "Red" Grange, the All-American from Illinois. Pyle kept trying to see George and Elmer Tesreau about signing up for a game against Grange's team to be played in Los Angeles on January 15.

I finally had to get to Pyle to tell him that we were preparing for the Rose Bowl game and would he please leave our players alone until it was over. I told him I would then talk to George and Elmer about the deal. As it turned out, they decided to play for $500 each on a team to be called the Wilson Wildcats.

When the game started, Wilson kicked off to Grange and then went down and tackled him. The Galloping Ghost flew in about three different directions and he didn't play any more that day. Later he said it was the hardest he'd ever been hit in his life.

George never finished school but went on to play several more games with the Wilson Wildcats and one of the early professional teams in Akron, Ohio. After that he went on a wrestling tour to Australia with Gus Sonnenberg, the former Dartmouth tackle. He made good money Down Under, but unfortunately they wouldn't let him take it out of the country. Back home he got into some bad company on the wrestling circuit. We tried to get him back on his feet by getting him accepted as a rigger for Cliff Moores, a Washington grad who made it big in the Texas oil fields. George was doing okay until Cliff dropped dead of a heart attack. Wilson then lost his job and returned to San Francisco where booze got the better of him and he ultimately died.

Despite the loss at Pasadena, Bagshaw had one of his most successful seasons with his 1925 team. Because of the attention it focused on the Queen City, the Seattle Chamber of Commerce decided to honor him by giving him a new Buick. His support wasn't unanimous, however. Some older alumni – headed by Bill Horsley, an advertising executive and former yell leader at the University – had begun to chip away at Baggy and, as Torchy remembered, the coach always responded in a manner which wouldn't win him any public relations prizes. He was especially touchy as far as Horsley was concerned.

When the day came for the presentation of the automobile, Torchy accompanied Baggy to the new Chamber headquarters at Third and Columbia where a sell-out crowd was waiting to pay tribute to the coach of back-to-back Rose Bowl teams.

As we went up in the elevator to the luncheon, Baggy was cautioned not to get into any arguments but to accept the car with great appreciation, to say he would learn to drive and that he would cherish the thoughtfulness for the rest of his life.

Baggy promised that he would, but as we went in the door, we bumped into Bill Horsley who didn't acknowledge the coach at all. The snub – or whatever it was – infuriated Baggy so much that when it was time for him to get up and accept the gift, he started in on a tirade against the alumni who opposed him and just about wrecked the meeting. It was especially difficult for those of us who were close to him.

Baggy lasted four more seasons. He had three good years and developed another All-American, halfback Chuck Carroll in 1928, but after a disastrous 2-6-1 in 1929, he was asked to resign.

That just about killed Baggy. Before it happened, we got him an offer to coach at Idaho where he would have been a real asset, but he wouldn't take it and he decided to fight it out.

What ensued came to be known as the Battle of Bagshaw. Dr. Alfred Strauss, one of the University's most ardent supporters who sent numerous good athletes to Washington from the Chicago area, came out and argued in Baggy's behalf, but to no avail. In the end he accepted the inevitable, and Governor Roland H. Hartley appointed him state supervisor of transportation on March 24, 1930. Though he was originally educated as a civil engineer, the job was not at all to his liking, and less than seven months later – on October 3 – he died of a heart attack in Olympia. He was 46.

George Wilson, in Torchy's opinion, was probably the greatest individual all-around player in Washington football history, and he watched him on and off the field throughout his collegiate career.

George worked on weekends for Marky Lease who had a wholesale clothing business in downtown Seattle and was sort of an unofficial assistant coach for Baggy, sitting on the bench during home games and traveling with the team on the road. In the summer George went to Alaska where he earned good money with the fishing fleet.

In his senior year he came back from Alaska with a very bad social disease, and every now and then when he was playing, he would have to drop out of the game for a minute or two while he threw up under the grandstand. That didn't seem to affect his performance, however, and about the only time he wasn't on the field—either on offense or defense—was when he was momentarily sick.

Walter Camp, who was a star player for Yale before the turn of the century, had been selecting All-American teams since 1897. Mostly he favored players from eastern schools or the Big Ten, but in 1924 he had heard so much about George Wilson that he decided to take the long train ride to Seattle to see for himself.

Well, the only game he could make was against the College of Puget Sound in Tacoma. It was played in the Stadium Bowl behind Stadium High School where you sat on the cold concrete looking down at the players in sort of a pit.

On the day of the game the fog was so heavy that you could hardly see the field. You could hear the whistle, of course, and once in a while somebody would come out of the fog. Wilson had quite a day, making four or five touchdowns, I think, as the Huskies won 96-0. Camp only saw one score, but he was impressed enough with George's physical appearance and reputation that he included him on his 1924 second team. (That incidentally was Camp's last team because he died in 1925 and was succeeded by Grantland Rice, who named Wilson on his 1925 Collier's All-American first eleven.)

For Torchy there was an unfavorable epilogue to the story of Camp's visit.

On the way back to the Tacoma Hotel where we were to meet Dr. Henry Suzzallo, the University president, and other officials, Walter said he'd really like a shot of scotch. It was prohibition and we didn't have any liquor, but I called Phil Weyerhaueser out at American Lake to see if he had some. "Yes," he said. "Come on out and I'll give you a quart of Johnny Walker Red Label."

It took me twenty minutes or so to go out to American Lake and back, and I got to the hotel just in time to ride up the elevator with the official party. The last person to get in was Doctor Suzzallo, and when I tried to shove somebody a little bit to give him room, I dropped the bottle of scotch and it broke.

Everybody was very upset, of course, because Doctor Suzzallo was very much against liquor in the first place and certainly didn't want it around the athletic program. I think Walter Camp felt it worse than anybody because he really wanted a drink—but we had to settle for soda pop and near beer while we had a bullfest for an hour or so.

Seattle Mayor Hugh Caldwell (left) and Dr. Henry Suzzallo, the president of the University of Washington, participated in the ground-breaking ceremonies for the new football stadium on May 17, 1920. Several years later Torchy was twice a victim of circumstances which led to command appearances in the president's office. (Special Collections Division, University of Washington Libraries)

On the way out Doctor Suzzallo said: "Torchy, I'd like to have you stop in at my office on Monday morning." I had a pretty good idea what was coming; and, Walter Camp or not, he let me know that he didn't want to see me pull another stunt like that.

Unfortunately that wasn't Torchy's last run-in with the University president whom he considered one of the smartest men he ever knew. He was involved in an initiation party for Kappa Beta Phi, the reverse of Phi Beta Kappa and sort of a maverick organization where fun was more important than good grades.

We decided to have the initiation at the Butler Hotel, and William "Wee" Coyle, who had been captain of the 1911 football team, and I went down to mix the punch in the afternoon. Wee did most of the mixing of the pineapple juice and straight alcohol, and he tested it enough so that by the time the boys arrived, he was pretty jolly.

About half way through the affair the punch began to have its effect and some of the youngsters got a little obstreperous and noisy. Unbeknown to us, the hotel management called the University to have somebody come and pick up the unruly students. Well, the word got to Doctor Suzzallo and he sent taxi cabs out to bring everybody back to the campus.

Two days later I got another summons to the office, and this time he really gave me a going over! He informed me that under no circumstances would such a thing happen again, and he gave orders to disband Kappa Beta Phi at Washington. And that's what we did.

Torchy thrived on his job as assistant graduate manager. He was a good promoter, and he loved the institution he worked for. As a person who steered pretty clear of liquor himself (his father's early warning, no doubt), the two incidents with Doctor Suzzallo were quite out of character for him. He wasn't above a practical joke now and then, though.

When Dorsett V. "Tubby" Graves drove over from Montana to check on a coaching job he had been offered, I was the only one in the office. Dar Meisnest, who did the hiring as graduate manager, was gone on a fishing trip, so I ended up signing Tubby to a two-year contract (which, by the way, was to stretch out to almost four decades.)

When he joined us, he was told to park his car on a parking strip in front of Hec Edmundson's house. Well, I had some traffic tickets which I got from the police department to use as an occasional joke, and one day I put one on Tubby's windshield, checking off a number of things he'd done illegally, adding up to about a twenty-dollar fine.

I called the chief of police, William B. Severyns, who went along with the gag and gave Tubby a good lecture when he came in to pay up. The chief finally agreed to tear up the ticket, but he didn't tell him it was a joke. I had signed the ticket "Officer I. M. Keen"—which was a little obvious—and eventually Tubby figured out that somebody was playing a trick on him and the trail led to me. He was not too happy about it at first, but we managed to become good friends in spite of my shenanigans—and he waited a long time to get even.

It came when my freshman baseball team was playing his varsity and they were leading 2-1 in the eighth inning. However, we had a man on third base with one out and I was thinking about a squeeze play to tie the score. Tubby's catcher, Gene "Beaner" Walby, had a potato in his pocket which looked a lot like a baseball, and on the next pitch he caught the ball while he tossed the potato out behind him.

We all thought it was a passed ball, so my man came running home from third only to be tagged out. The varsity won, but the potato play caused a rhubarb which almost ended in a fight. I guess I deserved it, though.

Before Ruth and Torchy were married, he visited her at the Inkster ranch near Gardner, Montana. The trip included numerous flat tires. During his stay he assisted with ranch chores and lived in a military-type tent with a wooden floor. That was comfortable enough until one of Ruth's bottle lambs got inside, sprayed the place considerably in its fright and left a disagreeable odor which Torchy was never able to scrub out. (Special Collections Division, University of Washington Libraries)

In addition to his athletic responsibilities, Torchy was deeply involved in other A.S.U.W. activities. He helped promote campus concerts by such renowned artists as soprano Amelita Galli-Curci and contralto Ernestine Schumann-Heink, as well as appearances by the then popular dance team of Ruth St. Dennis and Ted Shawn. He also had a big hand in the success of a giant outdoor religious pageant titled "The Wayfarer." Among other assignments, he participated in the recruitment of the 2,000 singers in the chorus which was a major task in itself. The musical

Torchy and Ruth Doris Inkster were married on March 15, 1924. They had met at a dance during their high school days in Spokane. Ruth attended the University of Washington for a time but eventually received her degree from Washington State with a major in mathematics. Her three children remembered her as an excellent cook with a great sense of humor, but mostly that "she was always there" to provide the stabilizing force for a hyper-active husband and father. She was a good swimmer and diver, but didn't particularly enjoy golf which she played only occasionally. As their daughter Shirley recalled: "Mother and dad were wonderful dancers; they knew all the steps." (Shirly Torrance Lincoln collection)

spectacular played to an audience of eighteen thousand or more for seven nights, raising considerable money to pay off stadium indebtedness. It ran for two years in the new stadium.

———————

On March 15, 1924, Torchy Torrance and Ruth Doris Inkster were married at the home of her parents in Spokane.

Ruth was the daughter of James and Laura Inkster. Her father, a jaunty little Scotsman, was in the real estate business after moving to Spokane from Davenport. For a time he operated a fountain lunch establishment called "The Palms" which he eventually traded for a ranch in Montana.

After their chance meeting at a dance hall, Torchy and Ruth dated periodically, both at Lewis and Clark High School and at the University of Washington which she attended for a time. Later she transferred to Washington State College where she earned her degree with a major in mathematics.

Fortunately, Ruth knew Torchy well enough to recognize his restless spirit which seemingly compelled him to be involved in many things. She accepted the challenge of a husband on the go, realizing that she, too, would have to keep pace.

Shirley, their first child, was born on September 8, 1925, six days after her father's 26th birthday. Less than four months later, Ruth bundled her up in a basket for the long trip to southern California. After all, the Washington Huskies were playing Alabama in the Rose Bowl. There was no question about it: life with Torchy might never lead to great riches, but it certainly wouldn't be dull!

———————

With a new family to consider, he had to give some thought to the direction his career was taking. Granted, he had what he considered an ideal situation. He was doing what he enjoyed and getting paid for it, but as the assistant graduate manager, he faced a limited future in the shadow of Dar Meisnest who gave every indication of being a permanent fixture at the University.

It was a difficult decision to make, but when Foster and Kleiser, an outdoor advertising company, offered him a job as lease manager, he accepted. He knew he'd miss the day-to-day excitement of the work at the University—and especially in the athletic department—but, he had to face it, there were other ways to stay involved with his alma mater while he tried his hand in the world of business.

The Torrances' first home was at 25th Northeast 60th Street in Seattle. Pictured were daughter Shirley and son Bill shortly after Torchy left the University and went to work for Foster and Kleiser, an outdoor advertising company. (Special Collections Division, University of Washington Libraries)

Chapter 5

Disappointment, Depression
and New Horizons

Torchy's decision to join Foster and Kleiser was based on his assumption that there was little chance of succeeding Dar Meisnest as graduate manager. Then, after Torchy had left his University job, Dar suddenly resigned to take a position with Pacific Coast Coal Company.

In the meantime, there was a major shakeup on the campus. When the state legislature overrode Governor Hartley's veto of the 1926 appropriations bill, the angry chief executive placed much of the blame on President Suzzallo and the alumni pressure groups he had organized to restore funding for the University. The governor attacked Suzzallo for his intellectualism, his extravagance and – inappropriately – for his place of birth. (It wasn't Italy, as Hartley inferred, but San Jose, California. Instead, it was the governor who was foreign-born, having come originally from Canada.)

As it turned out, Hartley stacked the University board of regents with members loyal to him, and when Suzzallo refused to resign, he was summarily dismissed. There was an immediate reaction, and demands were made for the governor's recall. Torchy remembered attending one of the protest rallies, but Hartley survived the storm, and M. Lyle Spencer, former director of the University's School of Journalism, was named president.

With the vacancy in the graduate manager's position, Torchy just took it for granted that he'd get a call to return to the University as Meisnest's successor. After all, he had the experience, and he was already well known in the areas where it counted. It didn't happen, however, and he was sadly disappointed when he was never contacted and the announcement was made that

Earl F. Campbell, manager of the University bookstore, had been appointed.

It was some time later that he met Doctor Spencer on the street, and the president said: "I'm sure sorry that you didn't want the graduate manager's job, Torch, because we thought you would be a natural. Dar told us you weren't interested, so we didn't bother to call you."

This revelation added to his disappointment, but there was nothing to do but swallow the bitter pill and go on with his work for Foster and Kleiser. Typical of him, he adjusted quickly and, in time, became an effective salesman of outdoor boards. He did so well, in fact, that Jerry O'Neill, the general manager, recommended him for a better job in the firm's main office in San Francisco, which Torchy turned down.

Not only was he making a satisfactory wage in the advertising business, but he continued to supplement his income on the baseball diamond, making as much as a hundred dollars a game on the weekends.

At various times in his career Torchy played against the traveling Boston Bloomer Girls, the bearded House of David nine and the all-black Kansas City Monarchs, featuring the incomparable Satchel Paige. "I managed a foul tip and laid down a bunt in four trips to the plate against him," Torchy recalled.

Then, when Babe Ruth and Bob Meusel of the New York Yankees were barnstorming across the country appearing in exhibition games against each other with teams supplemented by local players, Torchy had the fun of playing second base next to the Babe on first. He also could include among his unusual experiences the fact that he had to get Ruth out of bed on game day after the Babe had celebrated too much the night before. It was after that—in the late 1920s—that Torchy finally hung up his spikes for good.

One of his fellow employees at Foster and Kleiser was William Culliton with whom Torchy was to develop a lifelong friendship. Financially their relationship started off with the promise of great fortune, but then disaster struck.

Bill, his wife Helen and I started what we called the Triad Investment Company with just a few dollars in 1926. You could buy stock then on margin for ten percent down, and gradually we built up our holdings until we had an equity of some $115,000. It seemed all too simple, and our goal was to make a couple hundred *thousand apiece and then get out of the market. We were so confident we thought President Hoover might even call us for advice.*

In the fall of 1929 the three of us decided to go deer hunting in Canada. Ruth wasn't much interested in that sort of thing, so she stayed home with our children, Shirley and young Bill who had been born on March 18, 1928. On the way we stopped for a game of golf at the Shaughnessy course in Vancouver. We happened to pair up with a couple of stock brokers from New York who were also going hunting. We played with them while Helen walked along, and as we did, they told us that they were concerned about the jittery market and had sold all their stock.

That made us a little nervous, so as soon as we got back to the hotel, we called Charlie Adams, our broker, and the people at Pacific National Bank to tell them what we had heard. They assured us that we had good, solid stocks and that everything would by okay. With that, we went on up beyond Ford's Landing where there wasn't any communication with the outside world.

When we finally got back to Ford's Landing, we checked by phone and telegraph and learned that our stocks had dropped clear off the board. We had lost all the money we had made, plus $15,000 we had borrowed from the bank.

We weren't a very happy threesome as we headed for the border at Blaine. We got there at about two a.m., and the guards wouldn't let us go through with the deer on top of our car until eight in the morning. So we dumped the deer and hurried on to Seattle so we would be there as early as possible to try to salvage some of our holdings, but it was no use.

Very shortly Electric Power and Light began to show some signs of rebounding, so we tried to get the bank to lend us enough to buy about 5,000 shares, but they turned us down. Well, that stock went from three to 117 before it stopped and we could have recovered some of our losses. Instead, all we had was the fifteen thousand dollar debt, and it took me until 1939 to pay off my share.

In calling on advertising agencies and other potential buyers of space on outdoor boards, Torchy invariably would run into William H. Seifert, a salesman for a competing firm. On one occasion, while they were waiting their turns to see a buyer at Puget Sound Power & Light Company, they struck up a conversation.

Bill said, "Why don't we get into some business together instead of battling each other for outdoor advertising accounts?" I agreed that that would be fine, but what did he have in mind?

He then went on to say that he had a friend in the printing business who was ready to get out and that we could probably work out a deal to get into it for a reasonable amount. He was talking about E. L. Reber and the Western Printing Company. Associated with Reber was James A. Wood, associate editor of The Seattle Times, *and together they owned the Wood and Reber Advertising Agency. It was a good arrangement because whatever printing accounts the agency got, Western could do the work.*

It sounded very intriguing, and in 1931 we worked out a deal for me to get into the firm along with Bill. I would get a nominal salary, and for the investment of my time for five years, I would eventually get a one-third interest. I had set type for my brother at American Falls so I figured I knew a little something about printing. But after getting into it, I discovered I didn't know a thing, and to tell you the truth, I never did learn too much. My job was selling, and that I did fairly well.

What Bill and I didn't know at the time was that Western Printing owed about $75,000 and its total income for the previous year had been $78,000. That obviously didn't present a very happy picture.

The two of us went down to Peoples Bank to see Joshua Green, the president. We talked over the situation with him and he agreed to pay off our indebtedness and to give us a single note which we could pay off on a long-term basis. It was quite an undertaking, but we signed on the dotted line so that we could start out with more or less of a clean slate.

––––––––

About that same time I got involved in a brief gold mining venture. Laura Money Wardell, who helped us publish a racing paper called the Green Sheet, *told me about a claim her parents had on the Little Salmon River in Idaho. I went over to see it with my son Bill who was then about eight years old. The undeveloped mine was about five miles off the dirt road between Boise and Atlanta, and we had to go the last mile by pack horse because there was just a narrow trail with a mountain on one side and about a 500-foot drop-off on the other. We had big work horses with broad backs, so Bill's legs were spraddled wide as he held on for dear life.*

At the mine we learned that the Moneys needed power to operate a jackhammer to go deeper into the claim where they hoped to find gold. If they struck it rich, I was to get a share for providing the equipment. We thought the chances were pretty good because the St. Joe Lead Company had done fairly well with their claims around Atlanta.

Back in Seattle I went to the Washington Machinery Works on 4th Avenue South and bought a 2-kilowatt generator for something like $400, which was a lot of money in the 1930s. Shipping the generator to the mine was no easy matter because after it went as far as it could by truck, it had to be hauled in the rest of the way on the back of a horse. Unfortunately the 2K was in operation for only about two weeks when a defect developed and it soon became obvious that the equipment wasn't any good.

I thought I had friends at the Washington Machinery Company, but when I went back, they told me I had seen the generator and should have known what I was buying. It was one time I really got stuck badly. Besides that, it turned out that the claim didn't have enough gold to work profitably, so I missed another chance at riches.

Torchy and his partner fared better in the printing business. Not only did their company survive the economic woes of the Great Depression, but by 1938 Torchy and Bill were able to buy out Reber's share. That included Western Printing Company and the Wood and Reber Advertising Agency. Meanwhile, Torchy had other irons in the fire.

Having sold lemonade on the streets of Spokane and Indian souvenirs to railroad passengers at American Falls, it was only logical that he would eventually get into the concession business. Even in his role as assistant graduate manager at the University, he occasionally found himself selling peanuts or doing other odd jobs for Jim Boldt, the concessionaire at the stadium. But it took a strange set of circumstances to give him his first opportunity to become involved on his own in a sideline which thereafter would be a continuing source of income for him.

The Seattle Civic Auditorium was being built downtown during the administration of Bertha K. Landes, the city's mayor from 1926 to 1928. The grand opening was a fancy affair, with the women showing up in formals and furs and the men in their best bibs-and-tuckers.

Well, the committee had planned well, except for one thing. The entertainment was outstanding and the dance music fine, but the coat checking had been turned over to people with absolutely no experience. They gave out checks for hats, coats and umbrellas, but they forgot to leave a duplicate with the various items. The crowd was so big that all the borrowed racks were quickly filled, and good coats and hats ended up being piled on the floor.

When the party was over and the owners came to claim their belongings, it turned into a real disaster. People pushed their way into the check room, throwing coats all over the place trying to find what belonged to them. After a couple of hours, most of the guests got what they came with—but some didn't. The city was sued for lost furs and other items, but although just about everything was eventually returned, the bad feelings lingered on.

Earlier Torchy had been one of the candidates for the auditorium manager's job. After three days of interviews and a written presentation of the applicant's ideas on how to run the building for profit, he was number one of the final three which included Jerry Emerson and Wee Coyle, his Kappa Beta Phi buddy of the ill-fated punch-mixing experience. Because Coyle really wanted the job, Torchy and Emerson decided to withdraw in his favor, and the ex-Sun Dodger quarterback was appointed to the position which he held for almost three decades.

Torchy had known the mayor for a long time at the University where her husband was dean of the College of Sciences and once an interim president. She herself was a woman of boundless energy and deserves a place in history as the first of her sex to hold the top job in any major American city. She was extremely unhappy over the auditorium coat-checking fiasco, so she called Torchy and Wee Coyle into her office.

Mrs. Landes said, "I don't care what you do, but get that checking situation in hand so we'll never have another problem like that!" After our meeting I called Mike and Jane DePalma, who had worked in concessions with me at the University, and together we figured out a way to handle it.

Nothing was ever said about paying rent, a percentage or anything else because we had quite an investment in racks to handle crowds of up to five thousand people. This went on quite successfully for about seven years. Then, when I was away at a Rainiers' training camp, a big story broke on the front page of the Post-Intelligencer *saying that Torrance had been robbing the city of thousands of dollars over the past several years through concessions given to him by ex-mayor Landes.*

It was a disturbing situation for me, and I came home immediately. I sat down with the city council and the newspaper people and explained how the arrangement came about, and a few days later the P I printed a few lines of retraction, but of course nobody read that.

To make everybody happy, I worked out a ten per cent rental fee based on gross income, and the city picked up three or four hundred dollars a year. At the time the fee for checking was fifteen cents, but after paying Mike, Jane, the checkers and other expenses for a limited number of major events, I certainly wasn't getting rich on the deal.

In looking for ways to develop continuing printing business, Torchy got involved with Joe Gottstein during the building of the Longacres race track. Gottstein – like Marky Lease – had been one of Coach Bagshaw's unofficial "assistant coaches" – so Torchy was well acquainted with him. In 1932 he had gone with Joe

It was because of Seattle's lady mayor, Bertha K. Landes, that Torchy got into the concession business. A dynamic woman and the first of her sex to head a major American city, she was so upset over a coat-checking fiasco at the then-new Civic Auditorium that she called him in to straighten out the mess. She served only one term – from 1926 to 1928 – but she was active in civic affairs for more than a decade.

71

and Hugh Todd to meet with John Nelson, the farmer from whom the land was purchased. Special arrangements had to be made so that the farmer's cows wouldn't interfere with customers at the race track.

The Fiftieth Anniversary program of Longacres noted:

> In a remarkable 28 days the old Nelson farm, a 106-acre parcel just south of Seattle, was transformed into the state's largest racing facility. Renowned theatre architect B. Marcus Priteca, whose credits included Seattle's Paramount and Coliseum Theatres, was enlisted to design the grandstand and original clubhouse. Over 3,000 laborers were put to work to erect the complex and carve the mile long racing oval out of the rich bed of alluvial soil. On the backstretch 37 barns went up to house the 500-some horses that moved in for the first season.

During that time I worked closely with Joe, handling the ticket sales, advertising and parking. I received no salary, but I did get the printing of the various forms necessary to start pari-mutuel betting. I also printed the program and had a verbal agreement with Joe that I would have that particular concession as long as he had an interest in the race track.

Torchy's involvement with Longacres was complicated when Dr. Mark Matthews of the Presbyterian Church asked him to print petition forms and set up an organization to collect signatures in opposition to a state racing act.

I told the reverend that I'd be glad to do that, but, for myself, I couldn't work against the legislation because I felt the industry would be good for the state in the long run. The petitions were distributed around the state in good fashion, but the people didn't seem to be too enthusiastic about signing. Consequently, the legislature passed the act authorizing a racing season, and the race track opened for the first time on August 3, 1933.

During those early years the Green River used to flood quite regularly and the whole Kent area south of the railroad tracks running through Renton would be under several feet of water. Reverend Matthews, who was chairman of the Red Cross, appointed me to head the disaster relief program, and there were times we had to use rowboats to evacuate the residents. I even remember horse barns floating down the river.

As might be expected, Torchy also got involved in politics, not as a candidate but as a manager or member of various campaign committees. Like his namesake – Senator Roscoe Conkling – he became an avowed Republican, straying only rarely from the fold when an individual Democrat appealed to him.

He came out on the short end of the vote in two senatorial campaigns he managed.

Senator Wesley L. Jones ran for a fifth term in 1932 against Homer T. Bone. The senator was 70 years old at the time and not in the best of health. The day before the election we took him to Radio Station KJR in Seattle for an important presentation and he fell asleep before the broadcast. I had to wake him up so he could go on the air, and instead of making a good speech, he talked for about two minutes and that was all. We lost the election by 360,000 votes and Senator Jones died not long afterwards.

In 1934 Torchy worked for Reno Odlin, a Tacoma banker who had been both state and national commander of the American Legion. After a vigorous campaign Odlin lost by a narrow margin to Democrat Lewis B. Schwellenbach who had been president of the University of Washington Alumni Association in 1928-29.

In those days campaigns were always fun, and usually they helped me in business because I'd get most of the political printing. However, we didn't always get paid for what we did.

In the Wesley Jones campaign we ended up with a $28,000 deficit – which was a lot of money then. When I called Harry Jones, the senator's son, to ask for a little help, he said: "Well, Torrance, that was your doing, not mine. You'll just have to find a way to pay the bills."

That was kind of a jolt, and if it hadn't been for the help of Mark and Bill Reed, it would have taken me a long time to get everything paid off.

As for Reno Odlin, he was an impressive speaker, had a good military record and was an outstanding citizen of the state, but bankers didn't have a very good reputation in the early thirties after the crash. The Democrats had all the promises going for them, plus the help of President Franklin Roosevelt, so we lost that one, too, getting beat in every county but Chelan.

Finding time and energy to promote a race track, fight political battles, organize flood rescues, hunt for gold and pay off Western Printing's indebtedness was at least a time-and-a-half job for anyone, but somehow Torchy still managed to maintain an active interest in Husky football fortunes. For instance, in the late 1920s, as first president of the University Lions Club, he talked the members into signing a note to pay the college expenses of Thurle Thornton, a graduate of West Seattle High School.

He was the outstanding athlete in Seattle at the time and the University coaches wanted him very badly. The Lions Club agreed to the loan, with the understanding that some day Thurle would pay it back. He played during Baggy's final three years and we were happy with the way he conducted himself; but when he graduated, he went into the wrestling business, injured his back and spent the rest of his life in a wheelchair.

When he wasn't able to pay off the note, the bank carried it for four or five years until finally each member of the Lions Club had to divvy up twenty dollars to pay it off. I wasn't very popular with the organization for a while, but eventually most everybody considered it a small price to pay for helping a fine young man. Years later Thurle's son Jerry attended the University and was a good baseball player, so we got a belated bonus for our investment.

When James M. Phelan came from Purdue to replace Coach Bagshaw in 1930, Torchy was a member of the delegation which met him when he flew in at the Sand Point Naval Air Station. Phelan coached the Huskies for twelve years and compiled a record of 65 wins, 37 losses and eight ties.

Jimmy was a good coach, but he hit the bottle a little too hard. Probably his best year was in 1936 when his team won the Pacific Coast Conference and a trip to the Rose Bowl. At that time the host team selected the opponent, and most everybody wanted Jimmy to pick Louisiana State which had an outstanding record. However, Phelan had some kind of a grudge against Jock Sutherland, then coaching at Pittsburgh, so he invited the Panthers.

74

Before the game we had a big rally at the Biltmore Hotel in Los Angeles, and it was my pleasure to introduce two players from each team. Jimmy Cain and Byron Haynes were there for the Huskies, and when the Pitt representatives showed up, they were so much bigger than our boys that people just broke out laughing at the difference in size. I remember that one of the opponents was the All-American Marshall Goldberg.

The Torrances' second son, John (right), was born on October 1, 1936, in the middle of the Great Depression. It was a scrambling time for Torchy, with a printing business to pay for and a developing involvement in Seattle baseball. Ruth and Shirley were photographed with him and John in a post-World War II picture.

75

As it turned out, we didn't have a chance against them. They outplayed us in every respect and won 28-7. Jimmy was a little embarrassed, of course, because he really thought he was going to teach Jock Sutherland a lesson.

Ray Eckmann, who was captain of Baggy's 1921 team, replaced Earl Campbell as athletic director, which was a new title for the old graduate manager job. He didn't like Jimmy's drinking, and the board of regents finally agreed with him after the 1941 season and Phelan's contract wasn't renewed.

———

On October 1, 1936, John R. Torrance, Ruth and Torchy's second son, was born. Despite his busy schedule, Torchy still found time to take his family on Sunday drives in their Lincoln Zephyr (which had University of Washington colors for interior upholstery) and for an occasional skating party at the Civic Ice Arena. When he could, he joined them at the cottage he rented each summer on Puget Sound near the Fauntleroy ferry pier. "It was the closest he ever came to taking a vacation in those days," his daughter Shirley recalled.

Because he couldn't get it out of his system, he also took them to lots of baseball games (they had a box behind third base at Sicks' Stadium)—but that subject deserves a chapter of its own.

Chapter 6

Hooked on Baseball

Torchy simply couldn't stay away from a baseball park.

When he was a youngster in grade school, he retrieved foul balls to gain admission to the games and then hovered around the home team bench so much that Manager Bob Brown finally made him the bat boy for the Spokane Indians.

Wherever he went, his trail almost invariably led to a baseball diamond. When he finally quit playing regularly in the late 1920s, he turned his attention to the Seattle Indians, first at the old Dugdale Park and then at Civic Field which sportswriter Emmett Watson described as "a magnificent old sieve-like place . . . with a rattly tin fence, topped by barbed wire, with leaky entries that made it easy to climb over or wriggle through."

The Indians dated back to 1903 when the Pacific Coast League was formed as an outgrowth of the old California League. From 1907 to 1918 the Seattle team withdrew to play in the Northwestern League, then returned to the PCL where it was a struggling franchise in the mid-1930s. The club had been sold by Douglas E. Dugdale to William Klepper and John Savage who owned it for several years before they, too, decided to sell. Torchy, who was hooked on the game, had a nagging urge to get into management of a professional baseball organization and this looked like a good opportunity. He promptly got involved in looking for a prospective buyer who would be interested in his services in the front office.

On several occasions I talked to Paul and Bill Pigott of the Pacific Car & Foundry Company about getting into the baseball business. They were interested but the timing wasn't right for them.

Dave Beck, the founder of the Teamsters Union, had been offered a chance to take over the Indians, but he also turned the deal down. Meanwhile, Emil Sick, the head of Sicks' Brewery, went to a brewers' meeting in New York where Jake Rupert, who owned the Yankees, suggested that it would be a good asset for the beer business for him to buy the ball team in Seattle. Dave Beck also told him it would be a good idea.

When he returned home, he called a meeting and I was one of those he invited. He said he was ready to buy the Indians if he could get the club for a reasonable price. I was made executive vice-president and we worked out an arrangement to buy the franchise for $75,000, plus an additional $25,000 to be split between Klepper and Savage.

Well, several things happened.

After we closed the deal, we began to get wires from the baseball commissioner's office, the Pullman and railroad companies and from leagues around the country, all with bills against the Seattle ball club. You couldn't operate a franchise then until all indebtedness was cleared up, so instead of paying $75,000, it ended up something like $131,000.

The "new" Seattle Rainiers needed a better park to play in than Civic Field, so Torchy was soon involved in negotiations to build a stadium. The old Dugdale stands, erected in 1916, had burned down on July 4, 1932, and were never rebuilt, but after various sites were considered, it was decided that the location at Rainier Avenue between McClellan and Bayview Streets was the most suitable.

I finally acquired most of the land where the ball park was to be built. It included an adjoining vegetable garden on the north owned by Joe Desimone and Pre Vacca. Then we discovered that George Vandeveer, the attorney for Klepper and Savage, had sold a 90-foot piece for a Shell station on the corner where we had planned our entrance. Next we learned that Desimone and Vacca had held out about an eighteen-inch strip along Rainier Avenue which blocked much of the access to our parking area. (For several years we had to pay twenty dollars a month for an easement until we finally bought the narrow piece for something like three or four thousand dollars.)

Our next problem came when Emil Sick brought a contractor down from Canada to build the stadium. He knew nothing about baseball, but we told him we wanted two-thirds grandstand and one-third bleachers. We ended up half and half which really cut into our potential revenue. It was a nice park, though, but it was far too limited for major league considerations.

While that was going on, we also had to look for a manager. The Yankee organization recommended Jack Lelivelt who had managed their Los Angeles club. We hired him and he was a good one. His big problem was that he kept everything bottled up inside and would get terribly upset over a bad play or whenever the team lost.

Jack and his wife Ethel would go to supper with Ruth and me after almost every game and we'd go over all the reasons why we either won or lost. He was all baseball. Nothing else counted: no golf, no fishing, no nothing, just baseball.

We had some exceptionally fine ball players in and around Seattle in those days, and one of my jobs was to get them under contract. First to be considered was Edo Vanni, who besides being an excellent baseball prospect was also a good soccer player and football field goal kicker.

When I went to see Edo, I learned that Dutch Reuther, the manager of the Indians before we bought them, had advanced Edo $500 to sign. Dutch then wanted a thousand dollars to release him, but he finally settled for just what he'd paid and I was able to sign the young man. The bad part of it was that they almost ostracized me at the University where they wanted Edo as a place-kicker.

That was one of the few times in his life that Torchy didn't give his alma mater first consideration as far as athletes were concerned, but in his new baseball role he had his sights on making a pennant winner out of the Rainiers. Sicks' Stadium was opened to a sell-out crowd on April 15, 1938, with Torchy the master of ceremonies for the program. The date signalled a new era for Seattle baseball.

At that time Seattle's Franklin High School was a baseball hotbed. The center of attraction was a young pitcher named Frederick Charles Hutchinson. Torchy signed him for a $2,500 bonus, plus a clause in his contract which guaranteed Freddie twenty per cent of the sale price if he were sold to a major league club. (The latter was a feature of the old bonus rule which permitted minor league clubs to develop young ball players and get some return for the investment when they were sold to the majors.)

Freddie Hutchinson was a fireballing young pitcher for Seattle's Franklin High School when Torchy signed him for the Rainiers. In 1938 as a teenager he won 25 games while losing seven in the Pacific Coast League. It is an exciting part of Seattle sports history that on his 19th birthday he won his 19th game before an overflow crowd of 17,000. After a successful career with the Detroit Tigers, he returned to Seattle as manager of the Rainiers. (Dr. and Mrs. William B. Hutchinson collection)

The rule helped keep an independent franchise like ours alive. Without it no young player would think of signing with the Rainiers if he could sign directly with a major league club. I think it was the ruination of minor league baseball when the big owners went after the clause and finally eliminated it. I used to argue for reinstatement of the rule at every meeting until I was blue in the face. But men like Branch Rickey and Warren Giles had more power than I did and I would always lose by a vote or two.

Getting back to Freddie Hutchinson, the stone-faced youngster was exactly what the Rainiers needed. In 1938 as an 18-year-old he won 25 games while losing seven. The highlight of the season came on August 12 — his 19th birthday — when he won his 19th victory before an overflow crowd of 17,000.

Hutchinson, who came to be known as The Iceman, was too good to hold on a minor league team, so Torchy made a deal to sell him to Walter O. Briggs, Sr., of the Detroit Tigers for $50,000 cash, plus five ball players worth another $50,000. When it came time to complete the transaction, Emil Sick, B. N. Hutchinson and Bill Mulligan, the Rainiers' business manager, joined Torchy in a suite on the thirteenth floor of the Waldorf Astoria in New York.

I explained to Emil that Walter Briggs would call us at eight o'clock and we would go across the street and meet him at the Lexington Hotel. Well, eight o'clock came and there was no call. An hour went by and Emil was getting pretty upset, so at nine I called Mr. Briggs and he said he was sorry but that time had just slipped away and that we should come right over.

Mr. Briggs, who sat there in a wheelchair with a blanket over his lap, was very busy so he merely reiterated the deal and said we could go ahead and announce it in Seattle. With that we shook hands with him and his associates — Jack Zellers, the Tigers' general manager, and Del Baker, the field boss — and left.

As soon as we got out the door, Emil said: "We didn't get anything in writing. They can change their minds any time they want to. How can we announce it when it's not official?"

I explained to him that baseball was a lot like the stock market where people bought and sold with a wave of the hand. Similarly, when you shook hands with somebody like Mr. Briggs, you had a deal.

I called Seattle and made the announcement to the press, but Emil was nervous for two weeks before the paperwork and the check came through from the office of Kenesaw Landis, the baseball commissioner.

Emil was happy then, and he put his arm around my shoulder and said: "We couldn't do any of these things without your experience and know-how."

That's when I made a big mistake by replying: "And, Mr. Sick, I couldn't do it without your financial support." Well, from then on he figured that money was the whole thing, no matter what happened to the ball club. All the while he was in it, he never really understood the baseball business, but he was a great guy!

Two months after the Hutchinson deal, Torchy and Jack Lelivelt were summoned to the commissioner's office in Chicago where they learned that one of the five players included in the package didn't really belong to Detroit and therefore couldn't be delivered. When he heard about it, Walter Briggs promptly wrote out a check for $7,500 to make up for the loss and everybody was happy.

For the Rainiers the one important acquisition was Joyner Clifford "Jo Jo" White who was winding up his career after seven years with the Tigers. He reported to Seattle rather reluctantly after Torchy appealed to his wife. Once with the ball club Jo Jo performed lethargically in his first few games until Torchy gave him a pep talk. After that he became the sparkplug of the team that won three straight pennants in 1939, 1940 and 1941. He later managed the club.

Emil Sick made it possible for Torchy to stay involved in baseball after his playing days when he purchased the old Seattle Indians and needed someone to handle the details of management for him. Torchy was named executive vice-president of the club, a position he held for almost two decades. He considered the brewer a grand gentleman, but Emil occasionally complicated his work because he knew little about the game. (Rainier Brewing Company)

Tony Piet, one of the five players in the Hutchinson deal, decided not to come to Seattle. His full name was Anthony Francis Pietruszka, and he was a real good second baseman who had spent eight years in the majors. We could have used him, but he had an auto parts business in Chicago and didn't want to leave it. He also thought there were nothing but Indians in the Far West.

We invited him out to a game a year later, and it turned out to be a great one. There were sixteen thousand screaming fans in the stands as we beat Los Angeles 3-2, and Tony admitted that he had made a mistake in not joining the Rainiers. However, he felt he had layed out of the game too long to get back in shape for our league. Instead, we got Al Niemiec on waivers from San Diego after he had seen major league service with the Athletics and the Red Sox.

Another example of Emil's lack of knowledge of the game happened in 1939 when we were playing Hollywood. The pitcher for the Stars on the opening day of the series was Harvey Bittner. He was in great form and eventually beat us 3-2, but about the seventh inning I got a call over the loudspeaker to come to Mr. Sick's box. When I got there, he told me that Bittner was the kind of pitcher he wanted me to get for his ball club. I agreed that he would be an asset for any team, although I knew that the chances of getting him away from the Pirate organization were practically impossible.

Well, on Saturday night Harvey was on the mound again, only this time the Rainers shelled him out of there with about a four-run barrage. I was sitting next to Emil as Harvey was being taken out of the game, so I leaned over to him and said: "See that fellow going to the bench. I just bought him for you like you wanted me to." Of course, Emil insisted it wasn't the same pitcher—and the truth of the matter is that I didn't buy him because he wasn't for sale.

Another ball player whom Torchy was pleased to sign was Clifford Earl Torgeson, later to be known as "The Second Earl of Snohomish."

Earl was an all-around athlete at Snohomish High School and I had somebody watching him for several years. When he graduated, he came to me and said he didn't want a bonus to sign, he just wanted to prove himself as a ball player.

Well, I had been waiting to give him a chance for some time, so I sent him over to Wenatchee in the Western International League where Earl Jenner was the manager. The younger Earl wore big horn-rimmed glasses at a time when nobody in baseball wore specs.

Jenner called me and said: "Why did you send that kid over? He wears glasses!"

He was afraid Earl might lose an eye, but I assured him that everything would be all right. Sure enough, I think it was the first time up in his first game that Earl topped the ball, it hit the plate, bounced up and broke his glasses. He called me right away and I got his prescription and had another pair made and sent to him.

He sat out two or three games, and then Jenner put him back in the lineup and all he did was win the pennant for Wenatchee.

Torgeson was brought back to Seattle for the end of the PCL season and replaced Earl Averill in the Rainiers' lineup. Both Earls had been born in Snohomish 22 years apart. Averill was Torgeson's idol when he was growing up, so to take over for him was a young man's dream come true, but also a rather emotional experience. Torchy had played with Averill on the Bloedel Donovan Lumber Company team of Bellingham and remembered that he sometimes out-hit him then.

After Earl had played more than a dozen years in the major leagues with the Cleveland Indians, the Detroit Tigers and the Boston Braves, Torchy bought him for the Rainiers for $4,000 and presumably his last baseball hurrah. In his first game he blasted a line drive all the way to the centerfield fence and it looked like he'd be a real asset. Unfortunately, that was about the only time he really hit the ball, and he finally came to Torchy and said: "I guess I've had it. You'd better put one of the young fellows in for me."

Averill later was inducted into the Baseball Hall of Fame, and Torgeson's turn to make it big was to be delayed until after World War II.

In 1940 Jack Lelivelt won 112 games and lost only 66 as the Rainiers won their second straight pennant. Then one night as he and Torchy were driving home from a Harlem Globetrotters basketball game, Jack had a heart attack in the car and died after Torchy took him to Maynard Hospital. The Rainiers needed a new manager, and the choice was William F. "Bill" Skiff, head of the Yankees' scouting department. Torchy and B. N. Hutchinson, who handled the publicity for the team, thought they had worked out a deal with the Seattle sports editors—Royal Brougham of the *Post-Intelligencer*, Alex Schultz of *The Times* and Cliff Harrison of the *Star*—to break the story on Skiff's appointment in their late Saturday and Sunday editions. That way it would be fair to them all.

On Friday Torchy had a golf game with Eddie Peabody, the famous clowning banjo player. That night he and Ruth attended Eddie's opening at the 5th Avenue Theater. After the performance they were invited backstage, and when they finally left the theater, there on the newsstand was the morning *P-I* announcing that Skiff was the new manager. For whatever reason, Brougham had broken the story. The next day Torchy received a phone call from an angry Carl E. Brazier, city editor of *The Times*, who made the bristling pronouncement: "Torrance, your name will never appear in our paper again! We thought we were being double-crossed. Now we're sure of it."

Brazier couldn't make his threat stick for the long haul, of course, because through the years Torchy and his multiple activities were too newsworthy to be ignored, but for a long time he was shunned by the afternoon daily—and it wasn't really his fault!

For his "part-time" work with the Rainiers Torchy received $250 a month, but he also got the program printing business. Emil offered him the stadium concessions, but he turned it down because he didn't want to be accused of siphoning a big money-maker away from the club.

In a way, baseball gave him a much needed and much enjoyed change-of-pace from his other responsibilities. Occasionally he would suit up and shag fly balls with the team at practice, and the spring training sessions in El Centro and later Palm Springs provided a working vacation for him.

He was proud of the part he played in the successes of the young ball players he signed—but there were also a few who got away.

I wanted to offer a bonus to Earl Johnson, a fine left-handed pitcher who had been born in Redmond, but Emil and his board of directors thought I was spending too much money at the time. Joshua Green suppported me, but I was turned down. Earl then

85

went to the Boston Red Sox and had a successful major league career for eight years. His brother Chet, another lefty, had a brief try-out with the St. Louis Browns and later pitched for the Rainiers. He was a real crowd-pleaser with his crazy windups and contortions on the mound.

Always on the lookout for prospective young ball players in the area, Torchy especially had his eye on John Geoffrey "Jeff" Heath, a native of Fort William, Ontario.

Before Emil Sick bought the Indians, I got a call from Earl Mann, general manager of the Atlanta Braves, then a Triple A team. He was taking an all-star baseball team to Japan to play college teams just as we had done back in 1921. He needed help in filling out his roster and he wondered if I knew of any young outfielders I might recommend.

Jeff was playing ball in Yakima at the time, and when I asked him about a possible trip to Japan, he was real excited. In the back of my mind I figured that I might have something to do with the Seattle ball club when he got back, and he was my number

One of the many players Torchy signed to baseball contracts was Emmett Watson, a catcher from the Franklin High School team which included Freddie Hutchinson and Dewey Soriano. Watson's professional career was brief, but he claimed a lifetime batting average of .500: a pop fly single in two times at the plate. Later he became a popular columnist for the Seattle Post-Intelligencer *and* The Seattle Times. *(Special Collections Division, University of Washington Libraries)*

one prospect at that time.

Jeff did himself proud on the tour, and—to my loss and his gain—he signed with the Cleveland Indians before we had the Rainiers. I was happy for him and he did a terrific job for fourteen years in the majors.

Jeff eventually came back to Seattle where he continued an active interest in baseball, helping with Little League or doing anything else you asked him to do. He was probably the champion hot dog eater of the Pacific Northwest; at least he got that title from Keith Jackson, who was then beginning his broadcasting career at KOMO-TV and Radio. Jeff passed away in Seattle on December 9, 1975; he was 60 years old.

Along with Freddie Hutchinson of the successful Franklin High School team, Torchy signed Dewey Soriano, a fire-balling young pitcher. Roy Hamey, of the Pittsburgh Pirates, was in the stands one night when Dewey pitched an extra fine game. Hamey asked if he was for sale, and Torchy said, "Yes, for $40,000." The Pirates bought him, but he never pitched in the majors. He was sent back to Yakima where he began his career as a manager. Eventually he returned to the Queen City as general manager of the Rainiers—but more on that later.

On that same high school team was Emmett Watson, later a widely read columnist for both *The Seattle Times* and the *Post-Intelligencer* after he cut his journalistic teeth on the old *Seattle Star*. In his book, *Digressions of a Native Son,* he wrote of his own brief fling in professional baseball:

> The Rainiers called me in the summer of 1942. They got a catcher hurt and would I consider signing a contract? I was delirious. Torchy Torrance, long a dynamic figure in Seattle's civic affairs, was then a vice-president of the Rainiers. He called me into a back room beyond the showers in the main clubhouse. "We'd like to take you on the next road trip with us," he said. "You'll be gone three weeks. Can you make it?" A rookie can usually make it when they lay out an invitation like that. "We'll give you $250 a month," he said. "Sign here." I went out of there thinking, "This man's crazy! He's giving me a fortune to play ball."

Watson was released when the injured catcher returned. He

got another chance in a Rainier uniform in the early season of 1943. By then Torchy was gone, also in uniform, but in the gray-greens of a U.S. Marine.

Bad eye and all, 42-year-old Torchy volunteered for active duty in the Marines and opted out of a cushy job in Washington, D.C., for overseas service in a combat zone. He was twice the age of most of the "kids" he served with in the 3rd Marine Division, including Sgt. Van D. Bell, Jr., an Asiatic Fleet boxing champion. (Seattle Post-Intelligencer)

Chapter 7

Semper Fidelis!

On December 7, 1941, Ruth and Torchy were on a train on their way back to Seattle from a baseball meeting in Pensacola, Florida, with Earl and Mary Sheely when word came that the Japanese had bombed Pearl Harbor.

The train stopped for about twenty minutes in Atlanta, and during that time Torchy went to the Western Union office where he sent a wire to the Marine Corps in Washington, D.C., saying that he would be available if needed. He had been in the Marine Corps Reserves from 1926 to 1936, but because of the press of business, he wasn't able to attend the annual training camps and was forced to drop out.

At 42, married and with three children — not to mention his bad eye — he no doubt could have avoided military service, but that wasn't his nature. "I may have lost my left eye," he said, "but you only needed the right one to shoot." Shortly after their return to Seattle he received a telegram ordering him to report to the Marine Barracks at the Bremerton Naval Yard within ten days. Clearing up the loose ends of his various activities was no simple task, but he did what he could and then ferried across the Sound on the appointed day.

I was greeted by a Marine gunner named Tom Woody, one of the best men the Corps ever had. The first morning I reported, he said: "The troops are going out on a twelve-mile hike. Do you want to go with them, or would you rather take your time and break in gradually?"

I said, "No, I'd like to go with them," so he gave me the route of march and I went. Of course I wasn't used to that sort of thing, but I wasn't going to let on to the kids that I wasn't in shape.

The last two or three miles were something awful, but we finally made it back. I got in the bathtub and the skin came off both of my feet where I wore blisters. It was two or three days before I could do anything around the barracks.

From Bremerton I was assigned as sort of an aide-de-camp to Rear Admiral Charles S. Freeman, commandant of the 13th Naval District, with offices in the Exchange Building. He thought he was doing me a great favor by having me there where I could be at home and still look after some of my business affairs, but I didn't go into the Marine Corps to do duty around Seattle.

It was not exactly combat action, but it was a tough assignment nevertheless when Admiral Freeman sent him to Whidbey Island on a special mission. The Navy had selected Whidbey for a base and Torchy's job was to inform property owners that their land was being condemned for military purposes. It was a difficult public relations mission involving some people he knew very personally; but although a certain amount of unhappiness resulted, Torchy salved the wounds as best he could. His stay at Whidbey on the property detail and as officer in charge of the Marine detachment there was not all serious, however.

I became quite good friends with Admiral Ralph Wood who was commander of both the Sand Point and Whidbey bases. Even though he was an admiral and I was then a first lieutenant, there wasn't much difference in our ages.

We took over a house and made it our bachelor officers' quarters— a BOQ as they called it in the service—and six of us were billeted there. We had trouble finding a cook, but it happened that Mary Pearson, who worked for the Austin Company which was building the base, was handy in the kitchen and came over about once a week to fix us a good meal. She became a good friend of all of us, and one day—to pay her back a little—Admiral Wood suggested that we take her over to the Hope Island Resort for dinner.

I thought that was a splendid idea, so we commandeered a Navy crash boat, which was really a Gar Wood speed boat capable of doing about 45 miles an hour, and started for Stanwood. We planned to leave the boat there and get a car to drive over to the restaurant.

Everything was going fine until we entered the Stanwood harbor and hit a sandbar where the Army Engineers had been dredging. We got stuck, of course. Well, the admiral was all dressed up in his fancy uniform and I was in the best bib-and-tucker of a Marine lieutenant, so there was nothing we could do but take off our trousers, get in the water and try to push the boat off the bar. Mary sat in the stern, trying with all her 112 pounds to help us wiggle out of the sand. Unfortunately, there were people on the shore who discovered our plight and were having a picnic watching us struggle to get free.

The tide was about half way up, and it took us about 45 minutes to finally get loose. At Stanwood we put our pants back on and tried to straighten ourselves out as best we could. Then we went on to Hope Island for a very pleasant dinner despite the circumstances.

On the way back the boat didn't function very well and we just had to creep along. Later we discovered that the propeller was badly bent. Of course the admiral couldn't report that we had been on duty when we took Mary to dinner, so we decided to have the boat repaired and divide the cost. It came to something like nine hundred dollars which was a lot of money, but we finally paid it off and tried to forget the whole thing.

The trouble is the whole base heard about the episode and everybody thought it was very funny. All the while I was there we never did live it down.

In a way it reminded me of another incident a few years earlier when several of us went to an American Legion convention in Bellingham on a boat belonging to Harry Lewis who then was the undersheriff of King County. He called the boat Compensation because he bought it with his World War I bonus money. At any rate, on the way back we got off course as the tide was going out and ended up grounded on a sandbar about 500 feet from shore somewhere near the mouth of the Skagit River. We had to spend the night trying to prop up the boat with oars so it wouldn't tip over as the water receded beneath us. We finally got out all right when the tide came in the next morning, but it was a worrisome time for our families who expected us home about nine or ten the previous night, and they had no idea where we were.

———

After about three months at Oak Harbor where I was promoted to captain, I talked Admiral Freeman into getting me assigned to troop duty at Camp Elliott near San Diego. From there I was sent *to Green's Farm about twenty-five miles up in the hills for a refresher course as a Marine officer.*

I got along pretty well until one night we went out on maneuvers and the jeep simulating a tank I was riding in hit a big hole. I went up in the air and landed hard. It really wrecked my back and I stayed in bed a couple days without much relief. Finally the commanding officer let me go to the San Diego Athletic Club to take a few massages which helped.

About that time I was assigned to the 3rd Marine Division, soon to be shipped out to the South Pacific. I was to be the assistant athletic and morale officer for the division under Major Ernest Gould from New Orleans. When the day of departure came, I boarded the West Point *about noon, settled my gear in very nice quarters and was relaxing alone in the stateroom when an announcement came over the loudspeaker: "Captain Torrance report to the officer of the deck." I did and was told to return to Camp Pendleton prior to being transferred to Washington, D.C., where I'd be assigned to the Marines' Athletic Officers' Department.*

Torchy argued that he wasn't interested in going to Washington, D.C., but later that afternoon the *West Point* left without him. He found out that Dick Hanley, one of five Spokane brothers whom Torchy knew real well, thought he was doing him a big favor by getting him transferred to the Navy's special services department, then headed by Tom Hamilton, later commissioner of the Pacific Coast Conference. It took about two weeks to get the Washington, D.C., orders rescinded, and on February 23, 1943, Torchy eventually boarded the *Bloemfontein*, a converted Dutch motor ship, nicknamed the "Burp."

We had about 4,000 Marine troops aboard along with Brigadier General Allen H. Turnage, the assistant division commander, and we were headed to the South Pacific without any kind of escort. When I boarded, I was assigned to my quarters which turned out to be a cramped cabin with five bunks, about two feet apart from floor to ceiling. I was the first one there, so I thought I'd better wait until the others arrived so we could draw to see who got what bunks.

I set my gear down and went back on deck, and when I returned a half hour later, there were four officers there, and they had already taken the top four bunks, leaving the most uncomfortable one at the bottom for me. All the other captains were about twenty years younger than I was, but they were old enough to teach me a good military lesson. I slept in that lower bunk all the way to Auckland, New Zealand. One of the young captains was Jack Nordholt who became my close friend and took care of me like I was his father.

Torchy was designated troop commander on the ship which arrived at Auckland late in the afternoon on a Friday. Union longshoremen notified him after the gangplank had been lowered that there was only a half hour until quitting time and that there would be no unloading until Monday.

I reported that to General Turnage and he told me to go back and inform the longshoremen that we had to unload now. They refused and I went to the general again. He asked me what my orders were, and I said, "To unload the ship." He replied, "Well, that's what you do then. Take a company of men with fixed bayonets and tell those guys you mean business!"

That's what I did and we took over the pier. We noticed that the equipment was made in Des Moines, Iowa, and we had some kids who knew how to operate the cranes, so they took charge and we were debarked with all our gear by four o'clock the next afternoon.

On Monday General Turnage was notified by the mayor of Auckland that we had created a bad situation and would he please send somebody in to explain why we did what we did. The general told me to go, and I explained to the mayor that we didn't want four thousand troops sitting out in the water where the Japs could fly over and blow them all up in the ship. I told him I was sorry we broke the local rules but that our men were more important to us than the labor unions were to them.

It took a few days for everybody to calm down. Meanwhile, the Marines were disbursed in various camps, and – typical of American troops around the world – the young men were soon making friends with the New Zealanders, especially the young ladies.

Near Manurewa there was a large laundry which employed about 50 girls, mostly teenagers. Our kids discovered that the girls were getting fifty cents an hour on the job at the laundry, so they offered them seventy-five cents to take time off to be with them when they were not on duty. It upset the laundry business, but we finally got that situation worked out.

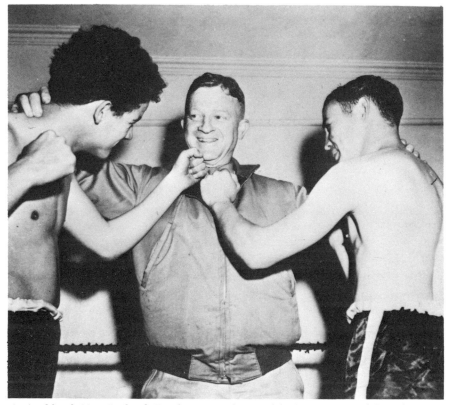

At Auckland, New Zealand, Torchy was in charge of the boxing team of the 3rd Marine Division. As a civilian he had been a member of the Seattle Athletic Commission which supervised boxing and wrestling in the Queen City. Once when he denied wrestling promoter Ted Thigh permission to stage a match unless he called it an exhibition, Thigh said he'd sue and run Torchy out of town. Needless to say, the threat never became a reality. (U. S. Marine Corps photo)

Many young New Zealand men had been sent off to the war in Europe which left a real void for the girls their age. Nancy Williams, who worked in her family's furniture business in Wellington and on a radio talk show, was a key figure in organizing several thousand young women to serve as hostesses in servicemen's clubs. She would bring bus loads of girls to the various camps to entertain the Marines. In his role as morale officer, Torchy became well acquainted with Nancy and they danced together on numerous occasions.

Once we sent a boxing team down to Wellington to compete against 2nd Division fighters. It was sort of a vacation, and on the first night we had a dance in a small ballroom which was just packed with our kids. Nancy was there and we were dancing together when General Barney Vogel sent his aide over to say that the general would like to have the next dance. Nancy replied: "You tell the general to get his own girl. I'm with Torchy tonight." Well, if he hadn't been a pretty good sport, I might have gotten into some real trouble.

Towards the end of the dance the aide came over again to tell us that the general wanted us to meet him at a restaurant down the street and he would buy us a hamburger. When we got there, the chef and the waitresses had all gone home, but the proprietor was still there. General Vogel, a huge man, got behind the counter, put on an apron and fried hamburgers for about fifty of us.

[Years later Lady Nancy Williams Kelly and her husband, Sir Theo Kelly, visited Seattle, and she and Torchy reminisced about their time together in New Zealand. "Torchy was the *best* dancer," she said. "It was fun, but a tragic time as well. You'd meet the young men, see them off, and when their contingents would come back, you'd ask for so-and-so only to find out that he'd been killed.]

I remember a particular incident during the Kellys' visit. One of the things Sir Theo wanted to do was talk to the Nordstrom people about their stores and their merchandising program. I was there when Theo asked Lloyd Nordstrom how many stores he had, and I believe he said 28. Then Lloyd asked Theo the same thing, and he answered: "Oh, about 4,000." The big difference brought a chuckle from all of us. It turned out that in Australia Sir Theo was president of the Woolworth Corporation which controlled department stores, shoe stores, drug stores, gas stations and just about everything else. It seems that Lady Nancy, my old dancing partner, had married very well.

On August 7, 1942, the Marines landed at Guadalcanal as the long road back began in the Pacific. The island was announced secured early in the following February. The 3rd Marine Division was involved in mop-up operations, remaining there until the invasion of Bougainville, the largest of the Solomon Islands, in November.

I didn't get sent up to Bougainville until the second week of the attack. Resistance had been pretty well overcome, and as morale officer, I went out to visit some of the troops on the front line. It almost turned out to be a bad mistake. The snipers were busy and one hit a tree about eight inches away from me. I ended up in a big foxhole with a half dozen other Marines on patrol who let me know it was foolish of me to be wandering around without a guide to show me where to go.

We had some wounded troops who needed extra attention, so our medical officer asked me to accompany the first group in a DC-3 to the mobile hospital on Guadalcanal. The Seabees had laid a steel mat runway over the swamp, working through the night to make it long enough for landing and takeoff. As it happened, I was reassigned to another plane which apparently saved my life. I heard later that the one I was supposed to be on went down and there were no survivors.

I got my kids to Mob 8, and one of the doctors there turned out to be Roger Anderson from Seattle who developed what came to be known as the Anderson splint for broken arms and legs. It was used extensively in the South Pacific.

The 3rd Marine Division was reassembled on Guadalcanal to begin training exercises for its next operation. Torchy organ-

Even on Guadalcanal Torchy didn't lose his interest in stateside athletics. Here he and Sgt. Karl Lipke perused an edition of The Sporting News *which found its way to the 3rd Marine Division's headquarters on the island recaptured from the Japanese. (U. S. Marine Corps photo)*

ized ball games and other recreational activities to help relieve the monotony and anxiety which always accompanied the long periods of waiting for the return to action. As part of his assignment, he was sent back to New Zealand to get sports equipment, sulfa drugs and other supplies needed by the division.

I was about to board the plane on which I was scheduled when a New Zealand army officer asked me if I'd switch to a second one. It was about a fourteen-hour flight to Tontouta on New Caledonia which itself was a stop-over on the long trip to New Zealand. According to the best information I could gather, the first plane apparently had gone down just like the one I had first been assigned to on Bougainville. It was my second lucky break.

On my return stop at Tontouta I traveled the twenty-five miles or so on the most precipitous road you ever saw to the town of Noumea. I had to stay over a day and a half, so I decided to visit the Mob 4 and Mob 5 hospitals which were there. At one of them I ran into Dr. Carl Jensen, an eye specialist and a close friend of mine from Seattle. He was doing an outstanding job of removing shrapnel and otherwise treating eye problems of young men so that they could either be sent home or back to their units.

I also went to see a nurse friend of mine I had known at Oak Harbor, and when I got there, who should be visiting with her but Admiral William F. "Bull" Halsey. In his gruff voice he said: "You young Marines can't take over for us old war horses. You better get on your way because this gal's my friend." When the nurse told him that I was a friend, too, I was invited to sit down with them and we had an enjoyable half-hour bullfest.

Later as we had been flying for about fifteen minutes on the trip back to Guadalcanal, smoke began to rise from beneath the catwalk between two 250-gallon drums holding extra gasoline for long flights over the ocean. We immediately notified the pilot who sent the navigator back to investigate. An electric wire had gotten crossed some way and was causing the smoke. We had to go back to Tontouta to correct the problem, after which we took off again and made it to Guadalcanal without further trouble.

Helping to maintain morale on Guadalcanal were various civilian entertainers for whom Torchy had to make arrangements for their appearances at 3rd Division units.

Ray Milland came out with a couple young ladies and they per-

(Top) Torchy posed with the "kids" who helped him in his duties as athletic and morale officer of the 3rd Marine Division on Guadalcanal. They were (left to right): Cpl. Ronald O. Usher, Sgt. Karl W. Lipke, 1st Lt. Arthur J. Manush and Cpl. Richard V. Anders. (Bottom) Lt. Col. Newton B. Barkley, at left, commanded the division's headquarters battalion to which Torchy was assigned. Other officers pictured were George DeFalco and Jack Nordholt. (U. S. Marine Corps photos)

formed at all of our battalion headquarters. After them came Ray Bolger and Little Jack Little. Jack had a miniature piano which he played while Ray danced, and they did a tremendous job for our boys. Bolger and I both had our bunks in the same tent, and early one morning a bomb dropped about fifteen feet away. Ray jumped off his cot and shouted something like "What in the world am I doing in a place like this?" It didn't affect his dancing, though.

Randolph Scott was another one who spent several days with us along with a two man vaudeville team. The kids really enjoyed them—but not all of our visitors were that entertaining.

Mrs. Eleanor Roosevelt arrived on Guadalcanal with an escort of fighter planes and then came by jeep from Henderson Field to our camp on Tetera Beach. A lot of our kids were bathing in the Tenaru River and were stark naked when the jeep came down the road. We were expecting an important person, but nobody thought it would be a lady. When the boys discovered who it was, they really scrambled for cover.

Mrs. Roosevelt spent a day and a half at the hospital, never leaving the premises because the Japs destroyed a large ammunition dump and there was some real fireworks on the island. She got back in the jeep the next day and that was the extent of her visit to our outfit. I guess she meant well, but she wasn't much of an inspiration to our troops at the time.

After the Bougainville operation, the first group of female nurses arrived at Mob 8 on Guadalcanal. I think there were about twenty-five of them, and they were quite a sight because our kids hadn't seen a girl from home for a long time. I took two or three of them to each battalion for chow where they had a chance to visit with the boys and they really gave them quite a lift.

It was during that period on Guadalcanal that a sequence of events occurred which was to linger in Torchy's memory for the rest of his life. A replacement battalion arrived from the States and with it was Bill Veeck, Jr., a Marine private, who was already prominent in the baseball world.

I had gotten the design for the concession stands at Sicks' Stadium from Bill's dad. I had met Bill at several baseball meetings and I considered us to be fairly good friends. When he arrived on Guadalcanal, he came over to headquarters where I was stationed and we had a good reunion. We even came pretty close to making *some baseball trades.*

Two days later Bill came back and said he would like to be assigned to the 3rd Division because he found out he was being sent to Bougainville as part of a defense battalion while we were going to invade Guam. I told him I was only a lowly captain and probably couldn't do much about it but I'd try. I went over to see Colonel David M. Shoup at Corps headquarters about the possibilities of getting Veeck reassigned. He asked me if I thought he'd make a difference in the landing on Guam, and I told him of course not but that he was an old baseball friend and was anxious to go.

The colonel explained that all of our orders and personnel records had already been processed for the invasion and that there was nothing he could do. Well, the next day he called about noon and said he'd worked it out so that Bill could come with us.

I hurried over to the replacement battalion to tell Bill the news but his unit had already been moved to Cape Esperance at the other

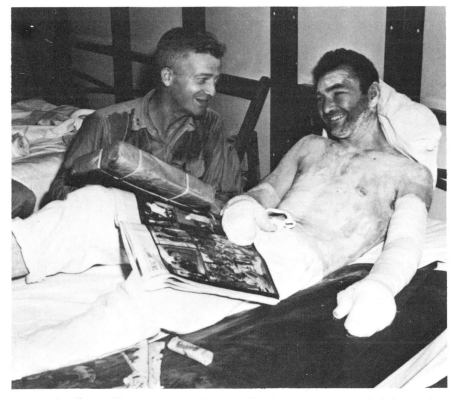

As morale officer of the 3rd Marine Division, Torchy's assignment included visitations to military hospitals to buoy the spirits of the wounded "kids," as he always called the young Marines with whom he served. This photo was taken on Guadalcanal. (U. S. Marine Corps photo)

end of the island. I tried all afternoon to get a communication through to his outfit, but with preparations for our departure and all the activities going on, I was never able to reach him. The next day we shipped out and Bill wasn't with us.

Veeck went on to Bougainville and during the course of his service there he was struck on the leg by the recoil of a 90-millimeter anti-aircraft gun. He spent the next eighteen months in military hospitals and eventually had to have the leg amputated. He became very bitter about his injury and had to blame it on somebody—but I'll tell you more about this unhappy situation later.

———————

Another coincidental thing that happened to me on Guadalcanal took place when I was trying to find Bill Veeck in the replacement battalion. I had gotten onto an impassable road and had to turn my jeep around, when all of a sudden I heard a commotion in the underbrush. I stopped the jeep, pulled out my .45 and out of the jungle stepped a bedraggled American.

He was a pilot and had been shot down over the island. He still had pieces of his parachute with him and had been wandering around two or three days with nothing to eat except the fruit he was able to find in the jungle. Well, he turned out to be Colonel Bob Haynes, the brother of Hanford Haynes, a classmate of mine at the University of Washington. Incidentally, Hanford, a center on the 1921 and 1922 football teams, had been chairman of the committee which gave the name Huskies to the UW athletic teams. I took Bob back to headquarters where we gave him something to eat after which he was flown back to his unit. That was the last I ever saw or heard of him.

———————

The 3rd Marine Division didn't go directly to Guam. American forces were already attacking Saipan, also one of the Marianas, so General Turnage's troops were kept in sort of a floating reserve. Being confined to a ship under the heavy tension of impending combat was hard on the men, so the division was temporarily diverted to Smith Island, one of the Marshall group. Torchy was deeply involved in organizing ball games, races and other diversions to keep the "kids" (as he always called them) active and reasonably relaxed.

While we were on Smith, I took off in an LCM to Kwajalein where I managed to get a thousand cases of Coke, a hundred cases of beer and one quart of scotch. When I got back to our ship, I reported to the officer of the deck and told him I wanted to talk to the general. When I announced to the general what I had, the Navy officer, a commodore, heard the word scotch and he immediately wanted me to bring the bottle to his cabin where he said he'd call in a few of the gang to have a drink. I told him no, the scotch was going to shore with the Coke and each of the Marine officers would at least get a sniff. The commodore was very unhappy, but when he realized he couldn't persuade me—and it was against Navy

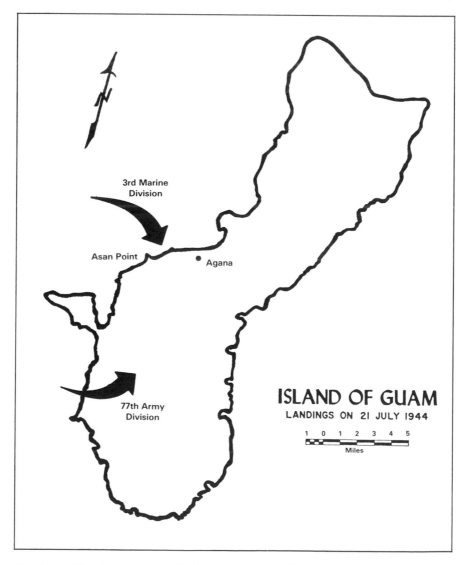

ISLAND OF GUAM

LANDINGS ON 21 JULY 1944

3rd Marine Division

Asan Point

Agana

77th Army Division

Torchy could easily remember the date the invasion of Guam began because it was on his wife's birthday—July 21, 1944. He landed with other members of the 3rd Marine Division just north of Asan Point.

rules to have hard liquor on board—he finally gave up.

Peanut-shaped Guam, the largest of the Marianas Islands, had been a minor U. S. naval station and was captured by the Japanese on December 12, 1941, less than a week after Pearl Harbor. In the summer of 1944 it was held by almost twenty thousand Japanese troops who, with the threat of imminent invasion, had confined most of the Guamanians in concentration camps on starvation rations.

The American forces assigned to the assault were the 3rd Marine Division, the 1st Provisional Marine Brigade under General Lemuel Shepherd, a unit of Corps artillery and the Army's 77th Infantry Division commanded by Major General Andrew D. Bruce. The 77th was well trained but had not yet seen action. Designated as the 3rd Amphibious Corps, the combined forces consisted of some fifty-five thousand men backed up by ships of Rear Admiral Raymond A. Spruance's Central Pacific Fleet.

Beginning on June 11, carrier planes began bombing the island, and two weeks before the invasion Navy warships opened up a barrage which, according to naval records, consisted of 28,764 shells of all sizes from five to sixteen inches. While Navy frogmen worked at clearing the landing beaches, the airmen returned to blanket the thirty-mile-long island with 1,131 tons of explosives. The 3rd Marine Division was to land just north of Asan Point where the Spanish explorer, Ferdinand Magellan, presumably first set foot in 1521.

It was easy for me to remember the day we began the invasion because it was July 21st, my wife's birthday. I wasn't scheduled to go in on the first wave, so as we lowered the landing craft and the kids went down the rope ladders to drop the last few feet into the boats, our information officer told me to get up on the top deck and give a running account of what was happening.

For the next hour and a half I talked about the landing operation and how to hit the beach until it was finally my turn to go. When I went down the rope ladder, the sea was very rough and I tried to drop into the LCVP on the up wave rather than the down. With sixty pounds on my back and not yet totally recovered from my injury back at Camp Green, I landed with a big crash, not knowing if I was going to recover in time to go ashore—but I did.

Because of the coral reef extending about two hundred yards out from the shore, we were transferred from the LCVPs to amphibious tractors which made a good target for the Japanese mortars and depressed anti-aircraft guns. With air support and overhead bombardments from the Navy ships, we gradually worked our way into the interior. One of the things we just couldn't explain to the kids was when one of the big shells would fall short and we'd lose a few of our youngsters, it was because somebody on an assembly back home had done a poor job and the shell was defective.

While we were crawling up the beach, a 60-millimeter shell from a Japanese mortar hit the sand beside me, bounced on my left leg and didn't explode. If it had, it would have been all over for me. Instead, it just caused my leg to swell. It didn't even break the skin, but it bothered me for several years afterwards.

The 3rd Marine Division moved inland with three regiments abreast. The Japanese counterattacked in various sectors with heavy losses to themselves; they did not give up easily. Eventually the Marines tied in with the 77th Army Division on their right flank and the process of clearing the island began. Guamanians freed from the concentration camps took up machetes and begged for rifles so they could join in the pursuit. As a result, not many Japanese stragglers survived to become prisoners.

Leathernecks of the 3rd Marine Division advanced behind a Sherman tank as they fought their way northeastward to clear Guam of the Japanese who had held the island for more than three and a half years. Torchy won the Bronze Star for his actions during the campaign which lasted just three weeks but which cost the U. S. some 7,800 killed or wounded. An estimated 11,000 Japanese died. (U. S. Marine Corps photo)

The army moved slower than we did and a gap developed on our right flank. The Japanese were able to pierce through to our rear echelon occasionally and that kept everybody on the alert.

One day our password was "Illinois." Well, about the middle of the afternoon we discovered that the Japs had broken through and were giving us trouble. One of our mess attendants had been taking food to our boys on the front lines, and when this happened, he came running back through the headquarters area screaming, "Illinois! Illinois! Here I come! Illinois!" He didn't want anybody to mistake who he was.

It wasn't long before we closed the gap, and we took a prisoner. He was bleeding a little so two of our kids took him to the aid tent. He was walking with his hands raised from the elbows up, and then suddenly he pulled a grenade out from his armpit, pulled the pin and blew up the aid tent. We also lost a medic. From then on I don't think we took too many prisoners.

Torchy (who had been promoted to major aboard ship enroute to Guam) was a headquarters officer, but in the Marines that didn't mean you were excused from reconnaisance missions or combat action.

While we were working our way across the island, Lieutenant Colonel Newton B. Barkley called Captain Bill O'Brien and me to his tent. He told us to pick two or three men each and to go out and take a look at our flank to see if we were in any trouble there. Bill's patrol started out a little ahead of mine and as we moved toward our perimeter, snipers opened fire. Captain O'Brien, one of the most popular officers in the division, was killed. We had found the gap in our lines which was closed, but it cost us another good man.

On another occasion, one of our Marines had an appendicitis attack and I had to rush him by jeep about ten miles across the island to a field hospital for an operation. There were Japanese snipers in the area, but the one shot I heard missed me. I made the trip all right, but then I had to come back the same way with lights on because it was dark. That made me mighty nervous, but I got through it okay.

People have often asked me if I was ever scared during my tour of duty. Well, as far as I'm concerned, anybody who was in the South Pacific and says he wasn't scared at one time or another has to be kidding himself. I think we were all that way on every

operation, but we had to do the job, frightened or not. Sometimes,
though, when things got really intense, you momentarily forgot that
you were scared.

The 3rd Amphibious Corps command announced the secur-
ing of the island on August 10. The victory had cost the United
States 7,800 killed or wounded: 6,716 Marines, 839 soldiers and
245 sailors. Something like eleven thousand of the enemy were
killed, with another seventy-five hundred concealed in caves,
ravines and the jungle. Many of them were ferreted out in mop-
up operations, some died of starvation and a few managed to
hide out until after the war was over.

Torchy had his share of close calls, but it wasn't combat
which eventually caught up with him.

On Guam I managed to get both malaria and the dengue fever.
The dengue is called the bone-crusher fever and it makes you feel
like all the bones in your body are broken. I wasn't in very good
shape and ultimately got down to 118 pounds as a result, but I
remained with the division for about three more months while we
were preparing for the invasion of Iwo Jima.

During that time Eddie Peabody, my old golfing and banjo-playing
friend, came to visit me in my tent while I was trying to recover
from the fever. He played a couple of tunes for me and we had
a good bullfest about our first meeting when he opened at the 5th
Avenue Theater in Seattle and the golf games we played on the
Jefferson course when he only used one club, an adjustable thing
which you could change from a putter to a nine iron by turning a screw.

Another interesting thing happened on Guam. We were sitting
in the headquarters tent having a cup of coffee (which I think they
made with one tablespoon of coffee and ten gallons of water) when
I noticed a young Marine coming toward us holding his neck. He
had been hit about a sixteenth of an inch from his jugular vein
and was bleeding pretty badly. I took him to the sick bay where
they patched him up.

Then I asked him his name and he said "Bill Gardner." And
where are you from, I wanted to know, and he answered "Seattle."

"You don't happen to be Ray Gardner's boy, do you?" I asked,
and he said he was. Well, Ray just happened to be our next door
neighbor in Windermere and a close friend—so you can see what
a small world it is.

Later I had him come over to the headquarters tent for a cup of coffee and we visited for a while. Now, in combat, officers don't wear their rank insignia to set them up as a special target for the enemy, so when Bill got up, thanked me and started to leave, he asked: "Who was that nice older man sitting next to you?" "Oh, that's General Turnage, the division commander," I said—and Bill just about fainted.

I wasn't doing too well with the dengue, so they finally shipped me off to the hospital on Kwajalein, then to another one in Honolulu where I stayed about six weeks and after that a third at Balboa Park in San Diego.

Not long after he arrived in San Diego, Torchy was called to Seattle where his father was gravely ill.

I arrived the day before he died. He was suffering from a severe carbuncle infection, but there was a flu epidemic going on so the hospital was full and they had him out in the hall in a draft. I

William Grant Torrance (at left) was born in Milwaukie, Oregon, in 1862. Following his wife's death in 1903, he was left with two other surviving children besides Torchy. They included Jessie Echo (center), an attorney who never married, and Kirby E., Sr. (right) who, like Torchy, was in the printing and publishing business. Kirby was instrumental in getting his younger brother enrolled at the University of Washington and into the Sigma Alpha Epsilon fraternity. (Shirley Torrance Lincoln collection)

107

was very upset about the situation, but there was nothing I could do about it by then. Dad always kept himself in good shape, and I'm sure he would have lived several more years if he hadn't caught pneumonia in the hallway. Although I didn't see him too much through the years, I treasured his counsel and paid attention to what he told me. This was his obituary:

William Grant Torrance, 83, Washington pioneer and father of Major R. C. Torrance, died last night [February 11, 1945] at King County Hospital of pneumonia.

In failing health for three months, he was taken from St. Vincent's Home to the hospital a week ago.

Born in 1862 in Milwaukie, Oregon, he lived with his parents in the first log cabin built on the Palouse River in Whitman County at the point known as Torrance Bridge.

For nineteen years Mr. Torrance, a veteran of Indian wars in the early days here, had lived in Seattle. Prior to that he had been a rancher and stock raiser in Eastern Washington and at American Falls, Idaho. During his residence in Seattle he was a member of the Old Men's Social Club.

Christian Science funeral services will be held at two p.m. Tuesday in the Arthur A. Wright and Son chapel. Interment will be in the family plot at Colfax.

I returned to San Diego and while I was in the hospital at Balboa, something happened that I've always regretted. Bing Crosby and Bob Hope came to entertain the servicemen there, and I was out on the lawn with all the others, only standing way back in the crowd. Bing caught my eye, but when the show was over, the boys all crowded around him and Bob—and before I could get to them, they were gone to another affair. Of course I got to know both of them very well later, but that would have been a good opportunity to renew Spokane memories with Bing and to reminisce about the first time I met Bob at Bing's house in Taluga Park at a New Year's Eve party in 1936.

When I was sufficiently recovered from the fevers and what they called combat fatigue, I was sent home to a temporary military hospital in Seattle where I figured my war service was over.

It didn't work out quite that way!

Chapter 8

Aftermath of War

At the military hospital in Seattle Torchy was in the office of Navy Captain Eugene Kline appearing before a review board prior to being separated from the service. They were trying to determine how much disability they were going to give him, but Torchy said he didn't want any. He just wanted to be discharged so he could save his printing business. That's when the call came.

It was from Emory E. "Swede" Larson, then chief of the Marine Corps Special Services Branch. Larson, a native of Monticello, Minnesota, had been a Walter Camp second team All-American selection at center when he played for the Naval Academy. He later coached the Middies, and one of his claims to fame was that he had never lost to Army, either as a player or a coach. Torchy had met Swede through his acquaintanceship with Coach Bernie Bierman of Minnesota, who was also a Marine.

Swede wanted to know what I was doing, and I told him I was just now getting out of the Marine Corps. "No you're not," he said. "Your orders are in the mail and you're coming to Washington, D.C., to be in charge of Marine Corps athletics around the world." Well, it sounded like something I should do, so I got on a plane and went.

At first I stayed at Dar Meisnest's apartment in the Shoreham. He was a Navy captain and was away on an inspection tour. Then when it began to look like I might be there for a while, I decided to bring my family back. I called Ruth, she gathered the clan and they arrived in June of 1945, one of the hottest summers you could ever imagine. I had rented a house in Chevy Chase by phone, but I neglected to ask if there was air-conditioning. There wasn't.

109

When the family got there, it must have been 110 degrees in the shade with the humidity almost as bad. We just about roasted in that house. In order to get any air at night, we pulled our mattresses out on the front porch—but even that didn't help much.

The war with Germany ended officially at midnight of May 8-9, 1945. Shortly after that, Admiral Ernest J. King, then head of naval operations, called Colonel Larson to his office and told him he wanted to send two officers to Europe to lecture to the troops who might be transferred to the Pacific. Larson told the admiral that he had two men ready to go at a moment's notice: himself and Major Torrance.

My family was tickled to go back to Seattle while Swede and I took off for a most interesting experience. We traveled all over Europe, doing our best to explain the difference in combat between the two theaters.

Very early one morning in Munich we came out of our quarters and ran into General George S. Patton, Jr., and one of his staff officers. The general turned around, saw us and said: "Well, I'll be a son-of-a-bitch, if the Marines aren't over here trying to take credit for this war, too!" We shook hands with the general and talked with him for a while. Then he invited us to visit his command in Bavaria to speak to his men, which we did.

Another interesting incident occurred when we flew into Tempelhof Airport in Berlin. We happened to be in Admiral Harold R. Stark's plane with three stars on it, and when we landed and they opened the door, I was standing by the exit and was the first one out. Actually I had backed out onto the portable stairs, and when I turned around, there was General Lucius Clay and the 82nd Airborne Division standing at attention and ready to present arms.

Swede Larson recognized the general and we went down to meet him. It had all been a big mistake. We visited with General Clay and he invited us to stay until the next plane came in a few minutes later. On it were General Ike Eisenhower and Vyacheslav Molotov, the Russian foreign minister. That's why the 82nd Airborne was there. Not for me! I got to shake hands with General Eisenhower, and he got quite a kick out of it when they told him how I got

(Opposite page) Torchy's family welcomed him back from the Marine Corps in 1946. With him, from left to right, were his wife Ruth, daughter Shirley and sons Bill and John. (Shirley Torrance Lincoln collection)

the first salute.

Torchy and Swede crossed paths with Bob Hope at Frankfort where he was entertaining troops with Hal McIntyre and his band at the Grand Hotel, or what was left of it after the bombing. They didn't get to see all of the show, but afterwards they visited with Bob in a makeshift dining room. From there they went to Nuremberg where the G.I. Olympics were being held. In addition to the big track meet for all American servicemen in the European theater, there was a baseball tournament, too. That attracted Torchy, of course, and he particularly enjoyed seeing pitchers Murray Dickson of the St. Louis Cardinals and Warren Spahn of the Boston Braves.

In his book, *The Last Christmas Show,* Bob Hope recalled:

The G.I. Olympics attracted a lot of *types* to the area. *Type,* that's the French version of the word "character" . . . [They] included Sergeant Jimmy Cannon and

MAJ. EMORY 'SWEDE' LARSON
Just completed a football grand slam.
He has never lost to ARMY-either as a player or coach for NAVY----
a SIX year sweep...

Torchy accompanied Emory "Swede" Larson —then a Marine colonel — on a tour of military units in Europe following the Allied victory there. Their mission was to lecture troops on the differences in warfare between the Pacific and European theaters. (U. S. Marine Corps photo)

112

Private Dave Gordon of *Stars and Stripes;* Corporal Billy Conn, who was a champion for thirteen rounds; Allan Jackson, the INS man (that's a news syndicate, not a branch of the Army); Sergeant Harold Grey; Colonel Swede Larson, ex-Navy football coach, then in the Marines; and Major Torchy Torrance, also of the Marines, who was at the meet with an eye to promoting a similar one in the Pacific theater.

Torchy and Swede were in Nuremberg when the war against Japan came to an end on the deck of the *U.S.S. Missouri* on September 2. For all intents and purposes their work was completed, too.

Swede suggested that we go to Paris to pick up some laundry we'd left there and then spend a few days on the Riviera before returning to the U.S. I told him that if we went to Paris they'd send us right home, but he disagreed and rank has its privileges, so we flew into Orly Field. Sure enough, not long after we landed, an orderly found us and said we had orders to return to the States the following afternoon. We missed our trip to the Riviera!

Just before we left, a bad thing happened. When we were being cleared for departure at Orly, I had the film of all the pictures I took in a separate bag. I had some good shots of General Patton, Warren Spahn, Murray Dickson and others and I told the guard not to X-ray the bag. Well, there was a delay of several hours, and in the meantime the security people changed and the new man ran my film through the X-ray machine and ruined it all. There was nothing I could do. I especially hated to lose my pictures of General Patton who, in my estimation, was a grand soldier. Four months later—on December 21, 1945—he died as a result of a jeep accident before he had a chance to go home.

Torchy remained in Washington, D.C., for several weeks completing the plans for athletic programs for Marines all around the globe. Then he returned to Seattle and was discharged in March of 1946. For his services with the 3rd Marine Division, he was awarded the Bronze Star with Combat "V".

The details of his decoration were revealed in a newspaper column by Alice Frein Johnson, a Washington correspondent and one of Torchy's college classmates:

Torchy, as his hundreds of Seattle friends know, will

talk for hours about the kids in the Marine Corps, especially the Third Division with which he served many months . . . but about himself—not a word. From Captain Raymond Henri, Marine public relations officer . . . I learned about Torchy's work in the Pacific. Said Captain Henri:

"During the invasion of Guam, Major Torrance, with three other officers, volunteered to stand in a patrol boat anchored on the reef to direct the unloading and transfer of supplies and equipment to the beaches. These four officers were under constant mortar fire for four days. None needed to have volunteered. It wasn't their job at all—one was a legal officer, one an interpreter, Torchy, the special services officer, and the fourth had a similar non-combat post.

"Once on the beach everyone was supposed to stay in his foxhole as protection against the Jap mortar fire. Torchy, however, wandered up and down the length of the beach for hours each night, directing medical corpsmen to spots where he had found wounded Marines lying.

"That's why he was awarded the Bronze Star!"

———————

For Torchy there were several residual matters left over from the war. One was quite humorous, thanks to an understanding wife.

At some time after the invasion of Guadalcanal, a small bag containing some of his clothes and other gear was lost. On it was his name and Seattle address, and when it was found by some unknown individual, it was returned to Ruth.

When the bag finally arrived, it was kind of sour because it had been soaking wet and ultimately dried out. Well, when Ruth dumped everything onto the living room floor, out came a box which broke open and a gross of condoms was scattered on the rug. It was terribly embarrassing obviously because there were one or two neighbors on hand at the time. My wife couldn't explain what the condoms were doing there, and I was a very unpopular guy when the story got around the neighborhood.

When I eventually got home, Ruth told me that she thought something might happen out in the Pacific, but she didn't expect me to take on all the natives in the area. It wasn't very funny, of course, until I had a chance to explain.

What we did was use the condoms for carrying supplies of aspirin, atabrine tablets and other items we wanted to keep dry. As the morale officer, I had picked up a quantity of the things to give to the other officers for our next landing—and that's when my bag was lost. Ruth understood, but I'm not sure the neighbors did.

A second incident could have had serious repercussions of another type for Torchy. Several months after his discharge, he received a letter from the Marine Corps asking him to explain the shortage of some two hundred thousand dollars in division recreation funds from Guadalcanal.

Early one morning Colonel Lacey Murrow—brother of the pioneer television newscaster, Edward R. Murrow—came to see me, a punk captain, on Guadalcanal. I was very flattered, of course. While he was there, I asked him if he'd take the 3rd Division money we'd accumulated back to the States along with a big order for athletic equipment and other recreational supplies for the troops.

(Incidentally, Lacey Murrow was the state engineer when they built the first floating bridge across Lake Washington.)

Lacey took the money to Fort Mason in San Francisco and turned it over to Major Earle Milliken and Colonel Malcolm Douglas there. They bought what we ordered and shipped it out, but they didn't include bills of lading, purchase orders, receipts or any other documents, all of which were filed at Fort Mason.

It was a nervous time for me, but I finally got in touch with Earle and he went to San Francisco and found the envelope containing all the papers to substantiate the purchases and shipping. I think Earle said there was about eighty five cents left over from the two hundred thousand dollars.

At any rate, the papers were sent on to the Marine Corps, and about two months later I received a nice letter of commendation from General Gates, the Corps commandant; and the situation ended happily.

The same couldn't be said about Torchy's relationship with Bill Veeck and the incident previously mentioned. When Torchy attended his first baseball meeting after the war, one of the major league owners reproved him for "the awful thing you did to Bill in the Pacific." The word had gotten around that somehow it was Torchy's fault that Veeck had lost his leg by going to Bougainville and not to Guam. He could have lost his life and

not just his leg in the invasion as so many others had done, but Veeck apparently didn't figure that.

It was a most unhappy situation for Torchy as he had to explain to everybody who had heard Veeck's version and not the other side of the story. He tried every way he could to get together with Veeck and tell him what he had tried to do on Guadalcanal – that he had finally arranged for Bill's transfer and then – couldn't get the message through to him.

Torchy thought he had a good chance to straighten things out when the St. Louis Browns manager came to Seattle for a meeting of the Puget Sound Sportswriters and 'Casters at the Olympic Hotel. He went to Veeck at the head table and told him he wanted to speak to him, and Bill waved him off and said very brusquely, "Later!" After the affair Torchy followed him out of the ballroom, but Veeck refused to talk to him.

That's the way the affair ended. Veeck died on January 2, 1986, without ever absolving Torchy of the blame which wasn't his at all!

It left bitter memories.

––––––

Like several million other returning servicemen and women, Torchy went to work to pick up the pieces of his disrupted life. In his case it was a multi-faceted task. There was his family, of course. Then came the responsibilities of Western Printing Company, the Seattle Rainiers and all the "extra-curricular" activities which his ebullient nature seemed to demand.

The printing business, which was the principal source of his income, was a major consideration.

While I was still in Europe, I got a wire from my partner, Bill Seifert, telling me that I had been gone so long that my half of the business wasn't worth very much and that I had better come home to protect what interest I had left. That upset me a great deal, and even though I probably could have done more for the Marine Corps when I returned to Washington, D.C., I finally went

(Opposite page) Torchy had to renew acquaintances with his growing sons – Bill (left) and John – following his return after more than four years in the Marines. (Special Collections Division, University of Washington Libraries)

to my commanding officer and explained my problem. After that I got my release in 1946.

I was truly disappointed in my partner. Apparently he and his wife were planning to take over the company without me, and the situation ultimately came down to which of us would buy the other out.

In the end Torchy bought Seifert's share for $50,000. It was a heavy financial burden coming so soon after four and a half years of military service, but, in a way, he had very little choice. The printing company was really his base of operations, while the concession business and his baseball work were supplemental to it, at least as far as revenue was concerned. However, it was quite obvious that he needed help to carry the load, so he sold a half-interest to George S. Douglas.

Gradually the printing volume picked up with Torchy back on the sales trail. In the summer the baseball program was a continuing account, but the Longacres program was a casualty of his war-time absence.

Because of my early involvement in the track, Joe Gottstein and I had a verbal agreement that the program would be mine as long as he had anything to do with it. Well, one day when I was already in the Marines, I got a call from Morrie Alhadeff, Joe's son-in-law who was well known in Seattle as Jerry Morris, a radio announcer.

He said: "Since you won't be able to handle the program for the track, I'm going to take it over." I told him that I had made arrangements so there would be no interruptions while I was in the service. He said something about blood being thicker than water, and with that I lost my job. I couldn't get it back after the war

Home base for Torchy's multiple activities was the Western Printing Company. Herb Mead, one of his young prodigies who worked for him at the plant, recalled that Torchy spent endless hours on charitable projects, often at the expense of his own business. (Special Collections Division, University of Washington Libraries)

either, and since I didn't have a written contract with Joe, there was nothing I could do.

The Wood and Reber Publishing Company subsidiary continued to operate. During the late 1930s it had published the *Ben Paris Fishing Guide* put out by the well-known Seattle sportsman who also ran a popular downtown establishment which included a restaurant, a barbershop, a sporting goods store and a billiards-and-pool hall.

Ben finally got tired of the guide, so Wood and Reber took it over. It wasn't an easy job because we had to sell enough advertising to pay for the printing and then hope we could move enough books to make a little profit. Later we had to have someone year around, so I hired Gordon Frear, who was quite a baseball player at Whitman College and an avid fisherman. He did a good job for

Torchy was not recruiting basketball players for the University of Washington when gigantic Yan Kruminsh of a touring Russian team came to Seattle in 1959. Instead, he was promoting Six Roads from Abilene, *the book John McCallum wrote with Edgar Eisenhower and which Torchy's company published. Also receiving a copy of the story of the Eisenhower brothers was Nina Eremina, a member of the Russian women's cage team. (*Seattle Post-Intelligencer *photo)*

119

us for several years and then took it over on his own, calling it the Fishing Guide of the Northwest. *When he got sick from injuries suffered in the war, he had to give it up and the book died a natural death.*

In the early days of racing at Longacres, Al Hardy came down from Vancouver to edit the Green Sheet *which we printed at Western until it was succeeded by the* Daily Racing Form. *Ellen McAvoy was the assistant editor. Later she married Severt W. Thurston who became head of Western International Hotels. Ellen herself worked tirelessly for many charitable and civic organizations, including the Seattle Symphony, the Chamber of Commerce, the Variety Club, PONCHO and others.*

We also got out what we called the Seattle Blue Book. *It included a listing of the leading families in the city, and it was considered to be quite an honor to be mentioned in it. Gertrude Mattheson Hazlett edited it for many years. Other editors included Elsie Kelleher, Mary Coyle Osmun, Helen La Doux Jones and Patricia Peabody Whitehead, who later became the fifth wife of Franklin Delano Roosevelt's son, Elliott. The book finally got to be too much trouble to put out, what with questions of civil rights and arguments about who should be in it. It was well received in the community, though, and for years after we quit publishing it, I kept getting calls asking when the next* Blue Book *would be out.*

Wood and Reber published two books by John D. McCallum. One was titled *Scooper* for Paul "Scoop" Conlon, a Hollywood gossip columnist and actors' agent. The book's success depended largely on the promotion Conlon could give it with his connections, but unfortunately he dropped dead of a heart attack the week it was released. The second venture was *Six Roads from Abilene.*

I was playing golf at the Tamarisk Country Club in Palm Springs with several foursomes, and included in the group was Ike Eisenhower whom I hadn't seen since the incident in Berlin with Molotov. After our game he visited with us for a half hour or so. It gave me the idea to publish a book about Ike and his five brothers (a sixth one had died as an infant). Back in Seattle I contacted John McCallum who apparently had been thinking about the same thing. We tested the idea with Vic Hurley, my friend from University days who had written several successful books by that time. He agreed that the project had merit, so we went ahead. The book was really dictated by Edgar Eisenhower and edited by John.

We printed about ten thousand copies and introduced it with a big party at the Tacoma Country Club. Edgar was there to autograph them, and we sold about four hundred copies that night. We had other autograph parties at the leading department stores, and then Edgar was going to get his other brothers—including Ike—to help with the sales.

Well, Edgar died, and then Ike was elected president so he didn't think he should be out promoting a book about the family. John tried hard to get the job done, taking a tour which included New York City. He had arranged for a front-page story in the Herald-Tribune, *and the day it was to appear, there was a sensational murder which took all the space.*

After President Eisenhower died, I met his wife Mamie at the Tennis Club in Palm Springs and asked her if she'd given any thought to helping with the promotion of the book. At first she said yes, but then she changed her mind. Later John and I tried to work out a deal with Doubleday and Company in New York to re-issue the book under that firm's name. They sounded favorable, but when they asked me if we planned to continue in the publishing business, I made a mistake by answering yes. For some crazy reason I guess they thought we were going to give them competition on the West Coast, so they turned us down.

Needless to say, we didn't get rich in our book publishing ventures!

Commercial television became a reality in the early 1950s, and a publishing phenomenon that came with it was the *TV Guide.* Some regional editions were being produced, and it was a lucrative printing job for anyone who was geared up for it. Torchy heard that the magazine company wasn't happy with the work being done in San Francisco, so he and George Bayless, Sr., owner of a Seattle bindery firm, traveled to the Bay Area to see what the printing situation was there.

When we got back, I called John Quinn at TV Guide's *main office in Philadelphia and asked him what kind of equipment we'd need if we wanted to be considered for the job. He told me that the plant which printed the magazine in Washington, D.C., had the equipment he'd recommend.*

I made three trips to Washington. On the last one I went over to Philadelphia where I was ushered into the office of Walter An-

nenberg, the publisher. He wanted me to know that he had checked me out, particularly with our Senator Warren G. Magnuson, and that he felt moving the Guide *to our plant not only would help distribution but would provide a better product.*

He told me that as a member of the TV Guide *family our association would last for years, and if there were any misunderstandings, I could call him and we'd discuss the matter. It would take something more than a ten or fifteen per cent price differential before they'd consider moving the work to another plant, he said.*

With that kind of assurance, I bought a 38x51½-inch Mann Perfector Press. With the other necessary equipment, plus the building I leased to install the press, the investment came to around $150,000, which at that time was almost more money than I could imagine. Jack Sullivan, the TV Guide *manager in Seattle then, was a good friend of mine and was very helpful in getting the job for Western. Everything went along fine for about two years until Jack got into some difficulty with the management. I guess they wanted him to move to another city and he wouldn't go. At any rate, they brought in a new manager named Dave Warmuth.*

I thought we were getting along pretty well, until one day I went down to Bob's Hamburger place for lunch and there I saw Warmuth and Ron Renny of Craftsman Press, a Seattle competitor of ours, in quiet conversation. They didn't see me, and I didn't let them know I was there. Then I went back to my office and called Philadelphia to find out what was going on. Craftsman had installed a big rotary press which was faster and could do more things than mine, but I wasn't too disturbed because Walter Annenberg had told me that I was a member of the family and if there were any questions, we would be able to sit down and work them out. Nothing like that happened.

One day I got a letter from the TV Guide *attorneys in New York telling me that we had been doing a good job but that they were cancelling my contract and moving to another plant. This was quite a shock because I had invested what I considered a small fortune and was still paying off at the bank. I called John Quinn in Philadelphia and he told me that Walter Annenberg had left for Europe and couldn't be reached. Consequently, I couldn't confront him with the verbal understanding I thought we had.*

I went to my attorney, Paul Ashley, and he said I could probably sue and win but that in the long run the costs would be so great that I'd probably be better off letting the contract go and trying to make up for the lost business in some other way. By then my partner was John S. Brinkley who had bought out George Douglas's share, and the two of us began looking for ways to solve the problem.

Metropolitan Press, another big plant in Seattle, was interested in our accounts, so we got together with the owners—Max Wells and George Hanley—to talk about a merger. We finally arranged to combine the two companies as Metropolitan Press and Western, with me as president and Jack going along in a sales capacity.

It was quite a job for the two of us to dismantle the old operation, but we eventually sold the Mann press to a printer in British Columbia and other equipment to various buyers around the country. We got back about a third of our original investment for the TV Guide work, but with the sales arrangement with Metropolitan we didn't come out too badly in the end.

There was an ironic sequel to the story. After about ten years of intense competition between the two large Seattle printing plants, Max Wells and George Hanley decided to sell out to Craftsman and retire from the business. This time Torchy became vice-president of the surviving company which, incidentally, was still printing the *TV Guide.* He was back as a member of "the family" again.

It might have been embarrassing, except that Ron Renny—a very high-class fellow—and I never discussed his meeting with Dave Warmuth or the moving of the Guide away from Western.

Eventually we lost the Guide to a California competitor because the magazine had grown from a small saddle-stitched publication to a bigger perfect-bound book like the Reader's Digest which required different equipment. It would have cost us at least two million dollars to keep the work, and even then they wouldn't have given us a long-term contract.

Another ironic twist of the amalgamation of the Seattle printing plants was that Dick Lea, the principal owner of Craftsman, was one of the people Torchy had to confront when he was notifying residents of Whidbey Island that the Navy was taking over their land.

This is getting well ahead of the story, but Torchy eventually retired from Craftsman, and George Prue—one of the men he brought with him from Met Press-Western—became president. As for the *TV Guide's* game of musical chairs, there was at least one unexpected repercussion.

123

In late 1954 we formed an organization called the Palm Springs Desert Senior Golf Association which had about 300 members from all over the country—including President Gerald R. Ford; Bob Hope; Don Hutson, the great football end; and other prominent businessmen, professionals and retired military officers. We played on the various courses in the area, and often when I was visiting, my son Bill would play with me.

On this particular occasion we were having one of our friendly grudge matches with Bill Edris from Seattle and his wife Marge at the Tamarisk Club. When we finished our game and were having lunch in the clubhouse, Walter Annenberg came over to our table and said: "I have to be careful about who I talk to because everyone wants to play on my golf course now."

He had built a fine layout with nine holes and eighteen tees next to Tamarisk to entertain business people and high public officials. Another reason I think he built it was because we wouldn't let him into the Desert Seniors.

Well anyhow, Bill Edris—who never pulled any punches—stood up and said in a loud voice you could hear all over the club: "Walter, you son-of-a-bitch, after the way you treated Torch, here's four people who don't ever want to play on your golf course!"

Torchy's post-war business activities included a revival of his concession interests. He and Walter Venino, the twin brother of Joe Gottstein's wife Louella, bought out Washington Concessions which was owned by Joe and B. N. Hutchinson and which had the University of Washington stadium contract at the time.

We called our company Universal Concessions and were able to renew the University contract every three years when the business was handled by Harvey Cassill, the athletic director, and the A.S.U.W. When the University took over the operation directly, the work was put out to bid and we were successful a couple times. In 1959 we got mixed up on the letting time and our bid arrived by taxi cab just as the committee was going into session. Ernie Conrad, who was representing the University in the matter, decided that our bid was late and he wouldn't allow it. Consequently, we lost the work to Dick Komen.

There were other concession ventures which occupied a lot

of Torchy's time. One was the Hyak Ski Area in Snoqualmie Pass, named after the small community of Hyak at the east portal of the railway tunnel through the Cascade Mountains.

Bob Block, one of the owners, called me to ask if I would be interested in operating the concessions in their ski resort. Again I arranged with Mike and Jane DePalma to run the business, although I was up at Hyak myself on most of the winter Sundays. We worked hard, but unfortunately the area didn't develop as expected, and we didn't make any money on the deal. Eventually Hyak went into bankruptcy, and I gave my stock—worth about four thousand dollars on paper—to the bankruptcy officials. Incidentally, Bob Block was

Bill Edris, Seattle real estate entrepreneur and man-about-town, popped in and out of Torchy's life as did so many other movers-and-shakers in the Pacific Northwest. Sometimes pugnacious, Edris was known to throw a punch now and then. Torchy witnessed this tendency on more than one occasion—but once, at a roadhouse north of Seattle, he himself was an innocent participant in an Edris embroglio. On a packed dance floor, an equally big fellow kept bumping into Bill and his wife until an argument ensued. The other guy took a swing at Edris, and just then an unidentified fist came out of the crowd and knocked the bully out. Torchy, who was dancing nearby with Helen Culliton, hadn't lifted a finger, but somehow he got credit for getting rid of the obnoxious character and people kept patting him on the back for his heroics. It was really Edris's bodyguard who delivered the blow, but he let Torchy enjoy the honor. (Special Collections Division, University of Washington Libraries)

125

stricken with polio about the same time Shirley was and I was able to get him to Warm Springs, too. Ironically, Robert J., Sr., a prominent Seattle shoe store operator, had been the largest contributor to my March of Dimes campaign even before his son got the disease.

About that same time the Pacific Raceways east of Kent was built and I was invited to handle the concessions there. On this one I had to go it without Walt Venino because Joe Gottstein thought it would be in competition with Longacres. Future prospects were bright with estimates of from ten to twelve thousand spectators coming for the weekend events.

Again Mike and Jane DePalma—two of the most loyal and dedicated people you could ever know—did their usual fine job, but—like Hyak—the expected crowds didn't materialize and sometimes we'd get rained out. It was a good experience and we had a lot of fun—but it was expensive fun as it turned out. One year I think we made about a fifteen hundred dollar profit. Later after the Raceways changed hands and we were no longer involved, the attendance picked up considerably and the new concessionaire did well.

For Torchy, "making a living" was one of the necessary evils of life. He worked hard at his various business enterprises, but amassing a fortune was never one of his top priorities. Service to his community, his University, to various charitable organizations, not to mention scores of individuals who needed help, took so much of his time and talent that his friends often wondered how he could keep so many irons in the fire—and keep them all hot!

Chapter 9

Into Extra Innings

After the war Torchy picked up where he left off with the Seattle Rainiers. During his absence player negotiations were handled primarily by Earl H. Sheely, a nine-year veteran of the major leagues with a .300 lifetime batting average, then the general manager. Bill Seifert, Torchy's partner at Western, took care of the printing needs, and the club fared as well as it could under war-time restrictions.

The ex-Marine was just getting back into the baseball swing of things when a terrible tragedy struck a Rainiers' farm team, the Spokane Indians. On June 24, 1946, a bus carrying the players over Snoqualmie Pass enroute to Bremerton swerved to avoid an automobile in the wrong lane and rolled 300 feet down a rocky embankment. Eventualy eight young men died as the result of the crash. *The Seattle Times* reported that "Roscoe (Torchy) Torrance, vice-president of the Seattle Rainiers, drove to the scene and kept an all-night vigil until the bodies were removed." Earlier, the life of Jack Lohrke, an infielder, was spared when he was sold to the Pittsburgh Pirates organization, and Torchy called to have him leave the bus in Ellensburg so he could join the San Diego Padres. Thereafter he was always known as "Lucky" Lohrke.

Returning servicemen brought renewed vigor to professional baseball, and foremost of the veterans on the Rainiers' roster was Earl Torgeson. Still in his early twenties, he was, in Torchy's estimation, a sure bet for the major leagues if he could overcome the effects of the war.

In Europe Earl was picked up as dead with other members of his artillery unit, but one of the graves registration people noticed some movement and Earl was revived without lasting damage.

After the war when I was touring with Swede Larson, I found out where Earl was stationed and went to see him. I discussed his potential with his commanding officer and how important it would be for him to be sent home in time for spring training. The officer

Torchy signed Earl Torgeson for the Seattle Rainiers out of Snohomish, Washington, High School prior to World War II. After the two of them returned from military service, the Rainiers' executive vice-president sold the ex-G.I. to the Boston Braves for $50,000 and five ball players which helped the Seattle team immeasureably in its post-war rebuilding program. Torgeson spent more than a dozen years in the majors and became known as the "The Second Earl of Snohomish." (Special Collections Division, University of Washington Libraries)

was sympathetic, but after I left, there was a change in command and Earl was detained because of his athletic abilities.

It was summer by the time he got back to the ball club, and he tried to play himself into condition too quickly. In about the second week he was going from first to third on a base hit to right field and he dislocated his left shoulder going into the bag. It was a serious situation, possibly an end to his career.

We had a fine team doctor at the time, but dislocated shoulders weren't his specialty. When I got to the clubhouse, he had Earl lying on the floor and was trying to adjust his shoulder. I told him "for gosh sakes, lay off" until we could get him to somebody who knew what he was doing. We had a big argument, but I finally got a call through to Swedish Hospital and we rushed Earl there where they took care of his shoulder in good shape. He was ready to play again in about ten days.

Both the New York Yankees and the Boston Braves were interested in him at the time, and I was anxious to sell him to the

The stands were full at Sicks' Stadium as the Rainiers met the Sacramento Bees in 1951 when the Seattle team won its first Pacific Coast League pennant after World War II under Rogers Hornsby. Torchy was deeply involved in land acquisition and planning for the facility which replaced the old Dugdale Field. (Special Collections Division, University of Washington Libraries)

major leagues in order to get some good ball players to help our club. Earl had indicated to me that he was interested in becoming a Yankee; and Bill Skiff, our field manager, was from the Yankee organization, so Bill and I went first to see Larry McPhail, the Yankee boss.

He asked me what I wanted for Earl, and I said a hundred thousand dollars. McPhail replied, "You're nuts! I wouldn't pay ten thousand for a player with a bad shoulder who has only had one year with a Triple A club."

I said, "Are you sure you're not interested in him?" And he answered that he wasn't, so I asked if I could use his phone. He told me to go ahead, so I dialed John Quinn in Boston and got him on the line.

With McPhail in ear-shot, I said: "John, remember our conversation about Earl Torgeson?" He replied: "Yes, and my offer still goes — fifty thousand cash and five ball players equivalent to another fifty."

I said: "Okay, he's your ball player. We'll send the papers to the commissioner's office tomorrow." Then I hung up the phone.

McPhail wanted to know what I was doing, and I told him I had just sold Earl to the Braves. He jumped out of his chair and raved: "You son-of-a-bitch, you had no right to sell him out from under me. We wanted him. I just thought your price was crazy!"

He made sort of a swipe like he was going to hit me (I don't think he really would have), but Bill Skiff stepped between us and said: "Listen, Larry, you had your chance, and now if you lay one finger on Torch, you're going to have to deal with me."

That's the way our conversation ended, but it had lasting repercussions for me. Always in the past I was invited to the Yankee press room after the games for food, drinks and good baseball conversation. The next time I went to a Yankee press conference at the Waldorf Astoria, I was told I wasn't welcome and I never visited the Yankee press room again.

The deal with Earl Torgeson went through, and he ultimately spent more than a dozen years in the majors, moving from the Braves to the Philadelphia Phillies, then to the Detroit Tigers and finally to the Chicago White Sox. Two of the players Torchy got for Earl were Tony York and Heinz Becker. Heinz, a big first baseman born in Germany, was skeptical about coming to Seattle, but Torchy told him it was a beautiful city and that

Attendance at baseball meetings was one of Torchy's responsibilities as executive vice-president of the Seattle Rainiers. He was one of the directors of the Pacific Coast League in 1953. Pictured, left to right, were: C. L. Laws, Oakland; Damon Miller, San Francisco; George Morgan, Portland; Bill Starr, San Diego; Clarence "Pants" Rowland, league president; E. J. Mulligan, Sacramento; Vic Collins, Hollywood; Torchy; and Dan Stewart, Los Angeles. (Special Collections Division, University of Washington Libraries)

he'd be happy to be with a team that was leading the league in attendance.

Heinz said the only thing he was worried about was that he'd heard that Seattle had earthquakes and he was scared to death of them. I assured him that he had nothing to worry about, maybe a slight tremor occasionally, but nothing serious.

Well, Heinz came out, and wouldn't you know, right after the season started we had one of the worst quakes we ever had in Seattle. Some of the buildings in the lower end of town were badly damaged, and the tank on top of Frederick and Nelson's burst and water ran down into the streets. Heinz was staying on the top floor of the Roosevelt Hotel and it shook pretty badly. When it was over, Heinz wanted to get out of town and never come back to Seattle again. However, he did finish out the season, but he was an unhappy ball player and finally left at the end of the year.

Developing young ball players and keeping them well for potential sale to the major leagues was one of Torchy's principal jobs in his role as executive vice-president of the Rainiers. He enjoyed following the careers of those he helped to succeed, and he shared the disappointment of those who didn't make it. Sometimes the difference came in freakish ways.

The 1952 Seattle Rainiers finished the season in third place in the Pacific Coast League with a record of 96 wins and 84 losses. General manager Earl Sheely (second row, left) died suddenly and was succeeded by Leo Miller for the 1953 season, the last in which Torchy was influentially involved. Miller lasted only one year and was followed by Dewey Soriano. Torchy's tenure as executive vice-president included pennant winners in 1939, 1940, 1941 and 1951. (Special Collections Division, University of Washington Libraries)

After World War II we had a fine young center fielder named Bill Ramsey who was a good prospect for the majors. Unfortunately, he developed a big bunion on the bottom of one of his feet. By using a lot of tape and padding his shoe, he could play without affecting his speed and base-stealing ability. I told him not to let anybody take the bunion off until we could get some expert advice. He listened to me and finished the season okay.

The following spring he still had the same problem and I told him he'd just have to live with it. Well, one day I came to the ball park and there he was on crutches. "What in the world happened to you?" I asked, and he said our team doctor had removed the bunion.

The doctor told him he would be able to play in about six weeks. The foot healed up all right, but it stayed so tender that Bill could never put his full weight on it and he was ruined for baseball.

Torchy was more successful in heading off some bad advice to Sammy White, the Wenatchee native who was burning up the Pacific Coast League as a hitter for the Rainiers. Before he sold the young catcher to the Boston Red Sox in 1951, Torchy luckily became involved in what might have been a critical moment in Sammy's career.

When the ball team was in town, I used to go out to the ball park and watch hitting practice two or three times a week. Sammy White was a rookie, but he was already hitting .415 and taking over on a pretty regular basis for Rollie Hemsley who was with us after a nineteen-year career in the majors dating back to 1928.

I got there just as Rollie was trying to change Sammy's stance at the plate. He thought Sammy looked awkward and that if he ever made it to the big leagues, the sportswriters would ridicule him for it. I told Rollie that I didn't care if Sammy stood on his head at the plate as long as he could hit .415.

Hemsley meant well, but it just didn't make sense for a batter with a .262 lifetime average to be trying to change the style of someone who was hitting the ball like Sammy was. [Ironically, after eleven years in the major leagues, White also finished his career with a .262 lifetime batting average, the same as Hemsley's.]

During Torchy's tenure with the Rainiers, various managers came and went. Field managers included Jack Lelivelt, Bill Skiff, Jo Jo White, Francis J. "Lefty" O'Doul, Rogers Hornsby, Bill

Rogers Hornsby (standing next to Torchy) relinquished his job as field manager of the Seattle Rainiers to Bill Sweeney (right) after the 1951 pennant-winning season. With them at a baseball meeting in New York was Earl Sheely, the club's general manager. (Special Collections Division, University of Washington Libraries)

Sweeney, Paul Richards and Freddie Hutchinson. The general managers were Bill Mulligan, Earl Sheely, Leo Miller and Dewey Soriano.

Rogers Hornsby was "all baseball"—a great player and a fine manager—and he might have stayed with the Rainiers for several years if it hadn't been for the pressure a couple Seattle sportswriters put on Emil Sick. After winning the pennant in the 1951 season, Rogers told Emil that if he didn't get an offer to manage a major league team, he'd be back. They shook hands on the deal, but during the off-season, with the reporters hounding him, Emil called Rogers while we were at a baseball meeting and insisted that he had to know if Hornsby was returning RIGHT NOW! Rogers reminded Emil of their agreement, but the owner was insistent. Finally Hornsby said: "Okay, if you've got to know right now, I'm NOT coming!" Then he hung up the phone.

As I said before, Emil never did understand baseball, and he'd

134

take advice from the last place he got a haircut. As far as the Rainiers were concerned, he was not supposed to commit himself on anything until we had a chance to talk it over, but it didn't always work that way. After Earl Sheely died on September 16, 1952, I was in New York to see a ball game when I got a call from Emil's wife, Kit. She said: "You'd better get a hold of Emil right away because I think he'd going to do something you won't like."

He was in Los Angeles and I tried to reach him by phone with no luck. In the meantime he had hired Leo Miller to be the Rainiers' new general manager. Leo was a nice fellow and a close friend of Clarence "Pants" Rowland, the league president, but, aside from that, he had no judgment as far as ball players were concerned and I knew he wouldn't do a lick of work. Sure enough, he just sat around all year, drew his pay check and had a good time.

On October 6, 1952, Torchy and Rogers Hornsby were attending the World Series between the Brooklyn Dodgers and the New York Yankees. They were at Ebbetts Field when the announcement came over the public address system: "Will Torchy Torrance please report to the office?"

When he answered the call, he learned that his daughter Shirley had been stricken with polio and was in serious condition.

I immediately went to the airport with Rogers, only to find out that there was no space available for a flight to Seattle. While I

Torchy's long-time involvement with the March of Dimes in Washington State led to a close friendship with Basil O'Connor, head of the National Foundation for Infantile Paralysis. He had a similar relationship with Dr. Jonas Salk, discoverer of the polio vaccine bearing his name. (Special Collections Division, University of Washington Libraries)

135

It was the height of irony when Torchy's daughter Shirley was stricken with polio in 1952 after he had devoted so much time and effort to numerous March of Dimes campaigns. He said a hopeful goodbye to her as she was about to leave for treatment at Warm Springs, Georgia. Stewardess Jean Sweet looked on. (Special Collections Division, University of Washington Libraries)

was discussing my problem with the reservations clerk, a little old lady stepped up to me and said: "I would be happy to have you take my ticket to Chicago."

I didn't know if I could get from Chicago to Seattle, but it was such a beautiful gesture that I accepted her offer and thanked her profusely. *Fortunately I made connections and arrived in Seattle the next morning and went directly to the hospital. Dr. Fred Plum, who was in charge of polio cases, put a mask and a white coat on me and took me to see Shirley. She was resting, but not in good shape with paralysis in both her arms and legs.*

At that time I was state chairman for the March of Dimes campaign and I knew Basil O'Connor, the head of the National Foundation for Infantile Paralysis, quite well. I called him and asked him if it would be possible to get Shirley into the Infantile Paralysis Hospital in Warm Springs, Georgia, and he arranged it for us.

They did wonders for her, but holding up under the tough treatment was not easy. She came through with flying colors, though, and after about a year I went down to get her. For the return trip I had arranged with Billy Patterson, then president of United Airlines and a friend of mine, to provide for a wheelchair and reservations from Chicago to Seattle. Unfortunately we ran into an electrical storm after leaving Atlanta and were delayed about half an hour as we flew around the bad weather.

When we got to the ticket counter in Chicago about ten minutes

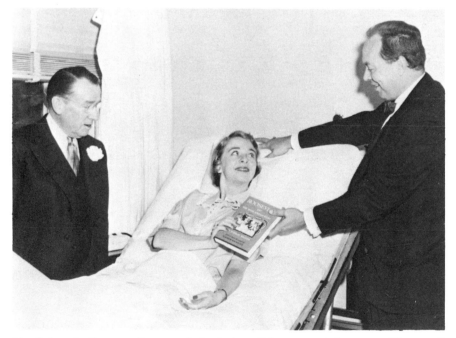

Dr. Robert L. Bennett, director of physical medicine, presented a copy of Roosevelt and the Warm Springs Story *to Torchy's daughter Shirley during her stay at the Georgia polio treatment center. With them was Basil O'Connor, who headed the national March of Dimes organization. (Special Collections Division, University of Washington Libraries)*

Torchy clowned with Seattle mayor Allan Pomeroy at the Rainiers' training camp at Palm Springs. The ball players (left to right) were: Ray Orteig, Nanny Fernandez, Merrill Combs, Don Lundberg and Al Stauffer. (Special Collections Division, University of Washington Libraries)

before loading time, we were told there were no reservations for us. It was too late for me to reach Billy Patterson or anybody else who could help us, so we had to go downtown and stay in a hotel until Shirley was well enough to travel again. Later, when I explained to Billy what had happened, he investigated and eventually fired the reservations clerks who were on duty that night.

I finally got Shirley home okay. After about five or six months she felt she was well enough to take care of her two youngsters with her husband's help. Although she and Jack Swanson were divorced later, I am happy to say that she bounced back well from both the physical and emotional setbacks.

In 1954 Emil Sick also hired another general manager, Dewey Soriano, the son-in-law of Royal Brougham, the *P-I* sports editor. Soriano, whom Torchy had signed out of Franklin High School years before, didn't develop as a pitcher but as a manager at Yakima and Vancouver, British Columbia. As a youngster he had sold peanuts in the stands during the time of the old Seattle Indians, so it was a real homecoming when he took over the reins of the Rainiers.

From the beginning Dewey and I didn't get along. Part of the trouble stemmed from an argument we had over a knee injury he claimed he got from our pitching mound. He wanted compensation, and I didn't think he was entitled to it. We had the same doctor and through him I found out that he had hurt his knee in high school. Later his mother — a lovely person — brought him to my office and had him tell me exactly what happened. That embarrassed him, of course, and apparently he held a grudge against me all those years.

We released him but later took him back on a trial basis. That's when Roy Hamey bought him for the Pirate organization, as I mentioned earlier. Then when Dewey first came to see me about managing the Rainiers, I told him I didn't think he was quite ready for it. That didn't set well with him either, so he asked if he could go see Mr. Sick and I told him it was okay with me. Emil was scared to death of the press, so when he had a chance to hire Brougham's son-in-law, he jumped at it.

He was involved in bringing his old teammate, Freddie Hutchinson, back to Seattle as field manager, and the two of them did a tremendous job of putting a team together — and I was out in the cold. Soriano locked me out of the clubhouse, and Hutch refused to let me in on Dewey's orders. Even though I remained as executive vice-president for a while, my active involvement with the Rainiers came to an end on a rather sour note.

In later years we patched up our differences to some degree before Hutch died of cancer on November 12, 1964, at the age of 46, and Dewey went on to become a ships' pilot.

It was the end of an era for Torchy. He continued to enjoy baseball, of course, but a new generation had succeeded him in his management role. During his years with the Rainiers, he became well known in both minor and major league circles, and one of his closest friends was Albert B. "Happy" Chandler, the former governor of Kentucky and baseball commissioner who will be mentioned at greater length later in this story.

In addition to Freddie Hutchinson, Jo Jo White, Earl Torgeson, Sammy White, and other players he signed, Torchy had at least a slight hand in the careers of such Rainier notables as Louis Alexander Novikoff, "The Mad Russian;" "Kewpie Dick" Barrett, the pudgy curve-baller; "High Pockets" Bill Lawrence; Bill Schuster, "The Rooster;" and Hal Turpin, "The Yoncalla Farmer." There was another individual, too — not a ball player — whose associa-

Sports announcer Leo Lassen helped generate enthusiasm for the Seattle Rainiers for more than a dozen years. Despite a strident, nasal voice, he had a loyal listenership of fans who appreciated his encyclopedic knowledge of the game and his unabashed favoritism for the Seattle club. (R. C. Torrance collection)

tion with the Rainiers generally paralleled the same years as Torchy's. His name was Leo Lassen.

A former managing editor of the *Seattle Star*, Leo began broadcasting the games of the Seattle Indians in the mid-1930s. With a withered left arm, he was denied the opportunity to participate in sports, but with his nasal, high-pitched, staccato voice, he became a radio pioneer and an institution in his own right as far as Seattle baseball fans were concerned.

Youngsters imitated his pet expressions: "Oh baby" and "back, back, back and it's OVER," the latter his oft-repeated description of a Rainier homerun. He was an encyclopedia of baseball facts and his memory of baseball lore was phenomenal. His dramatic broadcasts helped the Rainiers set attendance records because he created interest and always urged his legion of listeners to go to the ball park whenever they could. Like Torchy, Leo lasted until the Soriano era.

When they broke his contract, they also broke Leo's heart. He lived with his mother out in the Wallingford district, tending his rose garden. He loved classical music and could play and compose on the piano despite his handicap. Then one day when his mother went down to the basement to get their laundry, she slipped and fell and broke her hip. She died several months later, and Leo was really alone after that. I finally got him to come downtown to lunch with me just once after his mother passed away. He had a lot to offer, but he just hibernated. Leo died in 1975.

In a way it was almost a good thing that Torchy phased out of the baseball business when he did. The management of the game was changing considerably, and coming from a pre-television era when love of the sport was considered at least as important as the money, he would have had a lot of adjustments to make.

Except for an old baseball man like Cal Griffiths, most of the new owners seemed to be on ego trips. The money they've spent and the salaries they've paid is just ridiculous, and that goes for the other big-time professional sports, too. The owners are scared to death that somebody else will get a good ball player so they make crazy offers. Money doesn't always buy championships. Gene Autry, a nice guy, spent millions on his California Angels and came in fifth!

You can't blame the kids for taking all that money if somebody wants to give it to them—but it certainly has changed the game a lot.

One of the things I did when I went to the annual baseball meetings was to take pictures of all the greats of the game—players, managers and owners. I had pictures of Connie Mack, Babe Ruth, Lou Gehrig, Ted Williams, Lefty Grove, Mel Ott, Bill Rigney, Larry McPhail, Paul Waner, Cal Griffiths, PeeWee Reese, Casey Stengel, Gabby Hartnett, Rogers Hornsby and many others.

When I moved out of my office at Western Printing, I had them all packed in a box marked "Do Not Touch," "Don't Move." Well, the movers came, thought it was junk and hauled it to the garbage dump.

It was a terrible loss, but at least I had my memories left!

141

Torchy and Bill Benswanger, general manager of the Pittsburgh Pirates, enjoyed a conversation with the "grand old man of baseball," Connie Mack, owner of the Philadelphia Athletics. Twice Torchy lost valuable pictures of baseball greats, once when his films were X-rayed in a security check and another time when movers hauled his collection to the dump. (Special Collections Division, University of Washington Libraries)

Torchy's pattern hadn't changed from his pre-war busy-ness. Any reduction in his baseball involvement was quickly replaced by a litany of civic, charitable, social, recreational and business activities. High among his continuing interests were the athletic fortunes of the University of Washington. He was a Husky fan — first, last and always — and his zealousness eventually got him into the limelight not of his choosing.

Chapter 10

Help for the Huskies

The best way to stay out of trouble, to avoid ruffling feathers and stepping on toes is not to do anything.

That sort of inaction would have been an impossibility for Torchy. As Joshua Green, the city's patriarchal banker, once wrote to him: "You put more pep, energy, vim, vivacity and rarin'-to-go enthusiasm into a gathering of people than any man in Seattle."

With Torchy at the head of an organization, a project or a campaign, a bombastic effort was a foregone conclusion; and a prime beneficiary of his tireless support was the Athletic Department of the University of Washington. Dating back to his days as assistant graduate manager, his dedication to the promotion of Husky sports programs was almost without equal.

Despite his other multifarious activities, there was always time in his busy schedule for the needs of the Purple and Gold coaches and their student athletes. When he put away his Marine Corps uniform in 1946, he renewed—with extra vigor—his continuing commitment to his alma mater.

He remembered his own hand-to-mouth struggle as a Sun Dodger baseball player, and he resolved to help athletes of a new generation through some of their financial difficulties. Like any loyal alumnus, he was also interested in winning teams—especially on the football field! As a result, Torchy got involved in both fund-raising and recruiting.

Trying to talk athletes into coming to the University in the early

Torchy's involvement with the University of Washington football dated back to the early 1920s. Here he joined surviving members of the 1924 Sun Dodgers team which tied Navy 14-14 in the Rose Bowl. He was included in the reunion because he was assistant graduate manager at the

days was quite different than it was after the war. In the 1920s our program was sort of hit-or-miss. We recruited almost entirely in the state, and when we went after certain athletes, we'd work out a program so they could have part-time jobs with some organization in Seattle to pay their way through school.

Room-and-board at the dormitories and fraternities was about twenty-five dollars a month. Transportation by jitney bus or streetcar didn't cost very much and neither did books or tuition. There was no spring football practice, so that gave the kids more working time.

There were various kinds of jobs. The Standard Oil Company offered odd-hour work pumping gas at various stations. The Supply Laundry hired student agents to provide service to sororities and fraternities. Elmer Tesreau was one of those who did well in that business.

Many athletes worked as longshoremen on the Seattle piers. They could make from a dollar to a dollar and a half an hour on shifts of up to twelve hours on Saturdays and Sundays. That lasted until the late 1920s when conference officials decided that was not the best way for youngsters to earn their school money. After that the University would allow athletes to work as janitors and do other odd jobs on campus for from forty to fifty dollars a month which was not enough to cover their expenses.

During the 1930s there were a number of individuals who helped find additional jobs for the kids. They included Bill Culliton, Joe Gottstein, Joe Nuberger, Marky Lease, Bill Pigott, Al Kelly, Mort Frayn and others. I was active but I didn't head up the work at that time. Then came the war and the situation changed.

While Torchy was in the service, the football teams of Coach Ralph "Pest" Welch won 27 games, lost 20 and tied three from 1942 through 1947. In the meantime, Harvey Cassill—Torchy's friend from Lewis and Clark High School and their undergraduate days together at the University—became the athletic director. Torchy was one of those instrumental in the appointment; and with his close acquaintanceship with Cassill, he became involved more than ever. In his "spare time," whenever he wasn't looking for baseball players for the Rainiers, he was out beating the bushes for future Huskies.

Cassill, in the meantime, was searching for a replacement for Coach Welch. Clark Shaughnessy—best known for "re-inventing" the T formation at Stanford—was his first choice, but

145

when the latter declined the job, Cassill turned to Howie Odell, a graduate of the University of Pittsburgh and then head coach at Yale. Torchy played an important role in recruiting two of Odell's best known players – Don Heinrich and Hugh McElhenny – both of whom became All-Americans.

Don was the quarterback for the Bremerton High School team which won the state championship at the Seattle Civic Center field in 1947. He was a real inspiration to all the ball players on the squad, and we were able to get him enrolled at the University. I put Don to work on odd jobs at the Western Printing Company and later was able to give him some additional help in school.

As for McElhenny, everybody in the country was after him because he not only was a great football player but a potential world-class high hurdler. I went down to Compton, California, and visited with Hugh and his parents. I got along real well with both his dad,

Don Heinrich was an All-American quarterback for the Washington Huskies and later played professional football for the New York Giants. The "dream backfield" which included him and Hugh McElhenny was limited to just one year as each suffered injuries which kept them out of two seasons they might have played together. During his college days Heinrich worked for Torchy at the Western Printing Company. (University of Washington Athletic Department)

who was a littler shorter than I was, and his mother, a very lovely person. We had Hugh over to Palm Springs and did our best to keep ahead of the other coaches until we finally got him signed up in Seattle.

[Al McCoy, the University's chief recruiter; Paul Schwegler, a Husky All-American in 1931; and Lawrence "Doc" Sexton, a loyal alumnus of the Gil Dobie era, were especially influential in McElhenny's decision to play for Washington.]

We were all very happy about the situation, but in spring training, a potential problem developed. Here was the great Hugh McElhenny coming from Los Angeles and the other members of the squad weren't sure what kind of a guy he was or whether they would accept him. They didn't seem to block too much for him and they tried to tackle him extra hard—but it all changed as the result of a single play.

The team was practicing behind the swimming pool, and at the time there were some small piles of gravel just beyond the sidelines. Hugh was carrying the ball around end when one of the Huskies tackled him and both went sliding toward the gravel. When Hugh saw what was happening, he grabbed the helmet of the kid who had tackled him and held his face up off the ground so he wouldn't get cut up by the sharp rocks. Everybody on the squad saw what Hugh did, and after that there was no more trouble about his acceptance. He went on to become the greatest runner the University ever had and later an All-Pro halfback with the San Francisco 49ers.

I remember another incident which showed what kind of player Hugh was. We went back to Minneapolis to play Minnesota in 1949 and he ran the opening kick-off back 97 yards for a touchdown. Then we saw him on his hands and knees crawling off the field because of the pain caused by an old injury when he cut his foot on a piece of glass when he was in grade school.

I had known Dr. Danny Levanthal in Los Angeles for some time. He was considered to be the best foot, leg and knee man in the United States, so I called him and told him what had happened. He said to bring Hugh down, so we flew him to Los Angeles for an examination. After he looked at the foot, Levanthal concluded that if he operated, he might make the situation worse and that Hugh might never be able to play football again. "You're just going to have to play in pain," he said, and that's just what Hugh did, rewriting the record books in the process.

Unfortunately, Odell's three-year dream backfield combination of Heinrich and McElhenny was frustrated by injuries. They only played together for one full season when the Huskies won eight and lost two in 1950. The year before, McElhenny's foot injury kept him out of action, and in 1951 Heinrich was sidelined for the entire season with a separated shoulder.

When Harve Cassill took over, I contacted Doc Strauss in Chicago and told him we would like to have some more ball players from that part of the country since we hadn't had any for a few years. In the 1930s he used to arrange to have good players drive new cars out from Detroit to deliver to the Seattle agencies. The kids would get $50 or $75 dollars, and then we had to take care of them after that. Doc also would entertain the Washington crew on the way to Poughkeepsie with a luncheon or dinner. He was a great supporter. On this particular occasion he sent us a big fellow—about six-three, weighing 220 pounds—who could run pretty well. He didn't have a lot of desire, though, and one day in spring practice Odell hollered at him and said he wanted to see him actually make a tackle.

Well, the team was practicing on the same field by the swimming pool where McElhenny had saved the kid's face from the gravel. This time the boy from Chicago put on his helmet and really crashed into Heinrich coming around end on a broken play. He drove him into the embankment alongside the field, and everybody knew something bad had happened. They took Don to Providence Hospital and learned that he was done for the year, McElhenny's last.

The young man who tackled Don was so upset that he left school and that was the last we saw of him.

Hugh and Don went on to professional careers, but I wonder what kind of price they would have commanded had they played thirty years later than they did. I'm sure Hugh would have brought a million to a million and a half, and I think he signed with the San Francisco 49ers for something like $7,000. For eleven years he drew thousands of spectators in at the gates and I understand he never got more than $40,000 a year. Don signed with the New York Giants for a little more than McElhenny got, but by comparison with later contracts, he was very poorly paid. Later Heinrich at least got a little advantage from television when he became a color commentator for the Seattle Seahawks and then the 49ers. Hugh went on to a successful career in public relations.

The oft-repeated story that McElhenny took a cut in salary

when he signed with the '49ers is essentially true when the money earned by his wife is included. As Hugh recalled a number of years later.

"Torchy helped her get jobs at Friedlander's Jewelry and later at the King County Medical office. I had a summer job as a teller at Longacres, and when I turned 21 I was able to work for the Rainer Brewery. Every month when I was in school I got a check for $300 from 'somebody,' and it all added up to around $10,000. So figuring it that way, I did take about a $3,000 cut to start as a pro.

"I used to look forward to seeing Torchy come into the locker room after a game. We'd shake hands and when he'd let go, there'd be $25 for every touchdown I made. For some reason or other he didn't show up after the Washington State game when I scored five times. As for him or anybody else in Seattle giving me a new car when I came to school, that's not true at all. When I was a senior in high school, my dad promised me a car if I'd win the high hurdles, low hurdles and broad

"Hurryin' Hugh" McElhenny, also known as "The King," was the premier running back in the history of University of Washington football. Many of the stories about how he was subsidized to play for the Huskies were greatly exaggerated, but he did receive financial rewards from Torchy for scoring touchdowns. (University of Washington Athletic Department)

149

jump in the final meet. I did, and when I came out of the Coliseum, he handed me the keys.

"I did go to Torchy about a car once, though. I told him that Don Heinrich needed wheels and Torchy got him a 1941 Chevie, I think it was."

Besides his self-appointed, unpaid recruiting job, Torchy—as Hugh McElhenny implied—assumed the important function of raising funds and finding jobs to help athletes through school.

I organized a group—mostly of downtown business men—with the goal of putting Washington back on the athletic map as well as the academic one. At first we called it the Husky Club, but we soon changed it to The Greater Washington Advertising Association. Allen B. Morgan of the Seaboard Branch of the Seattle-First National Bank was my financial adviser. He kept all the books of the association, approved all the payments and signed the checks.

There was nothing devious about our organization. The leading citizens of our community participated in it, and it was of general knowledge to the newspapers because Charles B. Lindeman of the Post-Intelligencer *and Bill, Jack and Frank Blethen of* The Times *all contributed to it. We had nothing to do with the actions of the coaches. We never told them who to play, when to play or what athletes to go after. Our purpose was to support the program and the kids.*

There were seventy-five or more individuals involved at one time or another. Some gave money; some provided jobs or both.

The Greater Washington Advertising Association roster was an abbreviated Who's Who in Seattle business circles. The list included auto dealers Stan Nelson, Bill Ryan, Norm Dickerman, M. O. Anderson, Jack Blume, Sr., T. Dayton Davies, L. Leigh Savidge, Gene Feidler and William O. McKay; bankers Wilbur W. Scruby, Thomas F. Gleed, Joe Nuberger, Roy Taylor and Joshua Green, Senior and Junior; lumbermen Walter B. Nettleton, Harry "Mickey" O'Donald, Walter Shield, Charlie Stewart, Neil C. Jamison, Budge Summy, Ray Gardner and Bryan Lockwood; and hotelmen William Edris, Edward E. Carlson, Charles Hunlock and Severt V. Thurston.

Dave Beck of the International Teamsters Union was a big help to me because he could call people and arrange for part-time jobs for the kids. Walter F. Clark had as many as sixteen or seventeen athletes working in his restaurants.

Emil Sick, William H. Mackie and Lester R. McCash of the Rainier Brewery were great contributors and they also provided jobs. They hired Hugh McElhenny for public relations work; and Jim Warsinski and Milt Bohart—an All-American guard in 1953—took care of Emil and Kit Sick's house while they were gone for the winter.

There was Ole Lund of the Todd Shipyards, J. L. Heathcote of Safeway Stores, Frank McLaughlin of Puget Sound Power & Light, Jack McWhirter of the Fuller Brush Company, Paul Pigott of Pacific Car & Foundry, Gordon Prentiss of Sunset Electric Company, Irv and Victor E. Rabel of Star Machinery, Jack Salmon of Oceanic Sales, Roy E. Campbell of Arden Farms and Robert J. Acheson of the Blackball Ferry Lines.

I could always depend on people like restaurateur Vito Santoro, George Gunn, Jr., Douglas Ball, Ralph W. Barron, Warren H. Bean, Kenneth Colman, jeweler Paul S. Friedlander (who was Doc Strauss's son-in-law), Earl Jones, Howard Lease, Richard E. Lang, Gus Ledbetter, George Hardinburg, Charlton Hall, Waldo and Wendell Hemphill, Larry Ives, Ned Stone, Darwin and Kenneth Meisnest, Stewart G. Thompson, Ernie Rose, Gilbert W. Skinner, Ben Shearer, Joe Donnelly, John Boesplug, Sr., Eugene V. "Beaner" Walby, Charlie Adams, Joe Louis, Paul Mackie, Henry Broderick, John X. Johnson and Sarah E. Harris Johnson.

Men who ran department stores were a big help: Rex Allison of The Bon Marche, D. Roy Johnson of the J. C. Penney Company, Harry Perkins of Best's Apparel, William S. Street of Frederick & Nelson, Carl B. Williams of Rhodes, and the Nordstroms, Lloyd, Everett and Elmer.

I can't overlook Robert C. Hill of the Carnation Company, Frank West of Preservative Paint, Ned Thompson of Thompson Freeze, Stanley E. Stretton of the Standard Oil Company, Harold F. Navarre of Navarre Plumbing, Nat Rogers and George Van Waters of Van Waters & Rogers, Inc., Irving Green and Joe Bernbaum of Green's Cigar Store, Joe Brown of the Parrott Company, Roger Cutting of Northwest Lead, Irving Levine of K & L Distributors, Charles W. and Roy L. Maryatt of American Linen Supply, Kenneth Schoenfeld of Kraftsmaster, Inc., Lawrence and William C. Calvert of the San Juan Fishing and Packing Company and Frank Carson of Blake, Moffit & Towne Paper Company.

Then there were William Horsley, the advertising man; dentists

151

Leroy Goss, Aubrey Martin and Lando Zeek; meat-packers Henry Kruse, Harry Thompson and Willie Ristogi; Howard Keeler of the Overall Institution of Seattle; haberdashers A. A. "Bob" Littler, Clarence Klopfenstein and J. Jacobs; Don McPhee, the assistant county assessor; and a long list of attorneys: Claude Wakefield, B. Gray Warner, Ernest Skeel, Frank Meakin, Mark Mathison, John Ryan, Lawrence Bogle, Cassius Gates, George F. Kachlein, Jr., and Stanley Long.

That's not everybody, of course, but it's obvious that it was a pretty representative group, fine people who later were to be criticized for helping kids through the University. I should mention that we also supported students in the music school, in communications, engineering and medicine. Those who participated could be proud of what they did!

Actually, The Greater Washington Advertising Association was relatively short-lived. It and Torchy were to be caught up in a headline-grabbing hassle (see Chapter 11) which left a few scars and bitter memories in its wake. In the meantime, though, he continued his involvement in aid to the Huskies.

Through the years Torchy was instrumental in advancing—in one way or another—the college careers of more than one hundred and sixty students. Not all of them were football players. Some—like Joe Cipriano and Dean Parsons, both outstanding basketball players—lettered in other sports. Torchy took special delight in recruiting Dean Parsons out of Eugene, Oregon, home of the rival Ducks. Cipriano, from Mt. Vernon, Washington, later became head coach at the University of Nebraska. A few did not make the grade at all but were assisted nonetheless.

In addition to disbursing funds from The Greater Washington Advertising Association, Torchy signed notes, made personal loans and, on occasion, provided his own out-of-pocket cash. He later reported that of all the youngsters who borrowed from him, only two didn't pay him back. In some cases his relationship extended well beyond the college years as graduates went on to successful careers and growing families.

Recruiting in the late 1940s and early '50s was not the sophisticated process it later became—with computerized records, thousands of feet of game films, mounds of scouting reports and statistics without end. Sometimes mere happenstance was involved.

I was in Los Angeles and called Larry Crosby for lunch. Afterwards he said: "Bing's recording at the studio this afternoon; let's go over and watch for a while and in the meantime we can plan what we'll do this evening. [As high school students in Spokane, Larry had dated Torchy's future wife and Torchy had gone out with Elaine Cooper, whom Crosby later married.]

On the way to the studio we stopped at a large room where they stored all the costumes for various movies. Sitting at a table reading a book was a good looking black youngster who identified himself as Jim McCarter, the custodian of costumes. We visited for a while and I just happened to mention that I thought he was big enough to play football and should be in school some place. He said he'd played in high school and wanted to go to college but he didn't get a scholarship and couldn't go without one.

Jim McCarter was a noteworthy example of how Torchy got involved in the careers of young athletes. He met Jim just by chance in Hollywood, thought he was big enough to play college football and—in his inimitable fashion—pursued the matter until he had McCarter enrolled at the University and in a Husky uniform. After graduation Jim went on to a commendable career as a teacher and school administrator. (University of Washington Athletic Department)

153

I found out he attended Centennial High school in Los Angeles, so next morning I contacted his coach who said he believed Jim could play for any college team on the coast but somehow he had been overlooked. Besides that, he ranked well up in his class as far as grades were concerned. When I called Jim back to ask him if he'd be interested in the University of Washington if I could get him a job or a scholarship, he said he'd jump at the chance because he always wanted to be a teacher.

Next I called John Cherberg who was coach at the time, and he said: "Let's take a chance on him." Well, Jim gave them two weeks' notice at the costume shop; I paid his transportation to Seattle; we got him a job; and he ended up playing four years of football as a Husky. When he graduated, he went back to his original home in New York City where he went to work teaching disadvantaged children in the Bronx. When he came out to see me in Seattle, I was terribly proud of him.

———————

Then there was the case of Sam Mitchell and Joe Andrews who came out to Seattle from Fall River, Massachusetts. I got Sam a job at a construction site and arranged for Joe to play baseball with the well known Milkmaids semi-pro team of Mt. Vernon. Joe could hit a ball a mile, but he couldn't throw across the street because of a shoulder injury. Unfortunately, before he got started in school, his mother called to have him come home for his sister's wedding.

I couldn't talk her out of it, so I finally bought an airline ticket for him, hoping he'd return after the ceremony. He had turned down an offer from the Boston Braves when he was at Mt. Vernon, but when he got home, another scout offered him $20,000 to get his name on a contract. The family needed the money, so for their sake he signed, thus costing him the chance to play college football. He was a lot like George Wilson and might have become a real star and gone on to the pros. As it was, the Braves took him to their training camp, and that's when they discovered he couldn't throw, so they released him. The last I heard, he was going to work in a coal mine some place.

Sam Mitchell, on the other hand, stayed in school and did a very creditable job for the Huskies, both as a halfback and in the unenviable position of filling in at quarterback when Don Heinrich suffered his shoulder separation. (That year—1951—Sam completed 79 of 167 passes for 1,102 yards and eight touchdowns.) He then

154

got his degree and went on to make a name for himself as a teacher and school administrator.

There were two or three disappointments among the many young men Torchy recruited or aided, but mostly he enjoyed a feeling of pride with the others as he did with Jim McCarter and Sam Mitchell. To name a few, there were Jim Noe, the big center from Montana, who became a superior court judge; George Strugar, who played for the Los Angeles Rams and later did well in the trucking business; Steve Roake, a fine quarterback from Barrington, Illinois, who went on to a successful career as a pilot for Pan American Airlines; Dr. Karsten C. "Corky" Lewis, a halfback from Yakima who returned to the Yakima Valley to practice medicine; Dr. Jack Nugent and Dr. Gene

Among the scores of athletes aided in their college careers by Torchy and The Greater Washington Advertising Association fund were Dean Rockey (left) and Sam Mitchell. After their years at the University, Rockey became an ophthalmologist and Mitchell a highly respected educator. (University of Washington Athletic Department)

155

Because of a promise to their father with whom he played baseball in earlier years, Torchy helped brothers Tom (left) and Dick Sprague through school. Both became successful attorneys. Dick was an All-American defensive back in 1950. (University of Washington Athletic Department)

Hallock, both dentists; Dr. Dean Rockey, an ophthalmologist; and the two Sprague brothers—Tom and Dick from Spokane— who became prominent attorneys in Seattle. [Dick was an All-American defensive back in 1950.]

I played baseball with Severn Sprague, Tom and Dick's father, and I promised him I'd help the boys through school. In the case of Al Libke of Wenatchee, his dad played first base for the Rainiers when I was executive vice-president so I was anxious to get his son into the University. He had a great arm and would have been an outstanding quarterback, but unfortunately he developed mononucleosis and never really got a chance to play up to his capability.

I remember many, many more, of course, maybe a hundred and sixty or seventy of them. Some were stars and some just worked in the trenches. I won't be able to name them all, but some that come to mind are Don McKeta, Fred Robinson, Fritz Apking, Mike McCluskey, Bryan Zurek, Loren Perry, Bill Earley, Stan Kucinskas, Dick McVeigh, Don McCumby, Ed Sheron, Nat Davis, Frank Nelson, Fred Snyder, Corky Bridges, Dean Derby, Byng Nixon, Jimmy Cain, Bill Till, Bob Cox, Stew Crook and Bob Dunn.

I shouldn't overlook Phil Gillis, a good ball player who was the forgotten man in the Heinrich, McElhenny, Roland Kirkby backfield.

Then there was the Luther Carr family, a special case. The first time I went over to see them in Tacoma, Luther, Sr., had all nine of his children lined up according to height, a handsome sight. He told me then that he wanted all of them to have a college education. We started it out with Luther, Jr., who was a fine halfback despite the fact that he had to play under three different coaches.

Luther was followed by Gary and then Dave, the latter being an exceptional basketball player. The Carr girls also went on to graduate from the University of Washington. I was very proud to be in attendance when Luther, by then a successful businessman, was inducted into the Downtown Seattle Rotary Club Number Four. He made me feel my work was all worthwhile when he said he wouldn't have been there on the platform that day if Roscoe C. "Torchy" Torrance hadn't stood by him through all his trials and tribulations.

I have one regret, though. I made a special trip to Seattle from Palm Springs to attend the wedding of Luther and Frances. Then I got involved in another deal and missed the ceremony. I'll always be sorry about that.

Torchy had to admit that not all of his recruiting efforts were successful. He missed out on Dick Bass, who developed into an outstanding halfback for College of the Pacific. He was involved in getting Lee Grosscup to Washington for his freshman year, but he was unable to convince Jim Owens—then the new Husky coach—of Grosscup's talents, and Lee moved on to become an All-American quarterback at Utah. Jim wanted an option quarterback and Lee wanted to throw from the pocket. Many years earlier Torchy had tried to interest another Washington coach—Enoch Bagshaw—in a youngster named Herbert "Butch" Meeker, and what eventually transpired was later much regretted on the Seattle campus.

As a graduate of Lewis and Clark High School, I kept special track of the athletes there, and when Butch graduated, I talked him into coming to the University. I was the freshman baseball coach then, and he worked out with us for a few days while Coach Bagshaw was out of the city. Butch really wanted to play football even though he only weighed about 136 pounds, but when Baggy returned and I took Meeker over to meet him, Baggy opened and closed the conversation by saying: "You're too small to play for me, son."

With that we left the office and Butch was crying because he had his heart set on playing football. To help him out, I told him I would call J. Fred "Doc" Bohler, the trainer at Washington State College, to see what could be done for him there. I then got Doc on the phone and said: "I've got a good athlete for you. I hate to lose him at the University, but Baggy doesn't think he's big enough. If you can find a job for him, he'll be over to see you."

Well, that's just what Butch did. They got him a job in the gymnasium, and he finished his four years at WSC. In 1926 he almost single-handedly beat us in football, and he did the same thing in baseball, too. They eventually named the WSC cougar mascot after him. When Butch found out the cat was a female, he was quite upset—but he got over it. After watching Meeker perform for the third time on the football field, Baggy finally admitted: "That's probably the worst decision I ever made in my life."

In later years I visited Butch several times in the Veterans' Hospital in Seattle where he was dying of cancer. He was a great little guy, and I'll always be sorry he didn't become a Husky.

One of the football players Torchy wished he could have kept in a Husky uniform was Herbert "Butch" Meeker from Lewis and Clark High School in Spokane. Unfortunately, Enoch Bagshaw told the dejected youngster that he was too small to play for him, so Torchy sent the tiny scatback to Washington State College where he was to become a thorn in the side of Baggy's teams until he graduated. (Washington State University Athletic Publicity Department)

Chapter 11

The 'Slush Fund' Affair

Like Torchy, his close friend Harvey Cassill was not the type to be satisfied with the status quo. IIis goal was to establish the University of Washington as a major collegiate athletic power with facilities to match its men.

To focus attention on the Huskies, he was receptive to a suggestion for a home-and-home football series with Notre Dame. Torchy accompanied Cassill to South Bend, Indiana, along with Arch Ward, sports editor of the *Chicago Tribune*. Torchy was well acquainted with Ward through baseball connections, and Arch was very interested in promoting an intersectional arrangement. The three men met with Moose Krause, athletic director of the Fighting Irish, to work out the details for a game in South Bend in 1948 and one at Seattle the following year.

Unfortunately, the Huskies were not quite ready for that kind of competition. They lost the first game 46-0, with Irish reserves playing the second half to hold down the score. In what was to have been his first season, Howie Odell came down with a kidney ailment, and Reg Root, his assistant coach, took over for the year. Notre Dame won again in 1949 and the series was not renewed. The 50-50 split of gate receipts softened the blow, however.

In the meantime, Cassill had pushed through his idea to build a roofed upper deck on one side of the Husky stadium, and the board of regents backed him up with a $1,600,000 bond issue. The somewhat controversial stadium addition – known somewhat derisively as "Cassill's Folly" – had to overcome the fears many fans had of its seemingly unsupported cantilevered roof. Only 30,245 spectators showed up when it was first used on the opening day of the 1950 season as the Heinrich-and-McElhenny Huskies beat Kansas State 33-7. It took a little time, but in the ensuing years the expanded capacity of the stadium was sold out for almost every game.

Concurrently, Torchy and the other participants in The Greater Washington Advertising Association were doing what they could to help the coaches attract and support bigger, better and faster football players. However, even with the likes of Don Heinrich and Hugh McElhenny, the overall success on the field was moderate at best. The relationship between Cassill and Odell was strained almost from the beginning when Howie was the athletic director's second choice for the job; and after the 1952 season—despite a 7-3 record—the coach was let go with a year remaining on his contract.

Cassill wanted to promote Skip Stahley, one of Odell's assistants, to fill the coaching vacancy, but he simply couldn't ignore the clamor of fans, alumni and sportswriters in favor of John A. "Cowboy" Cherberg, the Husky freshmen coach. Cherberg, a graduate of Seattle's Queen Anne High School and a halfback for Coach Jim Phelan's teams in the early 1930s, had compiled a record of 22 straight wins with his frosh teams. Reticently Cassill offered him the job, and Cherberg became the eighteenth Washington football coach dating back to W. B. Goodwin in 1892.

Despite his earlier successes, The Cowboy's Huskies won only five games in his first two years, but he looked forward to the 1955 season with two of the West's most promising quarterbacks, Bobby Cox and Sandy Lederman. Then, as a harbinger of things to come, Cox transferred to the University of Minnesota, leaving Cherberg the task of dealing with the temperamental Lederman. Jim Sutherland, Sandy's high school coach in Santa Monica, was then on the staff of the University of California, and Cherberg thought that he might be able to get the most out of his former player. He discussed the possibilities with Torchy.

At John's insistence I went to see Pappy Waldorf at Berkeley. I asked him if it would be all right if we talked to Sutherland about coming up to Washington as an assistant. Pappy said okay, so I got Jim on a train to Seattle and he was hired.

The relationship between the two coaches got off to a bad start.

Apparently the first day Sutherland came on the practice field, he was smoking a cigarette which didn't set well with John at all. From that point on it was all downhill.

In the opening game of the 1955 season the Huskies fumbled eleven times as they squeaked by Idaho 14-7. Then it was discovered that Sutherland had changed the starting count between the center and quarterback. Cherberg wanted to fire his assistant immediately, but Harvey Cassill advised him to wait. Despite the discord, the Huskies won their first four games before the roof fell in. After a 13-7 loss to Baylor, Lederman skipped practice because he wasn't playing enough, and Cherberg promptly suspended him. The morale of both staff and players

Coach John A. "Cowboy" Cherberg of the Washington Huskies got caught up in a player revolt and the so-called recruitment scandal in 1955-56. Though charges and counter-charges flew back and forth and Cherberg was eventually fired, his statewide popularity didn't suffer particularly and he became a virtual fixture as lieutenant governor. (University of Washington Athletic Department)

161

deteriorated severely. Cherberg and Sutherland barely talked to one another, and—as Harvey Cassill later revealed—"three or four of the assistant coaches had me to lunch at different times to cry on my shoulder."

Torchy accompanied the team to Los Angeles for the next to the last game of the season against UCLA. Traveling with the squad to out-of-town games when his schedule permitted was just about the only bonus he got for all of his work. On this particular occasion, with the Huskies in an apparent slump, Cherberg turned to Torchy for help of a different kind.

At practice in the Coliseum on Friday afternoon before the game, John came to me and said that if I wouldn't mind he would turn the boys over to me for a few minutes before they went on the field the next day to see if I could whip up a little enthusiasm. He repeated the idea on the bus on Saturday as we rode out to the Coliseum. It was not an unusual thing for an alumnus to address a team before a game or at half-time, and I had done it before myself.

After the warmup exercises the team came back to the locker room, the coaches left and I gave what you might call a Knute Rockne speech. UCLA was a heavy favorite, but I told the boys "the Bruins put their pants on the same way you do, so if you play with pride and to the best of your ability, you can win the game!"

Well, they went out and really did a job. With about a minute left, our boys had a 17-14 lead, but when they were held on about their own ten-yard line, they took a safety so they could get out of trouble with a free kick. It was good strategy because they still led 17-16, but the Bruins got a good run-back and then a kid by the name of Jim Decker came off the bench and kicked a long field goal—the first of his career—and UCLA won 19-17.

After playing such a brilliant game and then losing in the final seconds, the kids were really downhearted and the trip back to Seattle was a sad one. It was when we got home that the trouble started, however.

A delegation from the football squad came to Torchy's apartment in the Grosvenor House during the following week after the UCLA game. The players said they wanted to talk about the coach, and Torchy told them if that's what they wanted to do, they should go see Harvey Cassill, not him. His best advice was for them to concentrate on the Washington State game and not their resentment of Cherberg.

Despite the impending revolt, the Huskies were at their best against the Cougars, winning 27-7. However, the victory over their cross-state rivals did not save what Husky football historian Dick Rockne called "the season of discontent." Instead, some thirty players—led by Corky Lewis and Bob McNamee—went to Harvey Cassill and told him that they could no longer play for John Cherberg. The player mutiny was quickly picked up by *The Seattle Times* and the *Post-Intelligencer*, and what should have been an internal affair became a big public hassle.

On Cherberg's recommendation, Jim Sutherland was let go shortly after the final game. Fans and alumni promptly chose sides—some defending The Cowboy and calling the mutinous players "cry babies," others backing Sutherland and the team members. Then *The Times* began to zero in on The Greater Washington Advertising Association, and a new dimension was added to the story.

Charges flew back and forth. The head coach was accused of having a short fuse and of trying to make his assistant the scapegoat for an unsuccessful season. Emotions ran high, and the A.S.U.W. board of control voted 12-2 to get rid of the coach, but on December 10 the regents rehired him.

On January 18, 1956, it was announced that Jim Sutherland had been named the head coach at Washington State. A day later John Cherberg held a team meeting to organize for the upcoming year, and afterwards Lee Grosscup and several other promising freshmen from California announced they were leaving the team. Among their reasons—as reported by columnist Mel Durslag of the *Los Angeles Examiner*—were such idiocyncracies as the coach's adamant decree against players chewing grass and whistling in the locker room.

By this time the kettle was really boiling. It all came to a head on January 27 when Harvey Cassill fired Cherberg, after which petitions were circulated by angry supporters of the coach to get the athletic director's scalp, too. Cherberg went on television and lambasted Torchy and the downtown supporters for meddling and called for an investigation of the Advertising Association's "slush fund." On February 9, Harvey Cassill yielded to the pressure and resigned; three days later Torchy appeared on KING-TV with a lengthy statement.

In his comments—which were also carried over KING Radio—

Torchy defended The Greater Washington Advertising Association and refuted charges made against him and the downtown supporters. A week later *Sports Illustrated* for February 20, 1956, came out with a six-page article titled "Boosters Mess It Up in Washington." The sub-title read: "The football fortunes of the Huskies mean a lot to Seattle and to Torchy Torrance, the city's hustling builder-upper. A report on how he almost loved his favorite team to death."

Torchy was labeled "Washington football's leading sugar daddy," and unidentified Husky players were quoted as receiving everything from free theater tickets to automobiles and monthly paychecks of as much as $175 a month. The story carried Cherberg's complaint that "the men who run the secret slush fund that pays his players extra-curricular salaries had used their checkbooks to turn his players against him."

The *Sports Illustrated* piece reported:

Corky Lewis was among the Washington Huskies involved in what eventually became known as "the season of discontent" in 1955. Torchy got caught in the middle between Coach Johnny Cherberg and disgruntled players; and when his so-called "slush fund" added fuel to the fire, the hassle made the national news. Lewis, a three-year letterman, later became a medical doctor. (University of Washington Athletic Department)

Torchy's fund is a big one—it has run in the past anywhere from $20,000 to $75,000—and he runs it pretty much as he pleases . . . Now and then he sees a chance to make an extra pile for the fund, such as an exhibition pro football game last summer between the New York Giants and the San Francisco 49ers.

He talked the teams into coming to Seattle. He sold the directors of Greater Seattle, Inc., on the idea of sponsoring the show. He persuaded the University regents to lend their 55,000-seat stadium (normally restricted to college events) for 15% of the gate.

It was a whopping success. Each team made $36,856; the Associated Students of the University of Washington received $28,361 for stadium rental and management fees; Greater Seattle, Inc., turned a profit of $7,021. After taxes, there was $28,000 left over, so Torchy, by previous agreement with Greater Seattle, Inc., tucked it into The Greater Washington Advertising Fund, the purse he uses to pay Husky athletes.

There was no way to refute all the untruths or to explain the questioned actualities printed in various publications. It was a bad time for Torchy, Harvey Cassill and their wives, Ruth and Florence.

It really hurt all of us, and it was something we never got over. The administration didn't stand behind Harvey. Chuck Frankland was on the board of regents and did nothing to help. H. P. "Dick" Everest, the University vice-president and faculty athletic representative, was my friend but he took a neutral position.

The Times *came out with stories about the slush fund as if nobody knew about it, and the Blethens had been contributing to it for years. I was terribly disappointed in Royal Brougham whom I had known well since 1919. When* The Times *started to tear me apart, he did nothing in the* P-I *to support me, and he didn't even call to give me a boost when he knew that many things being written were untrue.*

John Cherberg was aware of the fund for many years. He attended our annual breakfast meeting and thanked our contributors profusely for the help they provided. He even borrowed a list of our donors and wrote a special letter of thanks to them at Christmas time.

I'm terribly proud of the time I've spent helping the University.

I imagine it took two or three months out of the twelve for this activity during some years. I worked my own way through high school and the University, and I knew the problems athletes have. It's a fact of life that a kid can't be a college athlete and make it through school without outside help if he's in any need at all. That's why there has been a fund like ours at almost every university.

You know how it works. A lot of people are interested, but try and get them to work. I had to get into all sorts of things with the kids, like accidents, maternity problems and everything else. For instance, when Sandy Lederman's wife fell and broke her leg and then later had to have it reset, somebody had to help.

They said we had $75,000 in our fund and that I made a lot of money on the pro football game. We never had $75,000 total in five years, let alone one. Before we ever played the pro game, we were $9,500 in the red; we had almost two thousand in checks outstanding; and I had personally signed a note at the bank for $7,500.

They even said that Western Printing must have made a lot of money out of the University connection. Well, we were just one of several concerns doing printing for the A.S.U.W., and we must have been about fifth in volume. The University work made up less than four per cent of our business, and in checking back, Western Printing did more work for the University before I joined the firm than after.

At one time I even got a call from Tom Harmon, the ex-All American from Michigan who became a national television sports commentator. He wanted me to give him an exclusive story on the slush fund. He was a pretty good friend, but I refused. Then I asked him how he got through school. Did he have a special job or did anybody give him any extra help? He didn't answer, and he changed the subject.

The controversy continued. Meanwhile, George Briggs, Jr., the 31-year-old assistant athletic director at the University of California, was hired to replace Harvey Cassill within six days after his resignation. Briggs, in turn, signed up Darrell Royal — a former Oklahoma University quarterback and then head coach at Mississippi State — to succeed Cherberg.

Then, on May 6, the Pacific Coast Conference cracked down on Washington, banning the University from Rose Bowl receipts for two years and at the same time removing any of the Husky athletic teams from consideration for all championships. The

166

football payment plan was cited as the reason, stipulating that some 27 players had received an average of sixty dollars a month over the seventy-five dollar conference limit. It was little consolation, but UCLA was also punished for similar violations and Southern Cal was put on probation.

The Greater Washington Advertising Association had been disbanded, but the wolves went on nipping at Torchy's heels.

The Times continued to harrass me for some time until Paul Ashley, my attorney who had written extensively on libel, told the managing editor to lay off or he could be subject to a heavy suit. Well, the paper sort of slowed down, but then another thing happened.

A new football season with a new coach was well underway when *True* magazine came out in October of 1956 with a scathing article which dredged up the entire story and reopened old wounds. The article – by Lee Schulman, a producer at KING TV – was so flagrant that Torchy sued for a quarter of a million dollars.

The suit, which was being tried in the courts of New York State, dragged on for about two years. Torchy and Paul Ashley were then called east by one of the judges who advised them to settle out of court because more years would pass before the case would finally be decided and that legal fees and other costs would eat up any judgment which might be granted – provided Torchy even won the case.

In the end Torchy received a cash settlement of six thousand dollars and the promise of a retraction in an ensuing issue of *True*. Almost three years after the original offending piece had appeared, the August 1959 edition of the magazine carried the following abbreviated apology in a column called "The Editor Speaking."

> And speaking of professional athletes, we'd like to make a correction . . .
>
> Mr. Roscoe C. Torrance of Seattle, Washington, has been in communication with the editors with regard to an article referring to many irregularities in football recruiting on the Pacific coast.
>
> *True* did not state that Mr. Torrance provided liquor and girls for entertainment of football recruits or that he had any knowledge of it.
>
> The editors of *True* magazine did not intend to convey

any impressions that Mr. Roscoe C. Torrance participated in such irregularities in football recruiting and if any reader of *True* magazine placed such interpretation on the article, which was wholly unintended, *True* magazine regrets such interpretation, and takes pleasure in clarifying the situation so far as it concerns Mr. Roscoe C. Torrance, who is an alumnus of the University of Washington, and a prominent citizen of Seattle.

———————

Throughout the unfortunate affair Torchy had his share of loyal supporters. The *West Seattle Herald* editorialized:

> It seems that Torchy Torrance has had to take more than his share of abuse during the recent football controversy.
>
> A loyal alumnus of the University of Washington . . . Torchy's heart is in athletics. He likes to see good teams represent his alma mater. Maybe he has been a little over-enthusiastic, but certainly his activities in trying to bring good football players to Washington are no different than that of booster groups in other schools in the Pacific Coast Conference . . . he was doing his bit to put teeth into the song "Bow Down to Washington."
>
> Let's give "Torch" a break and quit picking on him. He's too nice a guy to have to suffer the abuse that has been aimed at him.

Dink Templeton, the Stanford coach and great pole vaulter of the wooden pole era, wrote in a similar vein:

> Torchy is the kind of alumnus every school wishes it had. He'll work his head off to raise some dough to help the boys, ladle it out to 'em in small chunks when they need it and still try never to dictate to the coach. Yet, suddenly he finds himself charged as the man who incited the players to rebellion against Johnny Cherberg . . . The charge is so fantastic that Torchy can't quite realize that it's real . . .
>
> It is my personal belief that no school ever had a better, a harder-working, self-sacrificing or squarer guy than the likable Torchy Torrance.

Hal Wood of the United Press—whom Torchy had known

Torchy was more than just a rah-rah guy for his alma mater. He devoted endless volunteer hours to athletic recruiting and student aid. As Dink Templeton of Stanford wrote: "Torchy is the kind of alumnus every school wishes it had." (Special Collections Division, University of Washington Libraries)

earlier as a sportswriter at Twin Falls, Idaho—was equally complimentary in one of his stories:

> Poor Roscoe (Torchy) Torrance, as honest a guy as you'll ever meet, is caught in the middle of this one—caught doing about the same thing every other major college has to do to keep competitive in the world of sports . . .
> Torrance, a Washington alumnus and red-hot for more

than a quarter of a century is irked by all the bad publicity.

"What the heck," he said over the telephone, "they talk about corrupting our youth. Shucks, I know hundreds of men who were helped through college and went on to become first-class citizens. I've never run across any men who were injured by getting helped through school."

As Torrance points out, a lot of young athletes would end up digging ditches if they didn't get a boost on their way through college.

"Many come from homes where they never would get an education if they didn't get some assistance," says Torrance. "I think men who help young fellows through school are doing a fine thing . . . You aren't a man if you don't try to win. I'll be a supporter of the University of Washington as long as I live—and I'll always strive for a winner!"

The turmoil eventually faded away, but years afterwards there were still a few individuals who held it against Torchy for being responsible, as they thought, for John Cherberg's undoing as a football coach.

In the meantime, The Cowboy—who by that time had good statewide name familiarity—took advantage of the situation and ran for lieutenant governor on the Democratic ticket in the fall of 1956. He won handily and later was re-elected often to the same position. Coincidentally, Howie Odell, another ousted Husky coach, was elected a King County commissioner in the general election that year.

As might be expected, the relationship between Torchy and Cherberg was seriously strained by the events of 1955-56. However, both men were prominent public figures and their paths had to cross periodically at various civic and social functions. Besides that, a lifetime grudge can be a terrible burden— so they ultimately patched up the differences between themselves.

It happened at Sicks' Stadium. As lieutenant governor, John was scheduled to throw out the first ball to open the season for the Rainiers and it was my job to introduce him. We met in the parking lot and shook hands. John sort of apologized to me and I to him. Though we had our differences, after that we were always able to meet on a friendly basis.

I didn't want to bring the story up again, but if it were left out of my biography, there'd be an obvious void.

Chapter 12

One Hundred Republicans
and One Democrat

Husky football and Rainier baseball were not Torchy's only athletic interests. While he was still at the University, he became involved in the Amateur Athletic Union which, in turn, led him to active participation in the affairs of the U.S. Olympic Committee.

There had to be a focal point—a base of operations—for his many roles, and the Washington Athletic Club ultimately filled that bill. He was just emerging on the Seattle business scene when the idea for such a facility was first conceived by Noel B. Clarke, a Los Angeles promoter, who started a campaign to sell two thousand memberships in a non-existent building in the late 1920s. However, Clarke's controversial real estate practices soon got him into trouble, and it was necessary for someone else to pick up the pieces and an outstanding obligation of some $7,500 for newspaper advertising and office expenses.

The club's ensuing development was traced in a history booklet written by William C. Speidel, Jr., titled *The WAC's Works*. Speidel noted:

> The second major figure to take a whack at the project was William D. Comer, president of the Puget Sound Savings and Loan Association . . . Except for Clarke's costs, he bought control of the club for $500 . . .
>
> Comer allowed as how he would arrange the financing of the club if backers could show him 2,000 men who were interested . . . so they took up offices in the White-Henry-Stuart Building, set up a crew of salesmen on a commission basis and went to work . . . A total of 2,600 resident applica-

tions were secured in 90 days and when weeded to 2,000, the project went forward.

The club opened its doors on December 16, 1930. Three months later they were about to be closed permanently. The depression which had hit the East two years before now was in full force in Seattle. It wound up as the rock on which Comer broke his pick. Practically single-handed, he'd been financing a $10,000-per-month Athletic Club grocery and sundry bill . . . the majority of the club's bonds were owned by his bank . . . and, although he never believed himself guilty of any crime, a bit of emotion and his signature on the wrong piece of paper resulted in his trip to the penitentiary . . .

It was at this point, when practically any thinking man would have let his Athletic Club bonds go for about five cents on the dollar, that Darwin Meisnest, then a cement

This was an artist's conception of the Washington Athletic Club building drawn when a group of eager optimists—Torchy among them—overcame great odds to turn a dream into reality. Ground was first broken on December 16, 1929, and the structure was formally dedicated exactly one year later. The land at Sixth and Union Streets had been owned from pioneer days by Mrs. Hannah Newman, wife of John "Packer Jack" Newman, a famous sourdough of the Alaskan gold rush of 1897-98. (Washington Athletic Club collection)

company executive, stepped into the picture . . . Meisnest assumed management of the club in March of 1931. He was 33 years old at the time. He immediately employed his brother Ken, who was 27 and who chose to learn the operation of the club from the bottom up by beginning his work in the basement as receiving clerk . . .

After three months the club was some $38,000 in the hole. A series of bewildering financial gymnastics ensued; the National Bank of Commerce put up the $38,000; and Darwin Meisnest ended up in control. The doors stayed open.

Speidel's history wasn't exactly right. As I recall, Ned Skinner and Bill Edris first picked up the bonds with the help of Judge Howard S. Findley; then they hired Dar Meisnest away from Pacific Coast Coal. It was later that Dar eventually bought control. Jules Charbneau should be given special credit for acquiring memberships at the critical time. They were selling for $25 and he got a ten per cent commission. I think he must have sold a couple thousand of them which made it possible for the club to continue.

What happened to W. D. Comer; Ed Campbell, vice-president of Puget Sound Savings; and Adolph Linden, owner of Radio Station KJR and a director of the bank, was very unfortunate. Apparently they improperly invested funds of their depositors after the stock market crash, and they all went to prison. They and their institution had been very instrumental in keeping the Athletic Club going in the early stages, but when they got out of the penitentiary, they never regained their former stature in the community.

Torchy, obviously no stranger to Meisnest, served on the WAC's board of governors at this critical time. Other members were Royal Brougham, Earl F. Campbell, Jules L. Charbneau, I. F. Dix, Clarence S. Edmundson, Otto H. Eisenbeis, Don H. Evans, Charles F. Frankland, Lacy Hofius, Carroll S. Kellison, Roy J. Kinnear, Dr. Otis F. Lamson, Charles C. May, Fowler W. Martin, Charles P. Moriarty, Floris Nagelvoort, Dr. Don H. Palmer, Reginald H. Parson, James F. Pollard, Lawrence K. Smith, Dr. William C. Speidel, Thomas D. Stimson, Art Strandburg, John J. Sullivan and George M. Varnell.

Even before the WAC building was opened for business, the board of governors, on November 14, 1930, established the club's purpose: "to foster amateur athletics, promote physical

173

culture, athletics, sports, good fellowship, recreation and social entertainment." At the same meeting the members agreed to Article 33 of the by-laws which read, in part: "Both the playing of cards or other games for money is prohibited. The Board of Governors shall have the power to suppress any and all gambling games, cards or otherwise . . . THE GAME OF POKER IS STRICTLY PROHIBITED."

Despite Article 33, slot machines were introduced into the club and were instrumental in paying off debts and achieving solvency. The passage of the Steele Act, which permitted the return of liquor to the state of Washington in 1934, also helped improve the financial picture. From a low of 1,426 members in 1935, the club not only survived but began a substantial growth.

It might be interesting to note that, during the struggle in the midst of the depression era, the WAC's Grill in the summer of 1933 was offering a beef sandwich for 25 cents, boneless pickled pigs' feet and potato salad for 35 cents and cold prime ribs of beef for 50 cents. The Windsor Garage had a special parking rate for members: 10 cents for the first two hours and 15 cents for the next two. As soon as Prohibition was revoked, the WAC started selling martinis, old-fashioneds and manhattans for 30 cents, Western beer for 20 cents and Eastern beer for a quarter.

In the meantime, Torchy, Dar Meisnest and Jack Sullivan were among those who conceived the idea of a club-within-a-club. Speidel's WAC history described the genesis of the new organization:

> . . . in the beginning it was a gimmick for increasing the membership of the WAC. Somebody asked how many people Room 400 would hold. The answer was 100 . . . so, naturally, it was decided to add one more number, form a club called the 101 Club and get that many new members . . .
>
> On September 11, 1933, it was announced at the board meeting that the 21st floor had been completely renovated and headquarters were being built for the newly organized 101 Club . . .

Torchy remembered another twist to the naming of the club:

At that time we felt we had one hundred Republicans and one

*Democrat, Judge Hugh Todd, so the 101 seemed like a good designa-
tion for the organization. Jack Sullivan was elected first president.
Paul F. Glaser was the second one and I was the third.*

*The 101 Club went on to become one of the finest organizations
in the city, supporting athletics and civic promotions of all kinds.
The good things it has done are too numerous to mention, but I
can recall one example.*

*Doris Brown was competing in cross-country at Seattle Pacific
College and wanted to go to Wales for the International Cross-country
Meet there. Ken Forman, her coach, mentioned it to me and said
it would take something like fifteen hundred dollars to swing it.
I went to the 101 Club luncheon the next week and told the members
what the need would be and how urgent it was because the event
was just a month away.*

*We raised $1,350 that noon, plus $150 later in the day, and
Ken and Doris were on their way to Wales. She won the meet
and it started her on her way to becoming both an Olympic athlete
and official. Ken Forman went on to serve as a coach for the U.S.
teams in the Olympics and the Pan American Games.*

———————

It was much earlier than that, though, that the Washington
Athletic Club sponsored the first of its many champions. It also
marked the beginning of Torchy's greater involvement in the
Olympic Games.

Back in 1924 he had helped raise money to send Augustus
Pope to Paris where Gus placed fourth in the discus event with
a throw of 145 feet, 9 inches. Four years later he assisted in
the campaign which permitted Coach Hec Edmundson and two
of his track men to go to Amsterdam. Stephen Anderson got
a silver medal in the 110-meter hurdles with a time of 14.8,
and Herman Brix also placed second in the shotput with a toss
of 51 feet, 8¼ inches. [Brix later went to Hollywood where,
as Bruce Bennett, he was one of several ex-Olympians who played
Tarzan on the screen.]

Next came Helene Madison in 1932.

*Ray Daughters was coach at the Crystal Pool in Seattle at the
time the Athletic Club was being built. He had developed some fine
swimmers, and we got him to come over to the WAC as director*

of athletics and swimming coach. Of course he brought all his athletes with him.

Helene Madison was his star pupil. The Athletic Club sponsored her for the 1932 Olympics in Los Angeles which I attended. Helene took the gold medals in the 100 meter and 400 meter freestyle races and anchored the winning team in the 400 meter relay. Her medals later were placed in the care of the WAC and were on display there for a good many years.

Actually that was the beginning of a sad story for Helene, and I blame Royal Brougham for a lot of her troubles. He thought he was doing her a big favor when he went to Jack Warner of Warner Brothers Studios and suggested that she would be the next Annette Kellerman of the movies. [Kellerman was an Australian swimmer who created a vaudeville act known as "ornamental swimming" which she performed in a huge glass tank. She starred in a movie titled "Neptune's Daughter" in 1914.]

Well, Helene signed a contract, but when she went to Hollywood for an audition, they decided she wasn't a good prospect for the movies and they released her. In the meantime, Don Farris, secretary of the Amateur Athletic Union in New York, and I had worked together to arrange an around-the-world exhibition tour for Helene,

In the early 1930s Helene Madison held fifteen of the sixteen world freestyle swimming records and was a triple gold medal winner in the 1932 Olympics. However, misfortune dogged her later career and she ended up back in Seattle where Torchy befriended her and eventually was executor of her meager estate. (Special Collections Division, University of Washington Libraries)

176

with her mother as a chaperone. It would have taken her about six or seven months with all expenses paid, and she would have had some money left over when she got back. This all went out the window when she signed the movie contract and was stripped of her amateur status.

She then went into the swimming exhibition business, mostly in Florida, but there weren't too many places where this was in demand during the depression. She drifted through several marriages and eventually opened a swimming school in the basement of the Moore Hotel in Seattle. It was then that she developed cancer which she battled for several years until she could no longer function.

I had been on the board of the Northwest Memorial Hospital since the idea was first conceived, and I talked the members into taking care of her until her final days. This the board did without any idea of being repaid for the services. I went out to see her two or three times a week during the last six months of her illness. During that time she asked me if I would be executor of any estate she might have. This I agreed to do, and she passed away on November 25, 1970.

Royal Brougham and I decided we should have a memorial service for her at the Bonney-Watson Mortuary on Broadway. We called her daughter in Portland and she attended along with fifty or sixty fans who remembered how great Helene was as a world-class swimmer. I was in charge of the service, and Brougham delivered the eulogy. It was a pretty nice affair even if we did handle it ourselves. Later on, in going through her personal effects, I found an insurance policy which amounted to about four thousand dollars. With her daughter's approval, we applied this against her hospital bill even though it wasn't expected.

In her last few years Helene tried to paint a little bit to take her mind off her problems. Despite everything, she was a wonderful individual and, in my estimation, the greatest swimmer of all time.

[In 1932 the eighteen-year-old, six-foot blonde from Seattle held fifteen of the sixteen world freestyle swimming records for women. While her records were eventually all beaten, she remained unchallenged for her performances over the entire span of official racing distances. Her record times were:]

100 yards.....1:00.0s	400 meters.....5:28.5s	880 yards.....11.41.2s
100 meters...1:06.6s	440 yards.......5:31.0s	1,000 yards.....13.23.6s
220 meters...2:34.8s	500 yards.......6:16.4s	1,000 meters...14:44.8s
300 yards.....3:39.0s	500 meters.....7:12.0s	1,500 meters...23.17.2s
300 meters...3:59.5s	800 meters...11:41.2s	1 mile.............24:34.6s

In 1936 Torchy was again involved when the Athletic Club sponsored Jack Medica in Berlin. He won a gold in the 400-meter freestyle race at 4:44.5, a silver in the 1500-meter freestyle at 19.34 and anchored the U.S. team which finished second at 9:03 in the 200-meter freestyle relay.

Also in 1936 was the phenomenal performance of the University of Washington crew. Earlier the Huskies had swept the NCAA Regatta, winning the freshman, junior varsity and varsity races at Poughkeepsie. Then the varsity surprised almost everyone by placing first in the Olympic trials. Up till that time no preparations had been made to send the crew to Berlin.

I learned from Clifford Goes, chairman of the Olympic rowing committee, that we had to come up with $35,000 in a hurry otherwise the Vesper Athletic Club of Philadelphia would represent the United States as an alternate. With extra help from the old standbys— Deke McDonald, Ernie Skeel and William O. McKay—the money was raised practically overnight. One of the ways we did it was to hold a "Crew Tag Day" on the streets of Seattle, selling tags for a dollar. Not only did the Huskies go to Berlin, but in the eight-oared shell race they edged out the Italians by six-tenths of a second to win the gold.

[Members of the crew were Herbert Morris, Charles Day, Gordon Adam, John White, James McMillin, George Hunt, Joseph Rantz, Donald Hume and Robert Moch.]

In the early 1930s, while he was struggling to turn a profit at Western Printing, Torchy also kept getting deeper involved in the affairs of the Amateur Athletic Union. He was invited to New York to make a personal presentation as a candidate for the western vice-presidency of the AAU, one of three such regional offices in the nation. There was a problem to overcome, however.

My two front teeth which were damaged in the water fountain incident when I was a kid in American Falls were acting up, so Dr. Bill Stevenson decided to pull them and fix me up with a temporary partial plate for the trip east. He said he'd work on a permanent solution when I got back.

At the AAU meeting I didn't know whether I'd lisp or whether my teeth would fall out, but my speech must have gone fairly well because I was elected vice-president of the western region. I was on my way to the national presidency, it appeared, but my finances held me back.

Anyway, when I returned to Seattle, Bill took a look at my teeth and said, "Let's let the thing go and see how it works out." Well, I went through the war in the Pacific, and more than forty years later the original "temporary" set was still doing the job.

Always the inveterate promoter of Seattle and Washington State, Torchy believed that the Pacific Northwest in general and Mt. Rainier in particular would be an ideal choice for the Winter Olympics trials, if not the big event itself. The third Winter Games had been held at Lake Placid, New York, in 1932 and, as a result, a new interest in skiing had been created in the United States. The Federation Internationale de Ski, a worldwide ruling body for the sport, had been created in 1924 (when the first Winter Games were held at Chamonix, France), and ten years later the F.I.S. met in New York to select a site for the 1935 trials.

Dar Meisnest and I attended the meeting and took with us a motion picture film that the Mt. Rainier Park people had made. After waiting about three hours in the lobby of the Biltmore Hotel while the Lake Placid delegation made its presentation, we were invited to show our silent movie. (You've got to remember that moving pictures were still rather crude at that time and "talkies" were just emerging).

Dar and I both made preliminary remarks and then we presented the film which was a dandy. When the movie was over, Leib Deio, the international president from Switzerland, stood up and said: "It yust made tears come to my eyes."

After we left the room, they took a vote and we were awarded the trials, provided we would deposit $10,000 with the F.I.S. and arrange for proper housing for the athletes. This we agreed to do. Dar and I figured we could charge a dollar a head for admission to the Panorama area at Mt. Rainier where the downhill and slalom races would be held. To help draw a crowd, we invited Hannis Schroll of Austria, a well known skier of the day, to put on an exhibition before the trials.

Following their earlier association at the University of Washington, Torchy and Dar Meisnest became closely involved in the affairs of the Washington Athletic Club and its various activities. In 1935 the two of them went to New York City where they were successful in promoting the Mt. Rainier area as the site for the Winter Olympic trials. (Special Collections Division, University of Washington Libraries)

We had cleared everything with the National Parks people, of course, except that we neglected to discuss admissions. About three months before the event, the subject came up and we were informed that we couldn't charge people for anything in Rainier National Park. That really hit us in the solar plexus!

Finally we organized a committee and called on the Downtown Rotary Club, then headed by Ernie Skeel, to help us raise the funds for the guarantee and other expenses. Thanks to D. K. "Deke" McDonald, William O. McKay and others, we began to solve the problem. We sold the radio rights to KJR for something like two hundred dollars, and the Park authorities eventually gave us permission to ask for donations. Well, you know how it is with donations: some people do and some don't. Besides that, it was right in the middle of the depression and money was really tight.

Anyhow, when the big day came, Darrell Crooks and Don Fraser—two members of the U.S. ski team—took me up to the top of Panorama where I was to announce the exhibition by Hannis Schroll and the trials which followed. I made it up all right with a pair of leather "climbers" on my skis and then spent the whole day on the mountain.

It was a beautiful clear day, and the hot sun reflected off the snow so that by night time I was beet red—burnt to a crisp on my face and even down my throat.

Anyway, the day ended and I was left up on Panorama. The "climbers" wouldn't work going down, they told me, so I took them off and there was nothing to do but ski, which I had learned a little bit. Unfortunately, when I got about a hundred feet from the top, I fell. After that I rolled and bounced all the way to the bottom. I was a mess. I had broken one ski, but luckily my arms and legs made it okay. My face cracked open from the sunburn, and it was weeks before it healed up. Besides that, I had a real sore bottom for a long time. Believe me, it was the last time I ever went skiing!

When the trials were over, we had taken in a little over four thousand dollars in donations, and the Rotary Club had to make up the rest. I don't know if it was worth it, but we made a hit because the International Federation invited us to put in our bid for future trials—but we never did.

While I'm still on the subject, it was also in the 1930s that I appeared before the state legislature about getting an appropriation to support an application for holding the Winter Olympics in Washington. Whether it was the state of the economy or what, the *legislators didn't take too kindly to the idea and it never got off the ground.*

Years later—in the late 1950s—we decided to try again. I was with a delegation which was supposed to include Governor Dan Evans; but at the last minute the governor was detained, so I was chosen to make the presentation before the Olympic Committee. I was up against strong competition from governors of interested states, which made it pretty difficult, but in the end Squaw Valley, California, was chosen.

While his many other obligations kept him away from the 1936 Olympics in Berlin, Torchy at least had a small hand in the U.S. participation. Because of Adolph Hitler's professed anti-Semitism, there was mounting pressure for the American team to boycott the Games. As a representative of the Pacific Northwest AAU (which included Oregon, Washington, Montana and Idaho), Torchy had to cast his vote on the controversial issue.

I went to New York on the train with Aaron Frank, a close friend of mine and a fine Jewish gentleman who was president of the Meier and Frank Department Store in Portland. The Northwest AAU had voted in favor of sending a team to Berlin, and Aaron told me that's the way he'd vote at the national meeting.

We stayed at the Waldorf Astoria, and I didn't see much of Aaron the first day we were there. It was about two o'clock in the morning when he knocked on my door and said he wanted to talk to me. He was obviously quite distraught. "I've got some tough news," he said. "I know we all decided in favor of sending our kids to Berlin and I certainly intended to do just that, but today I was told that Meier and Frank could lose its credit in the New York markets if I didn't vote against sending the team."

There wasn't much Aaron could do with pressure like that because it could have ruined his business. It was a sad moment for him, but he wanted me to know the circumstances of why he was forced to change his mind. The next day he cast a no vote for Oregon, and I, of course, voted in favor of U.S. participation. The margin was very close, but we ended up sending a team.

[At the Berlin Games, Hitler snubbed what the German press called America's "Black Auxiliaries." Rather than shake hands with the black champions (including Jessie Owens who won four gold medals), Hitler did not publicly congratulate any of the winners.]

182

World War II caused the cancellation of the 12th and 13th Olympiads, as well as what would have been the 5th and 6th Winter Games. Not long after his return from the Marines, though, Torchy was soon back in the business of helping potential champions.

Karol Estelle and Peter Michael Kennedy decided they wanted to go to the Olympics in the figure skating competition for pairs. They practiced three or four hours a day at the Civic Ice Arena and entered skating events all over the country. It was a costly business, so I got the Athletic Club to sponsor them for several years to the tune of six or seven thousand dollars a year.

I'd go down to the Arena at about five in the morning to watch them, and occasionally they'd get into a little argument about one thing or another and I would have to step in and help them over the rough spots. The WAC's investment was worth it, though, because after placing sixth at the Winter Games at St. Moritz in 1948, they came within one-thousandth of a point of winning the gold medal at Oslo in 1952.

Torchy was to become deeply involved in the financing of the 1956 U.S. Olympic team, but first there were other cir-

Torchy was instrumental in raising funds to send Karol and Peter Kennedy to the Winter Olympic Games in 1948 and 1952. The Seattle figure skaters won the silver medal at Oslo in the latter year, losing first place by a fraction of a point on a controversial decision by one of the judges. (Special Collections Division, University of Washington Libraries)

cumstances and events which ultimately led up to that funding effort.

When I was a teen-ager in Spokane, I was fascinated by a puzzle contest promoter named Place Meyers. He bought expensive suits which he wore for about three months and then he gave them to me. As a result, I was the best dressed poor boy at Lewis and Clark High School. Well, after I returned from World War II, I was appointed chairman of a committee to raise funds for a new American Legion Memorial Building to be erected at Seventh and University in Seattle, and I guess my memories of Place Meyers and his contests caused me to favor an opportunity which presented itself.

I had met Gordon F. Gemeroy, another puzzle man, through Jack Sharkey of The Seattle Times *and was sold on his theory for raising money. Other members of the American Legion committee with me were L. A. "Bill" Williams, Cecil H. McKinstry and Joseph A. Sweeney, and they agreed to the puzzle program.*

We had to raise $15,000 to set up an office in the Old Lyons Building and to place our first advertisement in the American Weekly *for $7,500. Legion members signed a note for that purpose. Pretty*

Torchy and Winifred Hageman shared awards for service to Seattle's Northwest Hospital. He joined its board of directors when the hospital was just a hopeful dream and served until it became a functioning reality. In his busy lifetime, he received dozens of certificates and plaques in recognition of his contributions. (Special Collections Division, University of Washington Libraries)

soon the twenty-dollar checks started coming in to enable us to buy more advertising and increase the return. In the end we netted more than half a million dollars so that we could go ahead with the fine building to house Seattle Post No. 1.

There was a complication, though. The winner of first prize turned out to be a Canadian from Ontario. We had advertised that the contest was open only to U.S. citizens, so we had to send detectives to find out what happened, and then we took the prize away and gave it to the second-place winner. It was not a happy situation, but it eventually worked out all right.

The American Legion campaign was so successful that Torchy next worked with Gemeroy to raise funds for a hospital in Bremerton, Washington. That, too, produced outstanding results, so Torchy recommended a similar program to fellow board members of the Northwest Hospital in Seattle, which at that time was still just a "dream on paper." Again the puzzles produced as they provided the necessary start-up funds for the envisioned health-care facility which eventually opened its doors in 1960.

It was not easy to work with Gemeroy. I had to sober him up on several occasions and even had to cook breakfast for him to get him ready to appear at meetings. He was in and out of sanitariums because of his drinking, but he really knew the puzzle business and how to raise money.

Despite the problems of dealing with the alcoholic promoter, Torchy recommended him and his program to the U.S. Olympic Committee. The official Quadrennial Report of the USOC following the 1956 Games described the venture for posterity.

Several years ago Roscoe Torrance of Seattle, Washington, long associated with the AAU and the Olympic Association, informed us of a successful plan carried out under his direction to raise funds for an American Legion Memorial Building in Seattle. It consisted of a puzzle contest in which the contestants made donations to the fund for the privilege of competing and qualifying for substantial cash prizes.

We discussed the adoption of such a plan for the 1952 Games and it was approved by the Executive Board provided the cost of launching the campaign would be met by outside underwriters. Unable to obtain such funds, the plan was abandoned, but the idea was revived for the 1956 campaign. After considerable discussion of the merits of such a plan, including the possibility of criticism, the USOC Executive Board, although not unanimously, voted to include it in our 1956 fund raising plan. Accordingly, a contract was entered into with the G. F. Gemeroy Company of Seattle to conduct a contest in the name of the U.S. Olympic Committee . . .

At the outset some of the Olympic officials were of the opinion that such a contest lacked dignity, but it was conducted in such a high class manner by the Gemeroy organization that no more than a half dozen complaints or criticisms were received in the Olympic office. The net amount of

Because of his earlier successes with Gordon F. Gemeroy's puzzle contests as a fund-raising gimmick, Torchy recommended him to the U.S. Olympic Committee with favorable results. Here Gemeroy (seated) checked a puzzle layout with Robert A. Baker, who placed the extensive national advertising through the Frederick E. Baker Advertising Agency. (Robert A. Baker collection)

$180,000 received was less than we anticipated, but our yard stick was contests conducted for hospitals, churches and similar causes where the emotional appeal is the determining factor. Everything considered, the contest was satisfactory.

Concurrently with the Gemeroy contests, Torchy was involved with the Seattle Rainiers; The Greater Washington Advertising Association; University of Washington football recruiting; his various concessions enterprises; the *TV Guide* experience; the affairs of the Rainier Club, the 101 Club, and the WAC (he was elected its president in 1952); the printing business; fund drives for the Salvation Army and the March of Dimes; the Seattle Seafair (he was president of Greater Seattle, Inc., too); and his daughter Shirley's polio illness.

Oh yes, in his spare time he rolled a respectable average in the printing industry's Ben Franklin Bowling League, using what one sportswriter called "a sidearm motion reminiscent of

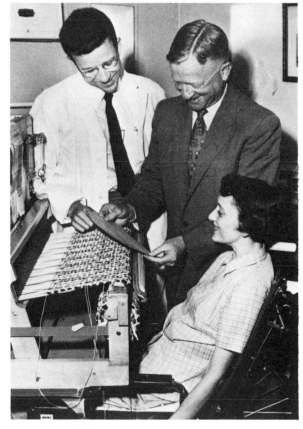

Torchy appeared in numerous publicity pictures during his many years of involvement in fund-raising for the March of Dimes. Here he and Dr. Fred Plum shared the good news of another sizable contribution with one of the polio victims his work aided. Doctor Plum treated the Torrances' daughter Shirley and later advised Torchy to return home from London prior to his open-heart surgery. (Special Collections Division, University of Washington Libraries)

187

The missing member of the Torrance family at Christmas time in 1954 was John who was away serving in his Air Corps medical unit. In the front row (left to right) were: William T. Lincoln, Douglas J. Lincoln and William S. Torrance with daughter Danna Ruth. Back row: Torchy; Shirley's husband, Gibbs D. Lincoln; Shirley; Ruth; Bill's wife June; and Winifred Inkster, Ruth's sister. (Shirley Torrance Lincoln collection)

a throw from deep short." In 1954 he was one of those instrumental in bringing the American Bowling Congress matches to Seattle. (As a youngster in American Falls he had been a pin-setter for ten cents a game when all of the pins had to be spotted by hand.)

As one of his friends said: "He was like a juggler with one too many balls in the air—but somehow he managed to keep all of them up there!"

Chapter 13

Time Out for Golf

Torchy's first golfing experience was not a happy one. As a youngster in Spokane, he lived across the street from a vacant strip of railroad property which was the scene of various athletic endeavors. In the first decade of the twentieth century golf was played by only a limited few, but one of the neighbors had some clubs and would practice occasionally in the large, open lot.

That was the first time I had ever seen or even heard of golf. I remember we were impressed by how far the ball would go when he hit it. One day I asked if I could try, and he let me. Well, I swung hard, hit a rock and broke the head off the wooden shaft. It took me quite a while to earn enough money to buy him a new club.

For the next eighteen years or so Torchy was more interested in baseball bats than cleeks or niblicks (as clubs were then called), but in Seattle he was introduced to the game on the University course where he discovered he had a natural aptitude for it.

The trouble is I started playing cross-handed, probably because I was a left-handed baseball hitter. One day I was in a foursome on the University course with Tubby Graves, George Varnell and Dick Hanley (who later became the football coach at Northwestern). We were having a fun game which started when Tubby whiffed a couple times on the tee. "I'm just practicing," he said. Then, on the third or fourth hole, Varnell asked me: "What's the matter? Have you got a bad left arm or something? Why don't you hold your clubs the way you're supposed to?" Well, from then on I started to play the regular way, although I continued to putt cross-handed

189

for a long time until they told me I looked so bad on the greens that I finally changed.

When Torchy joined Foster and Kleiser and his active baseball career was coming to a close, he became a charter member of the new Sand Point Country Club.

In 1926 I had the privilege of inviting Johnny Farrell and Walter Hagen, two top pros of the era, to play on the opening day. My big job was to get Hagen to the course on time, which I discovered was somewhat of a problem because he was staying downtown at the Washington Hotel and had been up late celebrating the night before. I finally got him out of bed, and our foursome — which included Hagen, Farrell and Hal Benton — eventually got off an hour late.

We had a great day. On the second hole — which was over a hill so you couldn't see the green — Farrell made a hole-in-one, the first in the club's history. Later, on the short 11th hole, Hagen teed off with his putter and got down for an easy two. If I hadn't been before, I was really hooked on the game after that.

I got so I was playing pretty good golf, shooting to about a 5-handicap. We went to the last hole before Hal Benton beat me for the club championship. During my Sand Point days I had given a trophy for the Captain's Cup, but before it could be presented, the clubhouse burned down and my trophy went with it.

As Torchy's life became busier and busier, golf became the diversion he needed. However, as a young man just starting out in business, he was limited financially and his chances of becoming a member of the prestigious Seattle Golf Club were decidedly slim. Then a stroke of luck gave him an opportunity he hadn't expected.

In the early 1930s Frank McLaughlin came to Seattle to succeed A. W. Leonard as president of Puget Sound Power & Light Company. One day A. W. said to me: "I wish you would take Frank around the city and introduce him to some people so he gets off to a good start."

That's what I did. I took him to the Athletic Club, the Rainier Club, the Chamber of Commerce and to various business places around town so he could meet some of the prominent people. Frank seemed to be very appreciative of my service, and I was glad to do it. While I was introducing him to our civic leaders. A. W.

recommended him for membership in the Seattle Golf Club.

I had pretty much forgotten my little favor to Frank when he called one day and asked: "How would you like to become a member of the Seattle Golf Club?"

Well, I told him that anybody would like to belong to the club but that I wasn't in that class of people and, besides that, I couldn't afford it.

"That isn't what I asked you," he said. "I asked you if you'd like to be a member."

I told him I would like it very much, and then I didn't hear any more about it for several months. Finally a letter came informing me that I was elected to membership and that my dues were paid for the first year. So, just doing a little favor for which I expected nothing in return, Frank got me into a position to meet a lot of

The most unique golf shot of Torchy's career took place at the Broadmoor Golf Club in Seattle in the mid-1930s when his ball lodged in a small tree. Kibitzing were his playing partners (left to right) Ernie Ketchum, Fred Burnaby and Alex Gray as Torchy resorted to his old baseball stance. (Special Collections Division, University of Washington Libraries)

191

great people and to have a lot of fun through the years. (In 1984 I reached my fiftieth year and became a dues-free member with all the privileges of the club.)

During his long golfing career Torchy played with scores of entertainment personalities, sports celebrities, political leaders and prominent individuals in various other endeavors. His score cards included names like Bob and Dolores Hope, Bing and Bob Crosby, Phil Harris, Fred Waring, Edgar Eisenhower, Paul Richards, Happy Chandler, Eddie Cantor, Ralph Kiner, Ed Sullivan, John Hodiak, Lloyd Mangrum, Horton Smith, Jimmy Dean, Tony Lema and others.

One game that I'm sorry didn't work out was at the Belaire Country Club in Los Angeles where I was scheduled to play with Gummo Marx, Edward G. Robinson and Dr. Danny Levanthal, the leg expert. It would have been an interesting round, I'm sure, but the rains came before we could tee off. As it turned out, Milton Berle joined us for lunch, and it was almost three hours before our unplanned party broke up.

As might be expected, Torchy also accumulated his share of golfing stories and experiences.

I never played with Bobby Jones, who was a fraternity brother, but I had the privilege of caddying for him when he came to the Seattle Golf Club in the early thirties for an exhibition. There were very few players who could get to the green of the old 540-yard 14th hole in two, but Jones did. I recall that he used his driver on the second shot from the fairway and dropped the ball on the edge of the green. He missed his eagle, but he settled for an easy birdie. Bobby won the U.S. Open four times. He was a real stylist and one of the greatest golfers we've ever had.

I played a lot of golf with my close friend, Anson A. "Bob" Littler, the dapper Seattle clothing store owner. We always had a standing 5-5-5 bet on every game—five dollars on the front nine, five on the back and five for final score. It also included $100 for a hole-in-one. We'd keep track all year and pay off at the end.

One year we went up to Victoria, British Columbia, late in the season to play in the annual Northwest Seniors Tournament. By this time I owed Bob $98, counting side bets. On the second day of the tournament I was in one of the last foursomes out, and on the second hole I made a hole-in-one. Bob had finished ahead of me and was at the clubhouse playing gin rummy when I came in. He wanted to know how I did, and very nonchalantly I said: "Just give me two bucks and we'll call it square for the year." [That hole-in-one was one of three in Torchy's career.]

In 1939 when I was vice-president and operations manager of the Rainiers, I also did occasional scouting of our farm club personnel. I decided to go over to Twins Falls to look at some of our players there, and I took Coach Tubby Graves of the University with me. While we were there, we decided to play a game of golf. The course was really a converted pasture and the fairways and greens were manicured by a flock of sheep which roamed the entire area. On about the sixth hole Tubby teed off and hit a sheep square on the head and killed it deader than a doornail. A few holes later

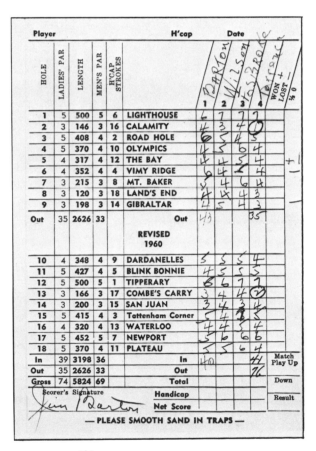

A scorecard from the Oak Bay Golf Club in Victoria, British Columbia, attested to Torchy's hole-in-one on the 146-yard second hole. It was one of three aces in his golfing career, and it earned him $100 from his friend Bob Littler in their annual competition.

193

Tubby also got a birdie, so I like to remember that game as the only time anybody got a sheep and a bird in the same round.

When we'd go to baseball meetings, Emil Sick would always play for high stakes against Walter Typel from Milwaukee who had the hops contract with most of the breweries. Afterwards they'd play gin rummy so that whoever lost could get even. It sounded big, but very little money ever changed hands.

On one occasion—in Sarasota, Florida—Emil said: "Walter get yourself a partner and Torchy and I will play you." It really put the pressure on me because with Emil I had to shoot about fifteen under par to make up for him. If he ever shot 110, it was lucky.

Anyway, Walter teamed up with Johnny Dell, and, with Emil shooting his usual game, he and I were six down coming to the eighth hole which had a big water hazard. There was no way Emil could get over it on his second shot, but he took out a wood and decided to go for it. Somehow he managed to hit the ball square; it sailed over the pond and onto the green, so we managed to pick up a couple strokes there.

After that, Emil parred seven holes in a row—something he'd never done before in his life and never came anywhere near afterwards. We won a lot of money from Walter, but then he and Emil stayed up all night playing gin until they were even again.

One time Ray Eckmann, Chuck Frankland, Mel Norquist and I took our wives to Vancouver, British Columbia, on a vacation, and while we were there, the four of us went out to the Shaughnessy Golf and Country Club for a game. Ray, who had become a haberdasher after his years at the University, always outdressed us by a mile. On that particular day he had on brand new knickers, plaid sox and a beautiful shirt and cap.

The starter at Shaughnessy was a huge heavy-set fellow with a beer-barrel stomach about four feet across. He stood about twenty feet away at right angles to the tee box when Ray got up for his drive. He took a big swing and the ball went off the toe of his club and hit the starter right in the stomach.

When it was obvious that the ball didn't hit him too hard to hurt him, we all broke out laughing. That was when the starter

REALLY got upset, and he kicked us off the course. We shouldn't have laughed, but the situation was so funny that we couldn't hold it back.

Another time in Vancouver my son John and I were out on the Capilano course as a twosome. John hadn't played much golf then, but he had a good swing. He got up on the first tee which was an elevated one with the caddy house at right angles from it. He took a big cut at the ball and hit it just like Ray Eckmann did. The ball went through the door of the pro shop, bounced around the walls, knocked goods off the shelves and scared the pro about half to death. He wasn't like the starter at Shaughnessy, though. He let us finish our game, and we had a real good time.

I remember another stray shot that wasn't very funny. Emil Sick, B. N. Hutchinson and I were playing at the Seattle Golf Club with John Boettiger (then the publisher of the Seattle Post-Intelligencer who married Franklin Roosevelt's daughter Anna). On the first tee John hooked his shot sharply and hit a caddy coming up the 18th fairway. He didn't apologize or check to see how the fellow was; he just went ahead with his game. Maybe that's why he was never invited to join the club? [Boettiger eventually left the P-I, failed in a newspaper venture in Phoenix, divorced Anna and finally committed suicide.]

I also remember another game when we didn't have much fun. Bob Crosby, Bing's younger brother, was also a good friend. Ruth and I had attended his opening show in New York on 42nd and Broadway, and he really was terrible. We talked with him afterwards and he said he was scared to death and knew he was off-key on everything he sang. It took him a year or more to develop his voice before he and his band ["The Bobcats"] caught on. Later, when I was in Washington at the end of the war to develop athletic programs for the Marines, Bob was there, too. He had tried his best to get into combat, but they thought he was doing too good a job in special services providing entertainment for Marine units. During that time we got quite well acquainted.

195

Anyway, on this particular day, I got a call from Bob who was in Seattle. "This is your Hollywood representative," he said. "How about a game of golf before I catch the 5:30 plane?"

Dave Warmuth, the TV Guide man who succeeded Jack Sullivan, was in my office at the time, and he said he would really like the chance to meet Bob. "Do you play golf?" I asked, and he said he played a pretty good game.

Well, the three of us went out to Broadmoor (which was closer to the airport than the Seattle Golf Club), and on the first tee Warmuth missed two swings before hitting the ball off at right angles. We knew then that he wasn't much of a golfer, and Bob and I were both upset because he had looked forward to a pleasant game before he had to leave for Los Angeles.

We played about 14 holes, and spent a lot of time looking for Warmuth's balls or waiting for him to get out of the rough some place. He seemed to think it was a big joke, but it really wasn't at the time. We never got to finish all 18 before Bob had to catch his plane, and, unfortunately, I never did get to play with him again.

I once caused a few heads to turn and tongues to waggle at the Seattle Golf Club when I invited a particular guest to play with me. The American Federation of Labor was having a convention in Seattle when George Meany was the president. He liked to play golf, so one day Dave Beck called me to say that the meeting schedule was a little light and could I arrange to take George out to the club for a game—which I did. You can imagine what some members thought (or said under their breath) when I walked in with the labor leader that Saturday.

Those who had lunch with George and later played with him ended up with a little different idea of the A. F. of L. Of course, there were still some people who called me up and let me know that the club was no place to bring a fellow like George Meany. I reminded them that he played at the best clubs in Washington, D.C., and around the country, so I figured we should show him the courtesy, too.

Like it or not, labor unions are here to stay. I had six of them in my printing plant, so I found it best to learn to live with them. Anyway, Dave Beck was pleased with the favor, and George had a good time. We corresponded for a year or two after that, and

196

he invited me to play with him in Washington, D.C., whenever I was in that neck of the woods.

I remember when another case of prejudice was overcome on a golf course. I was at a convention in Florida when Johnny Farrell was the pro at Hollywood. I called him to see if he could line up a game for me, and when I got there, he told me not to pay particular attention to the names of the men I'd be playing with. It turned out that "Mr. Anderson" and "Mr. Thompson" were a couple of fine Jewish fellows who would have been barred from the course if Johnny hadn't worked it out.

I ran into another kind of discrimination when Happy Chandler and I were playing on a fine course in Tampa, Florida. About half way around we came to a restroom. I started to go into a door and one of the black caddies stopped me. That one was for blacks

Bing Crosby was one of Torchy's long-time friends. They especially shared an interest in golf. Personal invitations to play in the popular Crosby Open Tournament were considered by Torchy to be highlights of his golfing career. (Special Collections Division, University of Washington Libraries)

only, he said; there was another one for the white folks.

It reminded me of the first time I experienced prejudice like that. Johnny Prim, a fine young black fellow, was playing baseball with us at the University. When we went to Berkeley, California, for a game they refused to let him into the White Cotton Hotel with the rest of the team. I then stayed with him at another hotel.

A person's color never made any difference to me. In some ways we're not all created equal; we have to work for the things we want, like Jim McCarter and Luther Carr, Sr., did.

Playing in the Crosby Open for two years was probably the highlight of my golfing career. Bing called me in 1951 and invited me to bring a pro and join the fun. I picked Ken Tucker from the Everett club who was a long-time friend of mine, and we had a real good time for six days.

We were there when Porky Oliver took his famous 16 on the 16th hole at Cypress, probably the toughest golf hole in the world. We were playing right behind him when his shot fell short of the beach and he then took all those strokes trying to get out of the sand. He was a good-natured guy and handled the situation well although it eliminated him from contention in the tournament. As for us, Ken put his tee shot on the green and got his par; and I chipped on with my second shot and ended up with a four.

In my second year at the Crosby, my pro partner was scheduled to be Ellsworth Vines, the great tennis player who was also pretty good with a golf club. At the last minute he had to cancel out to report to work as new general manager of the La Quinta golf and tennis complex between Palm Desert and Indio, California. It was too good an opportunity for him to pass up. I was then assigned a pro from Vancouver, Washington, whose name I don't remember. We didn't do too well, but we had a lot of fun. Phil Harris and I spent about an hour in the tower with Chris Schenkel and Jim Simpson who were broadcasting the tournament. I also played in the continuing gin rummy game we always had. I lost about a hundred and fifty dollars that second year, which was about what I had won the year before. I especially remember Phil Harris and singer Don Cherry in the card games. Cherry was a pretty good golfer, having played on the Walker Cup team. He entertained us with songs after Bing finished with his clambake on the opening night of the tournament.

198

I was invited for the third time, but I didn't make it. I was having trouble with the back injury I had suffered in the war and was taking shots for it. One morning I was having pretty bad spasms, so I called Dr. Barney McCallum at home and told him about my problem. He said: "Come to Providence Hospital at eight tomorrow morning and we'll give you a shot to see if that doesn't straighten you out."

Well, I got there at eight and nobody showed up till ten. Doctor McCallum and a nurse then came in and gave me a shot about half way between my rump and my knee. I felt a sharp pain but I thought it was just the needle going in. Geez, did it hurt! They had hit the sciatic nerve, and when I tried to walk, my leg crumbled under me.

Doc said: "Go lay on the bed for three or four hours and I think you'll be all right." But after three or four hours, I wasn't all right! I had to use a wheelchair to get to the front entrance of the hospital and into a taxi. Afterwards I went to see Dr. Fred Plum, a nerve specialist who had been taking care of Shirley after her polio attack. He told me that I had a bad situation because it would take years for the injured nerve to restore itself to normal. "You're just going to have to live with it," he said.

I lived with it all right, but that damned shot ruined my golf, my bowling, my dancing, my walking—and it didn't help my disposition either. I never played in the Crosby Open again.

While Torchy never lost his competitive spirit, the nerve problem took its toll on his physical ability. Fortunately, on December 17, 1954, the Palm Springs Desert Senior Golf Association was established at the O'Donnell Golf Club, with Ben H. Shearer as first president and George Howard, the pro at O'Donnell, as one of the key figures in its development.

Torchy was invited to join the select group, and in addition to his membership in the Seattle Golf Club, the Desert Seniors became an important part of his social and recreational life. He was elected to the board of directors and was a popular master of ceremonies for the annual awards dinner which usually took place at the Thunderbird Country Club. Many of Torchy's golf memories were to reflect his annual visits to Palm Springs before and after the founding of the Desert Seniors organization.

Jack Westland, with Torchy at the Thunderbird Country Club in Palm Springs, was national amateur champion in 1952 and also served as a United States Congressman from Washington's Sixth District. (Special Collections Division, University of Washington Libraries)

Long before the Bob Hope Desert Classic was created, we used to have the old Palm Springs Invitational which George Howard ran on the O'Donnell course. One year I invited Harry Givan down from Seattle to play in the tournament. He was one of the best amateur golfers in the U.S., but nobody in the southern circles had heard much about him. Well, not only did he win the tournament, but at the awards banquet afterwards his name was drawn for the big door prize which was a golf cart then selling for about six hundred dollars. My friends in Palm Springs told me "for gosh sakes, don't bring that guy down here again!"

Harry played on the U.S. Walker Cup team, and in 1952 he was both the trainer and campaign manager for Jack Westland of Everett who was running for Congress in Washington's Sixth District and also playing for the national amateur championship. Jack hadn't been able to play much golf because of campaigning, so he wasn't in the best of shape for the 36 holes on the final day. However, he and his opponent were all even after 18 when they came in for lunch. He had a sandwich, and Harry gave him a rubdown so he could at least walk the course the rest of the way. On the 16th green, Jack sank a curving downhill putt to win the title. The notoriety also helped him win the seat in Congress which he held for four terms until Lloyd Meeds, a Democrat, beat him in 1962.

Incidentally, I once was teamed with Anne Quast in a benefit match against Jack and Pat Lesser at the Everett Country Club. Pat was the U.S. amateur women's champion in 1955, and Anne won the same title in 1958. I played way over my head, and, as I recall, we came out about even.

———————

One of the features of the invitational was the Calcutta auction we held at the Desert Inn before each tournament. One year Emil Sick was there and wanted to get in on the action, so someone convinced him to bid for Bruce McCormick who was an exceptional golfer—when he was in shape to play. Bill Edris, the Seattle hotel man, got into a bidding war with Emil, and the price went to six thousand dollars before Emil finally won.

As play progressed through the week, McCormick built up something like a nine-stroke lead going into the final round. Edris, knowing a little about Bruce's weakness, invited him out to dinner. Bill served him four or five cocktails, and Bruce never got back to his room until about one a.m. He was not in very good shape for his 8:30 tee time the next morning. He was playing with Johnny Dawson, who was in second place, but nobody thought he'd ever lose his big lead with just 18 holes to go.

I think it was on the 8th hole that Bruce hit four balls out of bounds, and Johnny picked up quite a few strokes there. McCormick hit two more shots out of bounds later, and Dawson eventually caught up with him and won the match on the 18th hole. Needless to say, Emil was very upset as he watched about fifteen thousand dollars in prize money slip away from him. He had to settle for second place and a lot less. He also learned quite a lesson about amateur golfers—and a little bit about Bill Edris, too.

That, of course, reminded me of another Calcutta auction in which Edris was involved. On that occasion he and Rubin Fleet got into a heated competition for one of the players. Neither one *would give up, and finally Bill lost this temper and pasted Rubin one right on the jaw. Rubin didn't respond because he was so shocked. It really broke up the party, and it was quite some time before we were able to patch up the differences between the two of them. It was also the last Calcutta auction we had.*

Speaking of Johnny Dawson, I remember when he came to Seattle in the thirties on a promotional tour with Lawson Little, Jimmy Thompson and Horton Smith for Spaulding clubs. They were all great golfers, and Johnny had about the most perfect swing of anybody in golf. They played on the Jefferson municipal course, and I got up on a panel truck with a loudspeaker to explain to the gallery what was going on. It was quite unique in those days to have several thousand people follow the match. Years later there would be ten times that many.

After World War II Johnny Dawson and Jimmy Hines were involved in developing golf courses, including the Thunderbird at Palm Springs. Johnny offered Bob Littler and me a couple of lots and membership in Thunderbird at a very reasonable price. Bob accepted the offer and later made a nice profit on his lots, but I didn't have the money so I lost out on the deal. Johnny later followed Ben Shearer as president of the Desert Seniors and won the championship many times.

Horton Smith, who won the Masters in 1934, gave me a Tommy Armour putter when he came to Seattle and I really prized that club. It was stolen from me once at the Oahu Country Club in Hawaii, but I got it back. It was taken again at the Eldorado Country Club at Palm Springs, and I never saw it again.

When I was in France with Swede Larson, I went out to the St. Lo course where Horton Smith was teaching G.I.s how to play the game. Lloyd Mangrum, who later would win the U.S. Open in 1946, had been shot in the shoulder and was playing for the first time after being wounded. I played a few holes with him and Horton, and I was lucky that the course was dry and hard so I could get a long roll, otherwise I could never have stayed within shouting distance of either of them.

Ralph Kiner, once the National League homerun champion, was the longest hitter I ever played with. He hit the ball like he was still aiming for the centerfield fence. Probably the toughest competitor was Paul Richards, the former White Sox Manager who also was boss of the Rainiers in 1950. You never knew what his handicap was but he always played just good enough to beat you. He ended up running a newspaper down in Texas. Its slogan was: "Against the boll weevil and for an early spring."

One of the most unusual players was Fred Waring because he only used woods. He carried something like nine of them in his bag and he let me use them once when we were playing with Edgar Eisenhower at the Tacoma Country Club. In his book, Confessions of a Hooker, Bob Hope wrote that Fred failed to show up for a game once because he had termites in his clubs.

For a couple years I played in an unusual tournament Fred started at Palm Springs. Groups of eight teed off together and then played the best four balls, with partners alternating shots. I teamed with Al McCoy, who had been an assistant football coach at the University of Washington. In 1980 we came in absolutely last out of some 160 players and got a trophy with four jokers encased in plastic. The next year we reversed things and finished first. This time our trophy was four aces.

Torchy golfed occasionally with Fred Waring and played in tournaments sponsored by the well-known orchestra leader. Uniquely, Waring golfed only with woods, and Bob Hope once quipped that he had to cancel a match because of termites. (R. C. Torrance collection)

I can't leave the subject of golf without mentioning the games I had with Diane "Mousie" Powell, the wife of William Powell, the actor who became famous for his "Thin Man" role. George Howard would arrange the 18-hole matches, and we sort of took turns winning. George would always bet five dollars on Mousie and would have a lot of fun with me whenever I lost. It was no disgrace to lose to Mousie, though, because she was a fine golfer and played in just about all the tournaments in the desert.

Incidentally, it was through Dolores Hope and George Howard that I got to know Bill Powell. He was one of the actors who was able to make the switch from silent movies to talkies. His middle name was Horatio, which was very fitting because he was a real example of the Horatio Alger success story. I attended the service when he died on March 5, 1984, at age 90. It was a very informal affair conducted by Frank Bogart, the mayor of Palm Springs—no prayers, no tears, just a lot of people paying their respects to a great guy.

Speaking of George Howard, he was a special friend of all of us at O'Donnell. He knew all the Seniors by name, but he never called anybody anything except "Mr."—me excluded. He did call me Torchy. Madge and I were back at the Kentucky Derby when the call came to Happy's place on Saturday that George had passed away and that funeral services would be on Monday.

There was no way we could get a plane out of Louisville on Sunday because they had all been booked months in advance. We finally made connections through Cincinnati, and a state trooper we knew drove us all the way to the airport. We eventually arrived in Palm Springs Monday morning with just enough time to freshen up a bit before the funeral. In the anteroom after the services I heard someone say: "Oh, I'm so glad you got here." It was Dolores Hope, and I threw my arms around her as we shared our feelings over the loss of a good friend.

As much as he found time for his favorite game (after his earlier love affair with baseball), Torchy always had to return to the realities of his work and the extra-curricular activities he was involved with in Seattle. He had not been born with the proverbial silver spoon in his mouth, so he was never able to enjoy the frivolities of the idle rich.

I was never really a member of the "establishment" of Seattle. It was made up of about a hundred old-line families who could trace themselves back to the early years of the city which I have always believed to be one of the greatest in the nation.

It was hard to break into that circle, as far as society was concerned, and I guess Ruth and I weren't much interested. I don't think we attended any social activities of the real 400. I knew the establishment was involved when I was either recommended or turned down for a particular board or position or when I needed to borrow money. The one great exception was Joshua Green of the Peoples Bank. We became good friends and he was always ready to help me with loans for both personal and business reasons. I owe a lot of whatever success I may have achieved to that kind of generous support.

A Seattle wag once remarked: "Torchy's like God; he's everywhere!" In his role as state chairman for the March of Dimes (top) he presented a plaque to Evan M. Weston, president of the Washington State Labor Council, for that organization's 20 years of participation in the National Foundation for Infantile Paralysis campaigns. In 1955 (bottom) he welcomed Stewardess Burleene Van Wie with a Greater Seattle pin on the occasion of the opening of Western Airlines' first office in Seattle. (Special Collections Division, University of Washington Libraries)

Anson A. "Bob" Littler and Torchy, officials of Greater Seattle, Inc., received reporting salutes from Ed Crowley, Bing Crosby and Phil Harris when Crosby and Harris arrived to be grand marshals of the 1954 Seafair parade. Littler, a prominent men's clothing merchant in Seattle, was

Chapter 14

They Called Him Mr. Everything

The problem with putting the life story of Torchy Torrance into chronological order is that he was involved in so many diverse activities at the same time. As one writer put it: "He almost needed a scorecard to keep track of the committees he was on and what offices he held in which organizations."

At one of the busiest times in his career, he was among the original members of the executive board of Greater Seattle, Inc., which was created to help the city salute its hundredth anniversary in 1951. The early development of the organization was traced by Ralph B. Potts in his book, *Seattle Heritage.* According to Potts, Mayor William F. Devin had appointed a special centennial planning committee consisting of Torchy, Horace W. McCurdy, Victor Rabel, William G. Reed, Harold H. Hartman and other prominent men. Meanwhile, another group called the Seattle Salts was established to develop an annual maritime celebration. Among its founders were Jerry Bryant, a boat company owner; banker Frank Jerome; real estate pioneer Henry Broderick; and A. R. Lintner, president of the American Mail Line. To avoid conflict, the mayor's committee and the Salts merged to create Greater Seattle, Inc., headed by its first president, George Gunn, Jr.

The centennial celebration was the genesis of the annual festive event called Seafair. It featured a nautical theme with lavish parades, unlimited hydroplane races on Lake Washington, professional football exhibitions, the spectacular Aqua Follies at Green Lake, visitations by the U. S. Navy's Pacific Fleet and a long list of supporting activities throughout the festival which lasted a week or more.

Walter A. Van Kamp was lured away from the St. Paul, Minnesota, Winter Carnival to be managing director of the new organization; and creative promotion men—Jack Gordon, Guy Williams, Bill Sears and others—were hired to put zing into the gaudy show and to beat the publicity tom-toms. Torchy, meanwhile, was one of those who raised the funds and worked out the management details for an event which was to become an immediate and roaring success.

While plans were being developed for the first Seafair, an unexpected bonus opportunity came along. The Department of the Army selected Seattle as the homecoming destination for the first shipload of Korean War veterans, and Brigadier General Fenton S. Jacobs, commandant of the Seattle Port of Embarkation, was directed to prepare an appropriate pier-side welcome ceremony. A civic committee was formed to assist the military

Greater Seattle, Inc., got off to a rousing start at a meeting of corporate executives and other key people in the Seattle Municipal Building in 1951. With the ever-exuberant Torchy making the sales pitch, $60,000 was raised immediately to support the new civic promotion organization. George Gunn, Jr. (seated second from right) became the first president. With him was E. A. "Eddie" Black, one of the founding board members. (Special Collections Division, University of Washington Libraries)

Torchy received a commendation from Governor Arthur B. Langlie for his part in Seattle's "Welcome Lane" for returning Korean War veterans. The honor was repaid when Torchy presented the governor with a certificate of appreciation for his participation in the March of Dimes campaign. (March of Dimes photo)

establishment in staging the program, and Torchy, of course, was prominent among the members who included Alfred R. Rochester, Lamont A. "Bill" Williams and others. Instead of limiting the celebration to the port area, however, it was decided to treat the young men to a parade through downtown Seattle, complete with banners, confetti and party streamers.

The first ship – the *General M. C. Meigs* – arrived on June 10, 1951, with 3,828 G.I.s aboard. The gala reception on Pier 39 was so successful that the Secretary of the Army agreed to bring most of the other veterans home through the Puget Sound port so they could be greeted by what became known as Seattle's famed "Welcome Lane." Torchy, among others, received letters of commendation and thanks for this patriotic effort from Governor Arthur B. Langlie and Secretary of the Army Robert D.

Stevens. Unfortunately, Torchy's son Bill – a Marine officer like his father – returned from duty in Korea by another route, so he missed out on the welcoming parties which continued for months and included dozens of ship arrivals. Bill, incidentally was awarded the Air Medal and four oak leaf clusters for 80 flights over enemy territory as an aerial observer for the 1st Marine Division.

Torchy became president of Greater Seattle, Inc., and served from November 10, 1952, to December 15, 1955, during which time he directed a highly successful membership drive and saw the Seafair blossom as one of the leading civic celebrations of its type in the nation. During his involvement he also "killed two birds with one stone" by being instrumental in professional football exhibitions which were profitable both to Greater Seattle, Inc., and The Greater Washington Advertising Association, previously mentioned. No stranger to controversy, he was called upon to defend the running of Seafair's popular hydroplane races on Sundays. Ministerial groups and Bible-quoting individuals wrote critical letters to the editor and to the sponsoring organization demanding cancellation of the events which made Stanley S. Sayres' Slo-mo-shuns, Miss Bardahl, Miss Thriftway and other boats household names. As head of Greater Seattle, Inc., Torchy responded that the hydroplane races were recreational – like

(Opposite page) Torchy was a member of the civic organization which helped develop and support Seattle's famed "Welcome Lane" for returning veterans of the Korean War. Publicists Jack Gordon and Guy Williams deserved credit for maintaining enthusiasm for the downtown parade, with other dedicated participants including Al Rochester, Ralph Grossman and orchestra leader Jackie Souders. Torchy's son Bill, at right with his father, was a decorated Marine aerial observer in Korea.

*As King Neptune XIX, Torchy promenaded at the Seafair Coronation Ball and Royale Buffet with his wife Ruth and Karen Ann Brown of Kent, queen of the 1968 Seattle festival. It was a fitting tribute to the organization's past president and a key figure in the founding and development of Greater Seattle, Inc. (*Seattle Post-Intelligencer *photo)*

baseball, golf and fishing—so they should not be construed as being in conflict with the Lord's Day.

As a fitting climax to his involvement in Greater Seattle, Inc., Torchy was named King Neptune XIX to reign over the 1968 Seafair with Queen Karen Ann Brown and Prime Minister

Royal pages Wendy Arnold and Deanie Murtha received a regal hug from King Neptune XIX during a breather in their busy schedule of Seafair events in 1968. (Special Collections Division, University of Washington Libraries)

Dr. Jack Nichols, Seattle dentist and former University of Washington basketball star. Torchy and Ruth had a phenomenally busy schedule of social events to attend as part of his kingship.

We went to a number of parties, one of which was at Monte Bean's in the Windermere district. Included among the guests was Joan Crawford, the movie star who then was vice chairman of the board of Pepsi-Cola. Ken Kingsley, a friend of mine who had been

Movie actress and Pepsi-Cola executive Joan Crawford joined Henry Mancini and Leonard Nimoy as honorary grand marshals of the 1968 Seafair parade. She crowned Queen Karen Ann Brown and participated in other events of the gala celebration over which Torchy reigned as King Neptune XIX. (Special Collections Division, University of Washington Libraries)

213

Husky football coach Jim Owens (6′4″) and Dr. Jack Nichols (6′8″)—1967 and 1968 Seafair prime ministers, respectively—raised the ex-Sun Dodger shortstop to royal height after Torchy (5′7¾″) was named King Neptune XIX. (Special Collections Division, University of Washington Libraries)

head of the company which distributed Pepsi throughout the Pacific Northwest, had been promoted to the corporate level, so he and I extended the invitation to Joan. She crowned our queen and stayed for the entire Seafair.

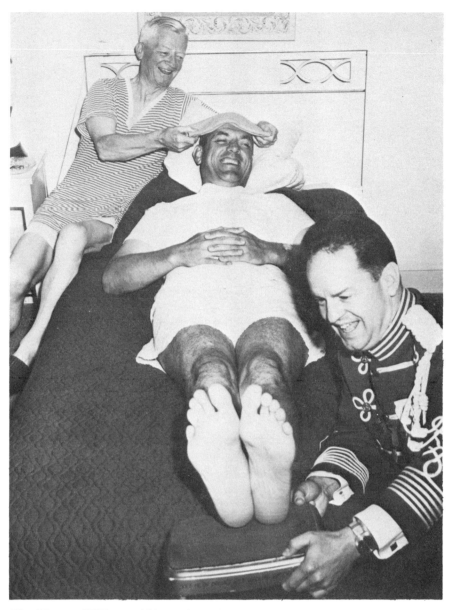

King Neptune XIX, out of his royal regalia, enjoyed a bit of relaxation with his prime minister, Dr. Jack E. Nichols, as Joe James, a member of their court, added an extension to the bed for the former University of Washington basketball star. (Special Collections Division, University of Washington Libraries)

At his party Monte Bean handled the program and announced that he had some celebrities to introduce, including special honored guests. Well, he introduced Ruth and me and Joan Crawford, but the honored guests turned out to be Joshua and Missy Green. Joshua, who had always been especially helpful to me, responded by saying: "We're not celebrities; we're curiosities." At that time he was 103 and Missy was 102.

A popular feature of the Seattle World's Fair of 1962 was the Plaza of States where each of the nation's commonwealths was honored on a particular day during the six-month exposition. As co-chairmen of the mayor's hospitality committee, Ruth and Tor-chy (standing at right behind the reversed chairs) watched as another of the states was honored with the raising of its flag. (Special Collections Division, University of Washington Libraries)

The Torrances handled the Seafair royalty role with ease because four years earlier they had enjoyed an unusual experience during the Seattle World's Fair of 1962.

Ruth and I were appointed by William Devin to be co-chairmen of the mayor's hospitality committee. It was our job to line up hosts and hostesses for celebrities from all over the nation and the world for the various events at the fair. We got a lot of help from Ben and Maxine Wheat. They lived out near the airport and I would call them all hours of the night to meet some dignitaries coming in when we couldn't be there. We also entertained these visitors at receptions and dinners in the Space Needle and elsewhere, often with Lt. Gov. Johnny Cherberg and his wife Betty representing the state.

Many a night Governor Al Rosellini would invite us to participate in one of the evening celebrations with heads of state or other dignitaries. They came in all sizes, colors and religions, and

In his role as the Seattle World's Fair hospitality co-chairman, Torchy presented a bouquet of roses to Alice Watts, Miss Delaware, during the state's recognition day at the Plaza of States. Governor Al Rosellini of Washington (center) regularly called on the Torrances to participate in various World's Fair events. (Seattle Post-Intelligencer photo)

it was very exciting and enjoyable to be involved like that for six months. Incidentally, President John F. Kennedy came to open the fair officially on April 21, 1962, so he and his brother Robert were two of our most honored guests.

I've got to admit that I was somewhat opposed to the World's Fair idea when we first started talking about it at the Rainier Club and in some of our poker sessions. At one of the early organizational meetings, it was proposed for 1961 and I argued that we couldn't be ready by then. I also figured a World's Fair would destroy Greater Seattle, Inc., which had developed into a good thing for the city. As it turned out, Greater Seattle made quite a bit of money handling the Century 21 souvenir coins which helped us finance our programs after the fair ended. That, of course, is another example of how I've been on the wrong side to start with but finally awaken to the fact that what someone else was doing was probably all right.

Between the World's Fair and Torchy's reign as King Neptune XIX, he and Ruth attended the 1964 Olympic Games in Tokyo with Bobby and Dorothy Morris.

It was probably the greatest single trip we ever had. We went first to Hong Kong and then to Japan. I can't say too much about Bobby Morris. He was such a good friend, and Dorothy was just like a sister to me. Bob didn't go to college, but he was a great athlete at Broadway High School. We used to play summer baseball on the same teams and we sometimes refereed together. In his day he was one of the truly great football officials working major college games, including the Rose Bowl.

Afterwards he went into politics and was elected King County auditor on the Democratic ticket. He was a terrific, popular fellow and always a cinch to be re-elected, so when campaign time came, he'd order a small poster with his picture, his name and what he was running for on it, and that's about all. Then he'd have dinner at the Roosevelt Hotel for about 75 to 80 men—mostly sports-related people of both political parties—and we'd all have a real good time. I think Bob Morris probably spent the least amount of money on a re-election campaign of anyone in the United States.

In Tokyo we stayed at the Hilton Hotel where we were met by June Ishii, who was the shortstop for Waseda University when we played against them in 1921. I had brought him to the United States to work for Piper and Taft, an athletic supply company in

Seattle, so he could learn the equipment business. He then went back to Tokyo and started his own company, manufacturing gloves, balls, bats and just about everything else. When we came into the lobby, there were Babe Herman, Lefty O'Doul and Hank Greenberg who had skipped the World Series to attend the Olympics. Ishii had his picture taken with those three baseball greats and it appeared on the front page of one of the newspapers. I don't think he got around to showing the picture to everyone in Japan, but he came close to it We enjoyed watching June—who was about five-feet-one—talking to those big American six-footers.

Lyman Bingham, Olympic vice-president and Avery Brundage's right hand man, provided us with a car and pass so we could drive right up to the entrance of the stadium. Bob wasn't in good health so we couldn't walk too far. Everything was fine until we loaned our car and driver to Irv Morgan, president of the Northern Life Company, so he and his wife Ruth could catch a train. The driver got them to the station on time, but he lost the official windshield sticker and the security people stopped him from coming back to the stadium to pick us up. They held him for about two hours before he finally got clearance. The long delay upset our evening plans, but the wait was better than the walking.

The Torrances enjoyed a Chinese dinner at the Four Seasons Cafe with Bobby and Dorothy Morris (center, foreground), two of their closest friends. Bobby (at Torchy's right) was a prominent athletic official on the West Coast and a perenially re-elected King County auditor. As young men, he and Torchy played baseball and officiated together. They were also partners in the ownership of a non-winning race horse. (Special Collections Division, University of Washington Libraries)

The Olympic Games were great and we had a wonderful time together, becoming even better friends than we were before. I'm glad we went because we never got a second chance. One Saturday—April 18, 1970—when I was in Palm Springs, Bob went for a short walk while Dorothy was at the grocery store. When he came back to the house, his heart just stopped on him. Dorothy called me and I caught the first plane back to Seattle. It was probably the only Saturday that winter that I didn't spend with Bobby. I would usually go over to his house and we would sit and talk most of the afternoon; then I would take off just in time for supper at home. I certainly missed my friend and those Saturday afternoons together.

Torchy had attended other Olympic games: the tenth in Los Angeles in 1932, the fourteenth in London in 1948 and the seventeenth in Rome in 1960. Ruth accompanied him to the nineteenth Olympiad in Mexico City in 1968; and while they were there, she—like many others—became ill. When they returned home, her problems persisted, and at first it was blamed on what American travelers to Mexico called "Montezuma's Revenge."

Her condition continued to bother her for about two years, but she didn't complain very much. Then one day we were attending a Littler's Style Show at the 101 Club when she told me she just couldn't stay for the rest of the performance and wanted to go home. She started to get up and then stumbled and fell. With some difficulty we finally got her to the car and I took her directly to Swedish Hospital.

The next morning Dr. William B. Hutchinson, Freddie's brother, operated on her and discovered cancer of the pancreas. When she was able to, she wanted to know exactly what the situation was, so Hutch and I sat on her bed and he explained the seriousness of her condition and that she had from six months to two years to live. She took the news like a Trojan and said she wanted to go home to the Washington Park Towers where we then lived and not spend her final time in the hospital.

One of the letters I got at the time was from Bing Crosby. He wrote:

Sorry to hear about Ruth. I hope that she goes into a steady convalescence and wins her way back to good health again. Tell her I'll say a little prayer that this takes place very soon, the next time I go to church.

I don't get down to the desert much any more, Torchy. Had to give up golf about a year ago because of this bursitis in my shoulder. Wasn't any fun playing with all that pain, and [I] didn't play well either as a result.

Bing

The end came for Ruth on Saturday, November 20, 1971. Ironically, it was the day of the Washington-Washington State football game, the annual event which always rekindled the friendly rivalry between her and her husband—because she was a graduate of one school and he of the other. Funeral services were held at the University Congregational Church of which she was a member. She and Torchy had been married for 47 years.

Three days after Ruth's death, Torchy's brother—Kirby E. Torrance, Sr.—also died in Seattle at age 78.

At 72—when most men were already retired—Torchy remained vitally active in the printing business and whatever organizations and projects could use his help. He was especially involved in fund-raising for the Salvation Army and received that group's coveted "Others Award." His service to the March of Dimes dated back to 1936 when he was vice-chairman under Seattle postmaster George Starr as they planned the first Roosevelt Ball to benefit polio research and treatment. He then became state chairman for the annual campaign, raising literally millions of dollars for that important cause. As a result, he included among his personal friends Basil O'Connor, former law partner of Franklin D. Roosevelt and president of the National Foundation for Infantile Paralysis, and Dr. Jonas Salk, developer of the polio vaccine bearing his name. O'Connor's second wife was Shirley Torrance's nurse when Torchy's daughter was undergoing treatment at Warm Springs, Georgia. Doctor Salk was one of the celebrities Torchy and Ruth hosted for dinner at the Space Needle during the World's Fair.

As Torchy got older, the honors began to pile up. In 1972 he received the Distinguished Alumni Service Award from the University of Washington. Highly cherished was the prestigious Pop Warner Conference Achievement Award for service to youth, established by the Northeast Philadelphia Chamber of Commerce and named in honor of the famed Stanford University football

The dapper and jovial Torchy was introduced as "Mr. Everything" when he received the coveted Charles E. Sullivan Award from the Puget Sound Sportswriters and Sportscasters at the organization's 24th annual Mid-Winter Sports Banquet in 1974. (Special Collections Division, University of Washington Libraries)

coach. Senator Warren G. Magnuson had been Torchy's chief advocate in having him recognized especially for his March of Dimes efforts and his assistance to young athletes.

Earlier he was presented the American Legion Award of Merit for his many contributions to that organization's programs, especially American Legion Junior Baseball.

Tubby Graves, "Pop" Reed of Franklin High School, Bobby Morris and I coached the Seattle Post Number 1 team sponsored by Gibson Carpet Cleaners. We were the transportation committee, too, hauling the kids to games all over the area.

Another prized recognition came in the Olympic Hotel's Grand Ballroom on February 4, 1974, at the 24th Annual Mid-Winter Sports Banquet of the Puget Sound Sportswriters and Sportcasters Association. On that occasion the master of ceremonies announced:

Tonight we pay tribute to Mr. Everything in Pacific Northwest athletics, Roscoe C. "Torchy" Torrance, the 1973 winner of the Charles E. Sullivan Award. His work at the collegiate, AAU and professional baseball levels is well known. Yet, it is the unrecorded help and encouragement he has so generously given over the years to young men and women in sports, the aid to ex-athletes down on their luck, his fireball enthusiasm for any and all projects aimed at the betterment of our community, and his warm, engaging personality – all these sterling qualities make Torchy Torrance a man among men.

While he was buoyed up by the honors he received, the period of adjustment following Ruth's death also brought its share of burdens.

I was determined to go to the 1972 Olympic Games in Munich. I was especially anxious because it would be an opportunity to spend some time with Avery Brundage. Not only had we known each other for a long time through the AAU and my membership on the Olympic Committee, but we were also fraternity brothers. He had lost his wife, too, so we were going to stay at Garmisch-Partenkirchen and fly back and forth to the Games each day by helicopter.

On the Fourth of July that year I was standing by the Civic Auditorium in Seattle watching a small patriotic parade. When the Stars and Stripes went by, a bunch of young people insulted the flag which upset me considerably. I let them know it and was going to take on somebody who was bigger than I was. Other spectators then interfered and told me to quiet down.

I was still churning inside when I went to Longacres that afternoon. I got to my box and when I started to sit down, I missed my chair. Joe Whitman, the track handyman, took me to the clubhouse, and, after Dr. Alexander Grinstein, the track physician, checked me over; the boys there said they would drive me home. However, I insisted I could manage myself, so with some effort I finally got to the Washington Park Towers and into bed.

I called Dr. James L. Wilson who came out and eventually determined that I had had a slight heart attack. He told me I would have to stay in bed for three weeks and that I'd also have to cancel my trip to the Olympics. It was especially disappointing because my son John was going to go with me and I was looking forward to a great time together. I ended up giving my tickets to Vic Markov, a member of Jimmy Phelan's 1936 Rose Bowl team and a fellow 101 Club member whose dad worked for Avery Brundage's construction company.

In December 1973 Torchy went to Los Angeles to spend a couple days with his sister Jessie on the occasion of her eightieth birthday. After the man she was engaged to lost his life in World War I, she never married. Then, following her war-time work in Washington, D.C., she moved to Los Angeles where she attended night school and eventually became an attorney. In July of 1974 Jessie was killed in a two-car accident near her home.

It happened on a Saturday, and I was at the Young Americans for Freedom convention in San Francisco where I first met Ronald Reagan and Barry Goldwater. Nobody could reach me there, so I didn't find out about Jessie until I returned home late Sunday night. I turned around and flew down to Los Angeles and Bill came over from Palm Springs to meet me. We tried to find out what happened. We talked to the patrolmen who eventually arrived on the scene, and supposedly there were no witnesses of any kind so they couldn't determine who was at fault.

There were no services because, as one of Jessie's friends told us, she probably would have preferred it that way. Jessie also left instructions for her final resting place, so at the time all I had to do was arrange for the sale of what few possessions she had which didn't go to nieces, nephews or other relatives. Unfortunately that wasn't the end of it.

Several months later the two ladies in the other car sued Jessie's estate, me and the rest of the family for something like $350,000. I think their attorney hired some witnesses to say they saw the incident, even though at the time the officers at the scene couldn't find anyone who had seen the crash. I was sure that Jessie didn't cause the accident because she was a careful driver, but we couldn't prove it. The suits dragged on for seven years before they were finally settled, one for $25,000, the other for $20,000.

High among Torchy's favored activities was the American Legion. He had served as commander of Seattle Post Number 1 and chairman of the committee to raise funds for the post's fine clubhouse at 620 University Street. Later, when the building had to be demolished to accommodate the new freeway, he became a member of the American Legion Foundation which managed the fund of some $350,000 derived from the sale of the headquarters. Then, in 1976 when Seattle was selected as the site of the national American Legion convention, he became a member of the committee to plan for the major event.

I wanted to get Bob Hope to put on a big show at the convention because he had done so much in three wars for servicemen. Then the idea was expanded to include Bing Crosby and Fred Waring. We even talked about having Kate Smith come out and sing "God Bless America," but she wasn't physically up to it. My plan was to let Vietnam veterans and their families in for a nominal admission because we were having trouble interesting them in the American Legion. Any profits we would make would go to charity.

I made this proposal to the committee, which, as I recall, included Jack Gordon, then the commander of Post Number 1, and Dick Klinge, the convention general chairman. I thought I had their approval and I went to work to arrange for the entertainers. I called Bob first and he immediately said yes. Bing and Fred were harder to get. Waring was having his 50th anniversary golf tournament at Shawnee-on-the-Delaware which he didn't want to cancel, of course, but after three or four months of letters going back and forth, he finally agreed to come. Eventually we got an okay from Bing, too. It was shaping up to be an exciting event because it would be the first time Hope, Crosby and Waring would be together, except on a golf course.

About 90 days before the convention, I decided it was time to get the publicity going and to make plans for the stage and other necessities at the new Kingdome which opened earlier that year. The management said it would take from 40 to 50 thousand dollars to build the stage and to provide the right kind of sound system to assure a good program. We figured about 35 thousand for advertising. It was my understanding that the American Legion Foundation would make this start-up money available out of our building fund, to be paid back from the show's receipts. In the meantime, I was also working with the University and others to arrange for the 2,000-voice chorus Fred Waring would direct.

I had to be out of town for a few days, and when I returned,

Bob Hope will headline American Legion Bicentennial Program here in Kingdome August 23rd — Watch media for details

The cancellation of a Bob Hope-Bing Crosby-Fred Waring extravaganza Torchy had planned for the 1976 National American Legion convention was one of the big disappointments of his life. He had already begun advertising the upcoming show in the dedication program for the Seattle Kingdome when the financial rug was pulled out from under him.

I learned to my dismay that my plan had been vetoed. I tried to get the action reversed, but I was unsuccessful. There were also some charges made by Joseph A. Sweeney that Western Printing had done something like $226,000 worth of printing for the last Gemeroy contest, which was untrue. At any rate, I was not only stunned but terribly embarrassed by the whole situation.

After that it came down to whether I would finance the whole program myself or cancel it. I talked the matter over with Bob Hope and his agent, and because the time was getting short and it appeared we might not have enough money to promote the event properly, maybe it would be best to call the whole thing off.

After some hard thinking on my part, that's what I did. Of course, it practically destroyed my relationship with Crosby, Waring and Hope. I had disrupted their schedules for a year and they were understandably upset. I never did get a chance to explain the situation to Bing before he died on October 14, 1977, while playing golf on the La Moraleja course near Madrid, Spain. My friendship with Waring was somewhat restored prior to his death in 1984, but it was never the same as it was when we used to play golf occasionally. I think Bob Hope forgave me because he and Dolores eventually invited me back to their home in Palm Springs.

Later, to refute the printing charges, I located the audit report prepared by the accounting firm of Griffiths and Wyles on the Gemeroy contest and requested an opportunity to present it before the foundation. It showed the printing was less than half of the figure mentioned by Sweeney, and that was over a two-year period which was certainly not out of line for a national contest of that type. However, the chairman refused to put it on the agenda, so I had no other choice but to resign from the foundation of which I was a founding member.

Because of his feud with Sweeney, Torchy also quit going to meetings of the Last Man's Club of Seattle, an organization established just before World War II by advertising man Anthony F. Moiteret, Don E. Douglas and others. Sweeney was one of the original 81 members still alive at the time. As one of the Legionnaires of Seattle Post Number 1 put it: "Torchy and Joe used to go at one another like two bantam roosters; it was better for both of them not to be in the same hall."

(Joe Sweeney died on March 28, 1988, reducing the roster of the Last Man's Club to less than a dozen, with Torchy elected Skipper in charge of the bottle of cognac from which the final survivor would drink a toast to all his departed comrades.)

Torchy considered the American Legion setback to be one of the biggest disappointments of his life, but at that particular time there was a new personal development to help take his mind off the unhappy situation.

One day I drove around in front of the Washington Park Towers in my Mustang where this lady was standing on the curb. I asked her if I could take her any place, but she sort of stuck her nose up in the air and said she was sorry but she had ordered a taxi. About a week later I saw her again at the Christmas party in the lobby of the Towers. We visited for a while, and I found out she knew my friends Harvey and Florence Cassill so I suggested we go visit them.

The Cassills had been telling me about a certain woman at the Towers, and she turned out to be the one. Her name was Madge True, and we both lost our mates about the same time. Both she and her husband—Cecil L. True, Sr.—were graduates of Lewis and

The gradually dwindling roster of the Last Man's Club of Seattle was printed during the organization's 25th anniversary year. Many more stars had been added when Torchy became Skipper and "keeper of the cognac" as the surviving membership was reduced to less than a dozen.

Clark High School in Spokane, so we all had something in common. Cecil was a very successful petroleum dealer, having succeeded his father in the business. He must have had 135 or more Rainbow gas stations when he sold out to Standard of Indiana. Later he and his son developed the Gull chain of stations which his grandsons eventually took over, making them the fifth generation in the petroleum business. Anyway, after visiting with Harvey and Florence, I took Madge out to eat. I really splurged. We went to Herfy's for hamburgers and coffee, and I think my expenditure was something like $1.80.

After that we continued to see each other quite often until she left on a seven-week cruise to South America. While she was gone, I wrote her a couple letters which I had my secretary type. Well, Madge didn't think that was very personal and she let me know it when she got back. Despite that momentary setback, we started going together until we faced the question of marriage.

I told her that the only thing that worried me was that she was well off and I wasn't, so money might come between us and cause trouble. She didn't think it would, so we went to see Dr. Dale E. Turner of the University Congregational Church. We decided to have some fun with him so we asked if he thought it would be all right if Madge and I lived together. Well, he hemmed and hawed and didn't really know what to say, but he finally remarked: "Maybe at your age it might be a good thing." Then we told him about our plans to be married.

On August 2, 1976, Reverend Turner performed the ceremony at the home of Madge's son, Cecil True, Jr. My son Bill came up from Palm Springs, and Shirley and John were there from Bellevue. It was the beginning of a new chapter in both of our lives.

In typical Torchy fashion, when he introduced Madge at a meeting of the 101 Club, he added: "Oh, by the way, we're looking for a baby sitter." She handled his teasing well, and the two of them began an enviable round of tours and other activities which included the World Series, the Kentucky Derby, University of Washington football games, a South America cruise and visits to Reno, Las Vegas, Palm Springs, Honolulu, Hong Kong and elsewhere. However, one series of trips did not end as planned.

We were on our way from Honolulu to Hong Kong, but we

hit bad weather and were late getting into Tokyo where we were informed that we'd have to lay over for the night because of a curfew on arrivals in Hong Kong after 11:00 p.m. and before 5:00 a.m. We had to get through customs and find a hotel, but we had trouble locating somebody who could speak English.

Finally a young Pan Am employee recognized our plight, got us through customs and into a taxi which took us to an all-Japanese hotel after midnight. Our room was so small we could hardly turn around. We had to get up at five to catch our plane, but the switchboard ladies couldn't understand our request for a wake-up call so we simply stayed up all night. In the morning we couldn't find any American food until we got to the airport where we had a cup of strong coffee and a little cookie. Eventually we got to Hong Kong.

The way it started, I hoped it wouldn't turn out like my last trip there in 1963 when Gordon Bass of the Western International Hotels and I had been invited on the Canadian Pacific's inaugural direct flight from Calgary. I had sent a wire to Don Ireton, a lumber company representative in the Far East, telling him that we could

Reverend Dale E. Turner of the University Congregational Church conducted the funeral services for Ruth Torrance and officiated at the wedding ceremony for Torchy and Madge. The Torrance family was decidedly ecumenical. Torchy's mother was buried with Baptist rites; his father, Christian Science; and his brother Kirby, Catholic. Torchy himself once taught Sunday School at the University Presbyterian Church, but when the minister insisted that he had to choose between that and Sunday baseball, his teaching days were abruptly ended. (Salvation Army photo)

Following their wedding in 1976, Madge adjusted quickly to Torchy's wide circle of friends, including celebrities like Bob Hope. Her generous contributions to charity and public service included a quarter of a million dollar endowment for athletic scholarships at the University of Washington. (Special Collections Division, University of Washington Libraries)

be there on a particular day. He and his wife Polly then planned a nice cocktail reception for us with Art Linkletter as a special guest. The only thing is, I forgot about the International Date Line, and we arrived the day after the party was over and Linkletter was gone. Don and Polly were rightly upset because they had gone to so much trouble. To try to make amends, Gordon and I took Polly to lunch at the Peninsula Hotel on the day we were going to leave — and that's when I ate something which tasted bad going down. I proceeded to get sick to my stomach, but they got me on the plane to Tokyo and I spent the entire flight in the men's room. From the airport I rode on the floor of a cab to the Hilton Hotel where they had sort of a hospital setup and I spent a week there recovering from the food poisoning, with Gordon Bass as my nurse.

As for Madge and me, we had a good time for several days

231

and then flew back to Honolulu where I developed some pains in my chest. I called Doctor Wilson in Seattle who didn't seem to think it was anything serious, so he told me to take some Tums and come see him when we got home. That's what I did, and he gave me an electrocardiagram and other tests which didn't seem to show anything wrong, so we decided to go to London as we had planned.

We flew from New York on the Concorde which took just three hours to cross the Atlantic. The speed makes up for the fact that it's not a very comfortable plane, having very narrow seats and aisles. I had called Bob Hope before we left and he was generous enough to arrange with his London manager to get us into several shows. The young man and his wife accompanied us to theaters on the first two nights, but on the morning of the third the newspaper headlines read: "Hospitals and doctors on strike!"

Right away the tight feeling in my chest got worse, so I called Dr. Fred Plum, a neurologist I knew at the Cornell University Hospital in New York, and he said: "Get on a plane and get here as fast as you can and we'll take a look." Well, I called the airport and was told that it would be six weeks before we could get on the Concorde. At first I didn't know what to do, but then I got hold of Eric Morley who was then president of Variety International. I had been a board member of the organization in Seattle, so I explained my problem to him. He asked me when we wanted to leave, and I told him as soon as possible. An hour later he called back and said: "You're on the Concorde's two o'clock flight tomorrow."

We got to New York in a hurry, and after Doctor Plum gave me a stress test, he advised me to go home to Seattle where I'd probably have to be operated on. I reported to Jim Wilson and he promptly referred me to Dr. John A. Mazzarella, a cardiologist. After about three steps on the treadmill, my chest began to hurt and I was sent to Swedish Hospital for an angiogram. It turned out that I had four arteries about 82 per cent blocked, so the next day I was in surgery for six or seven hours while they performed a quadruple bypass.

I stayed in the hospital about three weeks and then on Christmas morning they moved me to the Washington Athletic Club where they had two nice rooms for us on the 11th floor. We stayed their another three weeks and then we decided to go to Honolulu where I could recuperate and Madge could do a little swimming. About the end of March I finally was feeling well enough to go out for an evening, and it happened that Beverly Sills was there for a concert. She had been National Women's Chairman for the March of Dimes for a couple years and I had become fairly well acquainted with her. We attended the concert and afterwards went to see her. Well, I was wearing a white suit I had made for me prior to my surgery and in the meantime I had lost so much weight that it made me look like a scarecrow. I couldn't blame her, but Beverly didn't recognize me—until I explained who I was.

Our next stop was a fat farm down in Mexico. A year earlier we had been at a charity auction for PONCHO, an organization which supports the arts in Seattle, and I wasn't paying much attention as every now and then Madge would raise my hand off the table with the number I was holding. All of a sudden I heard the auctioneer yell "Sold!" and that's when I discovered we had bought a week at one of those weight-control places south of the border. We had to use our reservations by a certain time and we got there in the final week after they had given us an extension.

When we arrived, we were told they didn't have a room for us. Finally they ended up putting us in the owner's home, a fine Spanish-style house where we spent the week living on carrots, radishes and celery. I was there with 72 women for four days until several other men came later in the week. I didn't lose any weight because by then I was down to a point where I didn't have any more pounds to shed.

One night at the end of our stay another couple asked us if we would like to play some bridge. Well, at that time Madge and I had never played together so we sort of indicated that we wouldn't be much good at it. As it turned out, we got all the cards and really gave them a trimming. Our opponents thought we had lied to them, but, despite that, the four of us went to a little restaurant in the nearby village for something to eat, figuring we'd be the only ones there. We were wrong! All the hungry clients of the fat farm were there after a week of eating lettuce and other vegetables. Everybody started out with a pitcher of Margueritas and then had dinner after that. It was an enjoyable way to wind up an interesting week. We flew back to Seattle the next day.

I suppose we should get all the bad things that have happened to us out of the way in this chapter so we can finish on an upbeat.

Several years after we were married, Madge had to go to Honolulu on business, and while she was there she saw some people jogging in the hallway of the apartment building. Thinking it would be a *good way to get a little exercise, she tried it, too. Unfortunately, before she had gone very far, her knee popped on her. It didn't bother her too much in the beginning, but it turned out to be a serious problem. She had cartilage damage in the front and developed a cyst on the back so it was finally necessary to have surgery.*

Despite our mutual difficulties, we decided to take a cruise around South America, so we went to San Francisco to board our ship. When we got to the pier, the tide was in so we faced a steep gangplank of about 40 steps with Madge's bum knee. She made it okay, and after a little mixup in getting our quarters, the trip got underway. By the time we got to the Panama Canal, her leg was bothering her alot. We talked it over with the ship's doctor and finally decided that the wisest thing to do would be to leave the tour and return home, which we did.

About the only fun we had was in another bridge game. A tournament had been scheduled, and in the warmup games, we were matched against the chairman of the event and his partner. Again we told them that we had only played together once so we didn't know how good we would be. Well, just as it happened at the fat farm, we got all the cards and easily won the first two rubbers. Before we could start the third, the chairman got sick to his stomach— or so he said—and asked to be excused. It soon spread all over the ship that he had chickened out. It got to him, too, because when the tournament started, he came to us and apologized. After that our luck ran out and we were eliminated in the second round.

While I'm at it, I should tell you about another trip which had an unpleasant hour or so. We had gone to Las Vegas and were staying at Caesar's Palace where I was enjoying shooting craps and Madge had a good time pulling the slot machine handles. In fact, she stayed at it so long that I had to give her right arm a rub-down when we got back to the room.

One day I told her I was going to the bookmakers to place a few bets on the races at Santa Anita and Bay Meadows. It was late in the day when I decided to walk the half mile or so back to the hotel to get some exercise. When I arrived, I got into a crowded elevator and got off the first time it stopped.

Unfortunately, I was on the wrong floor. I went to what I thought was our room and was fiddling with the key in the door when a fellow across the hall said: "Didn't you get on the same elevator I did?" I recognized him and told him yes, and he replied: "You wanted the fourth floor, not this one." Then he suggested I use the stairway because it was a short walk and the elevators were busy. That's where I made my mistake!

When I got to the fourth floor, the door was locked. I then went back down to the one I had come in through and it was locked, too. There was nothing to do but go back and forth, pounding a little on each door—but nobody heard me. Finally I sat down on the steps to try to figure out what to do. I must have been there fifteen minutes before a maid came down the stairway with some towels, so I thought I was saved. Well, she wasn't going to let me in because it was against the rules, and she didn't know if I was trying to break into somebody's room or not. It took a while but eventually I convinced her that I was a registered guest and had the right key.

In the meantime Madge had called the police and was trying to reach Bill in Palm Springs. She didn't know if somebody had hit me over the head and taken what little money I had or not. Anyway, it all came out all right, but it wasn't much fun for either of us while it was happening.

In a way the lock-out incident reminds me of my most embarrassing moment back in World War II. I was staying at the Shoreham Hotel in Washington, D.C., when the temperature and humidity were both at a hundred or more. Air-conditioning was rather uncommon in those days so the hotel had double doors, the outside one being a lattice type so you could get a little breeze.

Well, on this particular occasion the wind was quite heavy and the lattice door blew open. I got up at about two a.m. in my birthday suit and went out to close it. About that time a gust came up and the door behind me slammed shut, and there I was out in the hall at two in the morning with nothing on and no key to get back in my room.

I looked down the hall and saw a tray with a napkin on it. I used the napkin to protect myself a little bit and went towards the elevators to try to get some help from downstairs. As you might have guessed, just then the door opened, some people came out and I ran smack into them. I think they were more startled than I was.

I backed off as best I could with my napkin and tried to explain what had happened—and would they PLEASE call downstairs and get the management! They finally decided I wasn't completely crazy and eventually a bellhop came up and let me back in my room—even though he could see I didn't have any pockets from which to get him a tip.

Earl Sande, one of the greatest jockeys of all time, was Torchy's childhood pal in American Falls, Idaho, and their relationship continued until Sande's death in Jacksonville, Oregon, in 1968. Earl rode 968 winners in his long career, including three Kentucky Derby victories, for a total of almost three million dollars in purses. (Special Collections Division, University of Washington Libraries)

Chapter 15

Race Horses and Inside Straights

Torchy and Madge shared an interest in horseracing, and his went back to boyhood days in American Falls when he and Earl Sands were dreaming their dreams of becoming a major league shortstop and the world's greatest jockey, respectively.

Earl and I roped and rode calves when we were kids, and I beat him once in a horse race. In American Falls they had built a new quarter-mile track which was about three inches deep in dust. The grandstand held 250 people or so, but we thought it was huge. In that particular race, which was a mile long, we had to change horses and saddles every quarter mile, and maybe that's what helped me win.

Or maybe Earl was just tired. His dad worked him 16 hours a day on their small irrigation ranch. He had to get up at four, milk cows, feed the stock, eat breakfast and then work on the irrigation system till dark. Finally, when he was still in his early teens, Earl came to my father and told him of his troubles at home and that he had a chance to go with a riding stable out of state. Dad told him if that's what he wanted to do for the rest of his life, and if the people were honest, he should take the job. He did, and that was the beginning of a fabulous career.

At age 18 Earl rode in 23 races in one day at Springerville, Arizona. He then went to New Orleans where in one year he started 707 races and brought in 158 winners. In 1920 he joined Harry Sinclair's Rancocas Stables and guided the great Man o' War to an easy victory in the Miller Stakes at Saratoga. Three years later he hit his peak when he rode Zev to his first Kentucky Derby win. That season he rode 39 stake winners for a total of $569,394 in purses.

His career almost ended in 1924 when he suffered a double fracture of the thigh, eight broken ribs and a broken collar bone in a spill at Saratoga, but he came back in 1925 to win the Kentucky Derby again on Flying Ebony. He retired briefly, but the lure of the saddle was too great and in 1930 he won the Triple Crown – the Kentucky Derby, the Belmont Stakes and the Preakness – aboard Gallant Fox. No wonder Damon Runyon wrote:

> Gimme a handy
> Guy like Sande
> Bootin' them winners in!

After that, though, Earl seldom rode again but became almost as successful as a trainer. Though they had gone in different directions in their careers, he and Torchy kept in touch.

I had told him that if he ever had a horse he'd trained in the Kentucky Derby, I'd be there to see it run. Well, in 1936 he won the Santa Anita Handicap with a horse named Stagehand. It was the top racing prize in the West at the time, so he took Stagehand and another horse named Chief to Kentucky.

As I promised, I arrived in Louisville at about four in the morning and went straight to the stables instead of the hotel because I knew Earl would be there. That's when I found out that Stagehand had had a fever for four or five days and hadn't been able to train. The veterinarian had just told Earl that the horse was ready to run, but because he loved horses the way he did, Earl scratched Stagehand and entered Chief in his place.

Chief was an exceptionally fine horse but had never been tested in such fast company. When the time for the race came, I walked around the track to the paddock with Earl and the horse. Just as we got in front of the grandstand, the University of Kentucky band started playing. Chief got scared, reared up and broke away from the swipe who was leading him. The horse ran all the way around the track before we were able to catch him. He then went out and ran a good quarter, but he was already tired and, of course, he faded and lost.

Despite the disappointment, I enjoyed being with Earl again. It was through him that I first met Albert B. "Happy" Chandler, then lieutenant governor of Kentucky who was to become one of my closest friends. He was serving mint juleps, which I drank, and they made me sick as a dog.

As for Earl, he continued as a trainer, but then at Belmont the New York papers came out and accused him of doping a horse and he was suspended for 30 days. Well, he never doped a horse; he loved them too much. Besides that, he was sick with the flu for about a week and wasn't even at the track when the so-called incident occurred. But that doping charge almost broke his heart.

Innocent or not, Sande was branded by the accusation so he never again was in great demand as either a trainer or a rider. However, at age 55 – after 21 years out of the silks – he rode ten races at Jamaica, New York, one of them being aboard a long shot named Miss Weesie. In a stirring drive down the stretch, he brought Miss Weesie home a winner. Up on the favored horse, Will Be There, was jockey Eddie Arcaro.

Earl ended up in Oregon where years back he had bought his parents a grocery store in Salem. He also had paid off the mortgage on their ranch at American Falls. I was involved in getting him hired as a judge at Santa Anita in 1968. He was really happy about getting back to the track when I talked with him, but maybe the excitement was too much because two weeks later he died in Jacksonville, Oregon, before he could take the job. He had gone to the post 3,673 times and rode 968 winners for a total of $2,998,065 in purses. Eventually he was elected to the Hall of Fame at the National Museum of Racing at Saratoga Springs, New York, an honor he certainly deserved.

Torchy's own involvment in horseracing came in 1933 when the sport was legalized in Washington State.

Bobby Morris, Mel Williams and I bought a horse named Bon Honest for $350. I had to borrow for my share because that was after my stock market losses and my investment in Western Printing. Bon Honest went nowhere at Longacres, so we sold him to Jack Atkins who took the horse to Caliente where he won four out of five races. That'll give you some idea of my luck at the track.

Like his golfing experiences, however, Torchy's horseracing ventures left him with a wealth of memories – some good, some bad.

One of the bad ones occurred when a jockey named Harrington came to Seattle from New York. He had gotten my name from somebody, (probably Earl Sande whom he claimed he rode against), and when he went around town looking for me, he managed to make contact with Cliff Harrison of the Star, *George Adams of Adams News, Hugh Todd, Herman Ross, Bob Littler and others, including Jerry O'Neill, my boss at Foster and Kleiser. He obviously was a good salesman because he got them all excited about a big horse ranch he said was going to be established on Whidbey Island. He also told them about a horse named Busy Bee running in Chicago the next day which he said was a sure thing. They all placed bets with him—about $400 altogether—and, just as he said, the horse won, paying something like $16 or $17.*

I had been out of town and by the time I returned and got down to the 101 Club on Saturday afternoon, everybody was happy over their good fortune. Cliff Harrison went right out to Littler's and bought a new suit with all the accessories, and I chided Bob for not putting $20 on the horse for me, too. But as it turned out, I was the lucky one. That night they called Harrington to find out when the bookie would pay off, and he told them either Sunday or Monday.

Well, I was interested in the horse ranch idea, so I went to see the jockey at the Olympic Hotel on Sunday afternoon, and we talked for quite a while about Earl Sande and the Whidbey Island venture. I got a little suspicious because of some of the things he didn't know about Earl, but other than that his story was very convincing. On Monday I went back to see him and to help the boys collect their money, only to find that Harrington had checked out, his suitcases were gone and so was the $400 (plus the winnings if he actually placed the bets). We never heard from him again, of course, and the Whidbey Island horse ranch was just a big come-on.

Then there was the time that Herman Ross, Hugh Todd, George Cruickshank, Lloyd Tindal and I went to the San Francisco for a weekend at the races. George Shilling, who had been the racing secretary at Longacres, was the manager at Tanfaran, so we looked forward to a good time. Unfortunately, on the first day none of us won a race and before long we were out of money.

We were staying at the Mark Hopkins Hotel where the manager (whom I only remember as Smitty) was a pretty good friend of ours.

At that particular time all his kitchen employees were out on strike so we volunteered to help him as dishwashers and general helpers — and we had a lot of fun doing it. Without telling the others, I arranged with Smitty to borrow $200 so we'd have some more betting money on Saturday. The boys were really worried about not having any funds, and I didn't let them know I had $40 for each of us until about 11:30 the next morning, an hour and a half before post time.

Once again our luck was bad in the first few races, so we finally asked George Shilling if he had any tips for us. He told us about a horse named Black Mammy which had just come up from the south and which he thought looked good in the ninth race. Well, we all jumped on that horse with the money we had left. It was a close race, and you should have heard us yelling as Black Mammy came down the stretch to win by a thick nose. She paid $38 to win, so we all got well, paid Smitty off at the hotel and went home on the train the next day, a very happy bunch.

I wasn't always that lucky, however.

In the spring of 1940 the Rainiers were training in the San Fernando Valley. Eddie Foy, the comedian, and Bing Crosby and his four sons used to come out and watch us. Anyhow, on the Saturday afternoon of our final workout, Jack Lelivelt and I decided to go to the races at Santa Anita. Just as we got to the Turf Club entrance, we ran into Joe Hernandes who said: "Why don't you come up to the caller's box and watch the feature race from there?"

I placed a bet on Porter's Mite, a horse owned by William Boeing, Sr., and then went to the top of the grandstand where you had to go out on a catwalk to get to Joe's box. Also there was Ethel Mars of the Mars candy family who owned Gallahadion which was running in the feature race against Porter's Mite. I got into a conversation with her and she said: "I'll tell you one thing, Torchy; I'm going to send Gallahadion to Kentucky and he's going to win the Derby. He's a big price in the future book, so get yourself a bet and make yourself some money. I promise you this is going to happen."

As I recall, Porter's Mite won the race that particular day and Gallahadion was second. However, the Santa Anita race was a mile and a sixteenth while the Derby would be a mile and a quarter, and Gallahadion was coming up fast at the finish. As I was leaving, Joe said: "Call Walter Marty at Caliente and make a bet in the

241

future book." When I got back to the hotel, I called Walter whom I knew when he was head of the mutuel department at Longacres. I told him I wanted to put $100 across the board on Gallahadion for the Derby, and Walter's response was:

"For gosh sakes, Torch, you're just throwing your money away. That horse will never be shipped out of California, and anybody who tells you different doesn't know what he's talking about. Gallahadion is not a good horse. Sure, he just ran a good race, but that was an unusual situation. I'm not going to take your money because you can't afford $400."

He was right about not being able to afford it, but I was going to go home and borrow the money and send it to him. Anyway, he talked me out of it, and I didn't think any more about the horse until later when I was in San Francisco where the Rainiers were playing. I called Bill Kine who had the books there and told him I wanted to bet $50 on Gallahadion across the board. He answered: "Where in the world did you get an idea like that? You're just throwing $200 away and that's a lot of money. You can bet somewhere else if you want to, but I'm not taking your money here. I've got lots of suckers without adding you to my list." So once again I didn't bet.

Well, Gallahadion was still 200 to 1 to win, 100 for second, 60 for third and 40 for fourth, so when I got home, I called Johnny Clancy who was running the books for Joe Gottstein and Bill Edris. "I want to put $20 across the board on Gallahadion in the Derby," I said. Just like the other two, John told me to take my $80 down to the dock, tear it in little pieces and throw it into the Sound. So I didn't bet with him either.

The week of the Derby a group of us from the Seattle Golf Club went up to Victoria for the annual tournament at Oak Bay. We were playing a practice round on Friday when Phil Taylor the pro there, asked if anybody wanted to bet on the race. He said he had to get the money down that day because the bookie would be busy on Saturday.

Well, I finally got $5 across the board on Gallahadion, but by that time the horse was already in Kentucky and showing well so the odds were way down. The rest is history. Gallahadion won the 1940 Derby and paid $38. If I'd have placed my first bet, I'd have collected something like $40,000 which would have permitted me to recoup my stock market losses and finish off paying what I owed at the bank. As it was, my winnings were less that $200.

But that isn't the end of the sad story. All the Seattle golfers knew I won, so when we got back to the Empress Hotel, they ordered ham and eggs, steak sandwiches and whatever else and charged it all to my account. The total came to about $120. On Saturday night the bookie didn't show with my money, and Phil Taylor said not to worry because I'd get it the next day. Well, our boat left for Seattle that afternoon and I still hadn't collected. About two weeks later I got a check for $65. The bookie had gone broke on the race and that's all the money he had left. What was worse, I got a telegram from Ethel Mars which read: "Along towards morning a sap got lucky." I was so upset by that time I never did answer her wire.

World War II curtailed Torchy's visits to the track, and afterwards he was too busy with other activities to get more than casually involved with the horses. However, when he and Madge married, they found that they had a mutual interest in the Sport of Kings.

We were attending the Kentucky Derby as the guests of Happy and Mildred Chandler when I mentioned to Happy that we were interested in buying a horse. He got us in touch with Lloyd Gentry, but he warned us to be wary "because when it comes to horses, Kentucky people will sell you anything." We went to Keenland the next day where Lloyd showed us a horse named Poor Old Johnny. When I tried to pet him, he reared back and wouldn't have anything to do with me. Then Madge went up to him and the horse gently nuzzled her on the chin. Right away—without worrying about pedigree or anything else—she said: "I'll take this one."

We shipped Poor Old Johnny back to Seattle by plane and turned him over to trainer Craig Roberts who said he wanted to give the horse about three weeks to fatten up a bit before he'd be ready to run at Longacres. Well, when the time came for his first race, we were scheduled to visit Madge's daughter Sally at her ranch over by Coeur D'Alene where there were no phones. Not only did we miss seeing Poor Old Johnny in action, we also didn't have time to place any bets on him.

On Saturday night we called Shirley in Seattle from the Spokane Club to see what had happened. Sure enough, Poor Old Johnny had raced and won, paying $68 to win, $38 to place and $15 to show. Appropriately enough, my son John was the only member of the family who made it to the track that day. He had bet $5

MAJOR TORCHY

1:18.1

6½ furlongs

405　Longacres　6/22/83
JILL'S MUD COURSE...Second
CHELAN RED........Third

Madge & Torchy Torrance.....Owner
Craig Roberts............Trainer
Jorge Aragon..............UP

FOUR FOOTED FOTOS

across the board on his namesake horse and won enough money to pay for a new sofa he had ordered for his apartment.

Poor Old Johnny won a couple more races that summer and then we sent him down to Bay Meadows where he developed a hoof problem of some kind. We even took him to a ranch where they had a swimming pool for horses in hopes that would cure him. Finally it was determined that he had a hereditary infection which had been passed on by his sire. It was one of those things Happy Chandler had warned us to be wary about. We were going to give the horse to the Stanford Riding Academy, but his condition was so bad that we eventually had to destroy him—which, true to form, happened after our insurance had expired. Poor Old Johnny was certainly an appropriate name for that horse.

––––––––––

It was some time later before we bought our second horse, a colt named Banchory Bimbo. The trouble is, he always wanted to run second and never first. After four straight seconds—two at Longacres and two at Bay Meadows—we finally lost him in a claiming race. However, by that time we had a pretty good case of horse fever, so we invested in a two-year-old named Speakeasy. He didn't do any better than Bimbo, so we traded him (and $20,000 to boot) for another horse which ran well in the morning workouts, but when it came to racing in the afternoon, he just didn't have it.

At Craig's suggestion we bought a coming three-year-old for $27,500 from Charlie Whittingham who was supposed to be one of the best trainers in the country. We called the horse Major Torchy. To go with him, we also bought a filly which we were going to name Madge E. Unfortunately, that name had already been used so we selected Fun and Magic instead. Well, all that filly wanted to do was hang around the pasture with the mares, so we never were able to make a race horse out of her.

As for Major Torchy, one of his races was particularly noteworthy. Our guests that day were Judy Biondi and her mother, JoAnne Patton, who had never been at a race track before. It's a special kind of thrill to see your horse come down the stretch in front or coming from behind on the outside with a chance to win—and that's

(Opposite page) Appropriately named, Major Torchy was a winner for Madge and Torchy on June 22, 1983, at Longacres. When it failed to repeat in its next few outings, the horse was sold and promptly raced to multiple victories against lesser competition at Spokane. (Longacres photo)

what Major Torchy did for us on that occasion. Madge knocked over two or three chairs and a couple people so she could get up to the window to see our horse come in first by almost a length. It was the most excited I had ever seen her get about anything. Afterwards we all got our pictures taken in the winner's circle with the horse and jockey. (Incidentally, I had met Judy on the day she was applying for a fund-raising job in the University's athletic department. She seemed a little bit nervous at the time, but I told her not to be because with her enthusiasm, she couldn't miss. Mike Lude, the athletic director, hired her, and she turned out to be just what the office needed. Her great-uncle, Harold Patton, was a member of Baggy's great teams of 1924, 1925 and 1926. In the latter year he was voted the Huskies' most inspirational player, winning the coveted Flaherty Medal.)

After that Major Torchy ran three or four more times with not much success, so we sold him. He then proceeded to win five out of six races in Spokane where the competition wasn't quite as tough as at Longacres. We didn't do much better with a horse named Bellwether which won one race and then got hurt. After we sold him for a dollar, he promptly won five races in a row for his new owner. By this time our trainer was Junior Coffey, who had been a fine running back for Jim Owens when the Huskies won the Pacific Coast Conference championship in 1963. We tried again with another horse named Andreas Emerald. Besides being very small, she had both poor legs and poor feet, so we sold her for a dollar, too.

Our next acquisition was Dynaglass, a three-year-old filly we got in a $25,000 claiming race at Bay Meadows. Like all the others, we thought she might be the real winner we were looking for—but, as everyone knows, hope springs eternal in the horseracing business. I just wish we could have had Earl Sande up on one of our mounts.

Through the years another of Torchy's diversions was poker. It started in his college days.

We had quite an illustrious group, as it turned out, most of them SAEs. There were Howard Lease, Budge Summy, Bob Anderson, George Comstock, Max Miller, Mike Mitchell and a few others. Howard became one the largest contractors in the Pacific Northwest, building the Seattle-Tacoma Airport and doing lots of work in Alaska and Hawaii; Bob was vice-president of Pacific Telephone Company in charge of the Seattle area; George developed a big neon sign business; Max, whom I'll mention later, became a famous writer; and Mike published the Ballard Tribune *and was a Seattle city councilman for years. I think we helped Budge Summy through school because he usually won the three or four bucks which changed hands during our sessions. Budge later became manager of the Seaboard Lumber Company.*

It wasn't until later when I joined the Seattle Press Club that I started playing regularly again. At that time the Press Club was headed by Earl Knight, who published the Alaskan Weekly *which we printed at Western. I remember one particular game when I was playing with Judge Hugh Todd; George Clark, manager of the Washington Farmers Association; Herman Ross, a real estate and insurance man and very high in Democratic circles; John Dore, who later became mayor; Bill Gains, assistant superintendent of the water department; and Lloyd Tindal, who published a weekly news and advertising bulletin we called a "three-sheet."*

It was about 9:30 in the evening when I got four cards to a royal flush. In those days we had a $5 limit with a three-time raise, so with that many guys in the game, you could build up a good-sized pot. Well, when we drew our final cards, I picked up the ten of hearts which completed my flush; Earl Knight had made a full house; and John Dore had three of a kind. We were set up for a real betting situation, and I was licking my chops when I thought about the big pot I was going to win.

We had just started raising and re-raising when the fire whistle blew, and everybody rushed to the window to watch the fire trucks speed by on 5th Avenue, letting me sit there with my royal flush. When they came back, the enthusiasm for the hand had disappeared. Johnny Dore dropped out, and I just got a call of my five-dollar bet. It was the only time in all my many poker games that I ever held a royal flush, and the fire department beat me out of a real killing.

———————

That reminds me of the time six of us were playing on Guadalcanal with about fifteen kibitzers standing around us. The stakes were pretty high because we didn't have any place else to spend the money we didn't send home. On one particular hand I had three tens to go in with, and everybody else in the pot seemed to have good cards too, so it made for a good build-up. On the last draw I filled my four-of-a-kind. Unfortunately, I spread my cards just enough so that one of the fellows behind me could see what I had. Without thinking, he blurted out: "My god, he's got four tens!"

Well, that brought the hand to a screeching halt. We didn't know what to do, but I finally suggested we all take out what we put in when we started raising and leave the rest for me. I ended up with about a ten-dollar profit when it might have been six or seven hundred. Of course, the kibitzer was embarrassed no end, and I don't think he ever got over it.

I was in two different poker groups at the Rainier Club. The first one included Emil Sick; insurance men Deke McDonald and Ned Thompson; attorneys Ernie Skeel and Frank Griffin; Frank Edwards, who owned several theaters in town and later became mayor; Carl Williams, president of Rhodes Department Store; and Alex Gray, who owned Gray's Auto Service. A few, like Emil, were a little reckless with their money and would draw on anything to stay in a hand. Not Alex, though—I think we helped build his company into one of the biggest in the city as the result of his poker winnings. I was sort of a neophyte with that bunch, but I was generally able to hold my own. Eventually most of them died or moved away, so a new group formed.

Those who played in our various once-a-week sessions were Budge Summy, Tommy Gleed, Everett and Lloyd Nordstrom, Paul Pigott,

Paul Pigott (left), head of the giant Pacific Car & Foundry Company, and Thomas Gleed, president of the Seattle First National Bank, were two of Torchy's poker-playing friends. He recalled that the card games produced important ideas and decisions for the betterment of the Seattle community. They also provided a diversion from the pressures of business and the multiple activities in which he and other civic leaders were involved. (PACCAR, Inc., collection)

248

Blaine Kennedy and occasionally Wiggs Campbell, Wiley Hemphill and Larry Lean, head of The Bon Marche. Tommy Gleed had a loud and infectious laugh, and I remember one time when he and Paul got into a real betting match. Paul had an ace-high full house and Tommy drew a fourth king. When the raising was over, Paul laid down his hand in hopeful triumph, and then Tom showed his four kings. You could have heard him laugh several blocks away, and it almost broke up the party.

Before that particular group began to erode away too, we also met once a month at one of our homes, and I'll never forget the night at our house in Windermere when Paul Pigott got up and said he had a splitting headache. I offered to drive him home, but he said he could make it. Later he went to the Mayo Clinic where they discovered an inoperable brain tumor, and Paul died shortly afterwards. It was a great blow to all of us because we dearly loved him and he contributed so much to the community.

When Paul was involved in developing Pacific Car & Foundry (which later included the Kenworth and Peterbilt truck companies), he wanted me to buy 500 shares of stock at five dollars each. Well, I didn't have the money at the time and told him I just couldn't afford it. Then he offered to give me 100 shares free. I wouldn't accept because I felt it wouldn't be cricket when everyone else had to pay. At any rate, had I taken the shares, they would eventually have been worth about a million dollars with all the splits and other accumulations. I really passed up a good one, but I was always noted for doing things like that.

One of the most interesting games I was ever involved in took place in Washington, D.C., when Senator Warren G. Magnuson invited me to dinner and a poker session at his apartment in the Shoreham. The players included Mon Wallgren, a former congressman from Everett; John W. McCormack, Speaker of the House from Massachusetts; Senator Scott W. Lucas of Illinois; Harry S. Truman, then the Vice President of the United States; and Clark Clifford of Kansas whom Truman appointed as his special counsel when he became President in 1946. They played all kinds of wild games, one of them being Seven-toed Pete which we called Low Ball in Seattle. In one hand I got a one, two, three, four and five which I believed we considered a cinch bet at home, so I kept raising until there was quite a bit of money in the pot.

Finally I was called and showed my cinch—only one of the others said: "You don't have a cinch; you've got a straight," and he picked up the pot. In their game a cinch hand was one, two, three, four, six. Well, my luck wasn't too good after that and I owed something like $300 when the game was over. I asked Maggie if he'd take care of it for me and I'd send him the money when I got home. That's what happened, and it was the only game I ever played in Washington, D.C.

There was more to the story, however. Several years later when Harry Truman was President, he came to Seattle when I was head of Greater Seattle and chairman of the reception committee for him. He had been at Bremerton for some occasion and arrived aboard the admiral's gig at Pier 91 where we were to meet him and escort him downtown. As he came up the stairs, he took one look at me and said: "Are you still trying to draw to an inside straight?"

We talked a little about the game as we rode into town, and I enjoyed him very much. For a Democrat he was a bit all right. If he hadn't authorized the dropping of the atomic bombs, there's no telling how long the war would have gone on, and we would have lost many thousands of our young men in an invasion. One of them might have been me.

I had another sort of indirect relationship with Harry Truman

Two former Husky football players—Senator Warren G. Magnuson and Lieutenant Governor John A. Cherberg—looked like they were getting down into a lineman's stance, but in reality they were participating in the placement of a Century 21 memento on the World's Fair grounds when this photo was taken. Though they were Democrats—and despite the unfortunate "Cherberg affair"—Torchy enjoyed memorable relationships with both public officials. (Bob Karolevitz collection)

in 1948 when I was chairman of the Governors' Day Parade in Seattle and Harry was running against Governor Thomas E. Dewey of New York for the presidency. Dewey was there, of course, and we had arranged for a youngster from every state to ride in a convertible with his or her respective governor. Dewey was real hard to deal with. He wanted to be either first or last in the parade, and we finally arranged for him to bring up the rear. Well, the parade sort of broke up towards the end like they sometimes do, and Dewey, for all his complaining, got lost in the shuffle. Despite our problems with him, I still voted for him—but he lost when Harry upset all the polls and prognosticators.

The thing about our poker games was that many important decisions and ideas grew out of them. It was at the Press Club, for instance, that we decided to run Johnny Dore for mayor, and he was a pretty good one. At the Rainier Club we had some of the preliminary discussions which resulted in the World's Fair and also got the Nordstrom brothers interested in a professional football franchise for Seattle.

That brings me to another subject. When I was still in the Marines in Washington, D.C., I used to get together quite often with Swede Larson; George Halas, renowned owner-coach of the Chicago Bears then serving in the Navy; and George Marshall, owner of the Washington Redskins. Burt Bell, commissioner of the league, joined us on several occasions and at one of them offered a franchise in Seattle to Swede and me for $25,000.

We could have managed that sum, so I contacted the University people about the use of the stadium, but at that time the regents were dead set against a professional team coming on the campus. We also talked about the possibility of Swede coming to the University as director of athletics since Al Ulbrickson apparently had indicated that he wanted out of the job. However, before any of this could happen, Swede suffered a heart attack while attending a football game in Atlanta. He died several days later on November 7, 1945, at the young age of 46.

It was many years later—in the early 1970s—that I again had a couple of opportunities to get involved. I had written to Pete Roselle, the football commissioner, telling him I would like to be notified when a franchise was available. About that time Don Adams—who managed apartments in the Seattle area for Judd Kussuba, a real

estate developer in Florida—came to me and said his boss was in-
terested in investing in a pro team in Seattle. I agreed to work
with them on the project. Then, when I was attending a Stanford
game at Palo Alto, Hugh McElhenny met me at Mickey's Restaurant
and wondered if I could assist him in working out a franchise deal
for a Minneapolis man who was willing to put up about twelve
millions dollars. I hated like the dickens to tell Hugh that I simply
couldn't help him at that time because I had already committed
myself to Kussuba and Adams.

Well, that's when the bottom fell out of the real estate market
and Kussuba got into a real financial bind and had to drop out
of the picture. Meanwhile, the twelve million dollars Hugh had lined
up wasn't enough to get the job done, so I went down to Los Angeles
to talk to Bob Hope. Bob was reluctant. He said he knew the enter-
tainment business but not too much about professional football, so
he declined. He told me he had already turned down an offer to
buy the Los Angeles Rams.

By that time another group—including Lloyd Nordstrom, Her-
man Sarkowsky, Ned Skinner, Monte Bean, Howard Wright and
Lynn Himmelman—had entered the picture and eventually got the
franchise which brought the Seahawks to Seattle. Even though I
was left out, that was fine because it was great for the community.
My only regret was that Hugh McElhenny and Don Heinrich were
not involved because they would have added a lot to the program.
The sad thing about the whole affair was that Lloyd Nordstrom
from our old Rainier Club poker gang died before he could see
his team play.

By this time Torchy was in his middle seventies, and Madge—
then his new bride—was urging him to slow down a bit. There
were trips to take, ball games to see, horse races to watch, as
well as a combined total of ten grandchildren and an increasing
number of great-grandchildren to visit.

They were at the World Series game on October 18, 1977,
when Reggie Jackson of the Yankees hit three homeruns to beat
the Los Angeles Dodgers. (Only Babe Ruth duplicated that feat
in a World Series game, and he did it twice.) They attended
the Kentucky Derby so Madge could become better acquainted
with Torchy's good friends, Happy Chandler and his wife Mildred.
They also traveled with the Husky football team occasionally

but finally gave it up after they got drenched while sitting on concrete seats in the old Syracuse University stadium. ("The Huskies got beat and Madge and I got lost trying to find our way back to the bus, so it was a miserable trip," Torchy recalled.)

At Craftsman Press Torchy didn't really retire; he just eased off the payroll without fanfare in 1978 but continued to make periodic stops at the plant to get his mail and to deliver tapes of his memoirs to be typed by secretaries Veronika Page and Connie Nicholson. His interest in politics, the Washington Huskies, the race track, sports in general, the 101 Club and other organizations never waned; he just assumed more of an emeritus role, well earned and widely recognized.

The Salvation Army was one of Torchy's favorite charities. He served on the Army's board of directors in the Northwest District for many years and was a continuing spokesman for its needs. Here he exchanged his King Neptune XIX cap with the Army's Colonel Don Barry. (Salvation Army photo)

253

Torchy, third from the right in the back row, participated in numerous annual meetings of the Washington Athletic Club's board of governors through the years. Past members and former officials were included in the dress-up affairs. He served as president of both the WAC and the 101 Club. (Washington Athletic Club collection)

Chapter 16

The Passing Parade

On August 10, 1955, the *Seattle Post-Intelligencer* carried the following story by the veteran political writer, Stub Nelson:

> The signs indicate that Roscoe C. (Torchy) Torrance, one of Seattle's better known citizens, will enter the contest for mayor.
>
> Torrance has been contemplating the race for some time, and it is no secret he would like to cap an illustrious career of civic activities with service as mayor . . . He has been very much "around" since his days (about World War I time) on the University of Washington campus where he first gained fame as a baseball player.
>
> Always he has been a good mixer – busy in many areas besides his own personal business – and he probably can say "Hello" to more fellow citizens than 999 out of 1,000 Seattleites. That is a valuable asset in a campaign for public office.

Frederick E. Baker, the Seattle advertising man who was active behind the scenes in Republican politics, approached me about running for mayor. Unfortunately, I was not financially able to consider it. Besides that, my family took a vote, and with me abstaining, the total was 4 to 0 against me.

Nelson was right about one thing, though: the gregarious redhead's unusual ability to meet people and make friends. The passing parade of intimates, casual acquaintances and a few detractors who became a part of his life included young and old, rich and famous, the unknown and needy, all of whom knew the Torrance grin, the hearty handshake and the ready guip. The relationships he shared ran the gamut from fun and frolic to tragedy and heartache. After eight decades, here are some of his memories:

I couldn't forget George Bailey, the blind man who played the University of Washington Chimes from the time he graduated in 1917 until fire destroyed the tower in 1949.

George got so he knew nearly everyone's voice on the campus and in the University district. I'd walk down the other side of the street and holler: "Hello, George," and he'd holler back: "Hi, Torch, how are ya?" For years he didn't miss a beat, always on time to ring the chimes at 7:50 a.m., noon and 6:00 p.m. He taught at the Lighthouse for the Blind for many years and sold Lighthouse brooms all over the city. He died in 1960.

———————

Lefty Gomez, the old Yankee pitcher and Hall-of-Famer, was the greatest story-teller there ever was—all clean, nothing off-color. If you could get Lefty together with Casey Stengel, the show would go on for a week. Incidentally, I told a few stories myself. I always got my biggest laugh when I said I wasn't really a power hitter. When I bunted, I had to take a full swing.

———————

One of the guys I played baseball with around the Pacific Northwest for several years was Bill Brown. He was a third baseman and I was a shortstop so we backed each other up on a lot of plays. In the '30s we talked about starting his son Bobby with the Rainier organization when he was old enough—but then the war came and we lost contact. Well, Bobby went on to finish college, got a medical degree, signed with the New York Yankees and eventually became president of the American League.

Another Brown I knew was the great comedian Joe E. We used to have a tournament for young high school ball players when we sponsored the Sicks' All-Stars. After it was over, we'd have a banquet at the Athletic Club and I'd have Joe come up from Hollywood to entertain us with his zany baseball routines. Everybody loved him. He visited our troops when we were at Auckland, and—like Bob

Hope—he was mighty good for morale. Unfortunately, after he lost his son Don in an Air Corps accident over San Diego, he was never quite the same. His other son, Joe W. Brown, was general manager of the Pittsburgh Pirates for quite a few years.

Another person I remember (although I never knew his name) was an Indian chief I met in Idaho when I was on the crew surveying a road through the reservation near Fort Hall. For good public relations we ate lunch with the chief and his people. They had a big kettle of soup held by cross-sticks over a fire, and we all got a bowlful.

It tasted pretty good, and then the chief told us to have some more. Unfortunately, he also said: "Dig down deep and gettum puppies." When we found out we were eating dog meat, it was awfully hard to keep our lunch down. We didn't volunteer to eat with the Indians any more after that.

I have a special memory of Larry Westerweller, a three-year Husky letterman in 1928-29-30. We were playing Oregon and Larry was out of the game at the moment, probably recovering from an injury, when one of the Oregon backs broke loose and was running down the sidelines with nobody able to catch him.

Well, Larry took care of that. He came off the bench like a shot and tackled the runner on about the 20-yard line, as I recall. Of course there were two really surprised people: Westerweller, when he realized what he had done, and the referee, when he saw what happened. Unfortunately, when the smoke finally cleared away, Oregon was awarded the touchdown that beat us, and poor Larry was destined to hear about his dumb stunt for years after.

When I was president of Greater Seattle, Inc., I had the privilege of welcoming Emperor Haile Selassie of Ethiopia when he arrived at the Seattle-Tacoma airport in 1954. It was my job to introduce him over the public address system, and I indicated that he would respond through his interpreter. Well, just then his son (who was an Oxford graduate) stepped forward and said: "I speak very good English and my father doesn't do so badly, so why don't you let me take over?" I guess I had a little egg on my face, but afterwards we got along just fine.

As president of Greater Seattle, Inc., Torchy was on the airport welcoming committee for Emperor Haile Selassie of Ethiopia in 1954. Later he was master of ceremonies for the Lion of Judah at the Rainier Club. Seated, left to right, were: John L. Scott, Lieutenant Governor Emmett T. Anderson, Princess Sybel Desta, the emperor, Mayor Allan Pomeroy and Prince Sahle Selassie. (Seattle Post-Intelligencer *photo*)

[Herb Robinson, editorial writer for *The Seattle Times*, remembered another incident involving Torchy and the emperor. Haile Selassie, at five-foot-one, was extremely touchy about his height. But Torchy didn't worry much about things like that, so when he introduced the Lion of Judah at the Rainier Club, he gave it his old cheerleader's flare and said: "And now I give you that great *little* guy, Emperor Selassie!"]

My other involvement with royalty was at Hugh McElhenny's last game against U.S.C. in the Los Angeles Coliseum. Queen Wilhelmina of The Netherlands was there and I was supposed to present her to the crowd at halftime. Unfortunately, it was raining cats and dogs and there was about four inches of water in the tunnel so we couldn't get out on the field. All I could do then was introduce her over the public address system. Of course, McElhenny became known as The King, but he was a different kind of royalty.

Whenever I could, I tried to help improve the situation of those

258

who were handicapped in any way. I remember Joe Kenney, a pretty fair catcher at Franklin High School and a good prospect for the University. Unfortunately, his front teeth stuck straight out and his family never had enough money to get them corrected. He was terribly self-conscious and bashful, so I took him to the dentist and when his teeth were straightened, he became an entirely new individual. His shyness disappeared, and he turned into an outgoing young man and a capable college ball player. He ended up running a successful restaurant and bar in Canada.

Another case was Earl Vashaw of Mount Vernon. He had been badly gassed in World War I and was crippled for life. He was crazy about baseball, though, so I had some cards printed up and made him a scout for the Rainiers. Although he didn't come up with any particularly good players, at least he had a purpose and was able to enjoy being involved in the game he loved for a few years before he died.

That brings me to Dave Kosher. After I got out of the Marines and was back with the Rainiers, I got a call from Jimmy Innis, the respected coach at Everett High School, telling me about a spastic youngster who couldn't feed or clothe himself but who, like Earl Vashaw, loved baseball. Jimmy wanted to know if I could do something for him and give him a reason for living. Again I had some cards printed up and made Dave a scout, too.

At first he had to have someone drive him around, but after several years he was able to take care of himself and operate his own car. One day Dave told me he had a ball player he wanted me to see, so I went with him to the Columbia Park Playfield where Ron Santo and his Franklin High School team were playing for the city championship. Ron had a good arm and I liked what I saw when he swung a bat. Dave and I talked about him as a good prospect, and when I got back to the office, I called Rogers Hornsby — who was then in a scouting capacity for the Chicago Cubs organization — and told him that I thought Santo was worth a $20,000 investment. Hornsby gave his okay, and I told Dave to go get Ron's signature on a contract, which he did. It was a feather in Dave's cap and made his reputation as a baseball scout. Ron played for eighteen years in the majors, mostly at third base for the Cubs.

When Rogers Hornsby managed the Rainiers, he took a special liking to Dave. He took him to the training camp at Glendale, California, and taught him a lot about the game. In fact, Rog was so interested in Dave that when he died in 1963, he left his World Series ring to him.

I wouldn't say that Jim Rivera had a handicap, but he came to the Rainiers out of the penitentiary in Georgia. Hornsby and I talked with Earl Mann about Jim at a major league meeting in New York. Earl thought Rivera would make a good ball player for somebody, but because of the circumstances, there was no way he could use him in Atlanta. We decided to take a chance on him, and he turned out to be one of the best outfielders we ever had and was instrumental in our winning the Pacific Coast League pennant in 1951.

I had a lot of trouble with Jim, though. When other inmates got out of prison and knew that he was making a success of himself in baseball, they began calling on him for money and other favors. He actually needed a caretaker when he wasn't on the field, so I arranged to have Orville Mills—a law partner of Stephen F. Chadwick, the club's attorney—look after him. Orville stood about six-five and weighed something like 250 pounds, so he was a good choice to protect Jim.

Things were going pretty well for about a year when I got a call from the Grosvenor House saying that Jim was having some kind of trouble in his apartment. Orville and I went right over and we found a guy accusing Rivera of taking advantage of a girl who supposedly was the fellow's wife. He was demanding a $500 payoff to let Jim go. It didn't take us long to find out it was a frame-up, so we got the guy out of town on the afternoon train.

When I sold Jim to the White Sox, I told him he should get a bodyguard or somebody to keep him out of trouble. I don't know if he did or not, but he lasted ten years in the majors. Baseball lost a very colorful character when "Jungle Jim"—as the sportswriters called him—finally bowed out in 1961.

———————

When I discussed Enoch Bagshaw's great Everett High School football team, I purposely left out Romeo Lauzon because I felt he deserved a little extra attention. He had a speech impediment, and because he and the coach had a disagreement of some kind, he decided to go to the University of Idaho instead of Washington.

He was given a summer job doing maintenance work on the campus in Moscow, but one day he called me and said, in his hairlip fashion: "Torch, the people over here are trying to kill me off. I've fallen off a roof twice, and now they're putting me on a steeper one. What are the chances of my coming to Washington?"

260

I told him to come over and I'd see what I could do about getting him enrolled. Well, at that time we had a registrar who was tough on freshman entrance requirements. After checking Romeo's credits—which had been accepted at Idaho—he was told he had to pass a special history test before he could enroll. I arranged for a date and time, and he took the exam, completing it without apparent trouble on the assigned morning.

That afternoon I got a call from the registrar's office saying that Romeo had been given the wrong test and that he'd have to take another one. He was understandably upset, but he calmed down and took the second exam. When I asked him how he had done, he answered: "I passed it like a damn!" He played center for the Huskies in 1925, 1926 and 1927 when Baggy's teams won 27, lost 5 and tied 1.

On Guam in 1944—shortly before Torchy left for the hospital on Kwajalein—he heard the voice with the unmistakable hairlip impediment. Sure enough, the G.I. looking for him was none other than Romeo, and they had a battlefield reunion. After the war Torchy gave the ex-Husky a handyman's job at Western Printing. Once when he was working on the loading dock, the hot-tempered Romeo heard a truck driver make a disparaging remark about Torchy, and he flattened him with one punch. When it was suggested to him that he shouldn't have done what he did, Romeo replied testily: "If he wakes up and doesn't apologize, I'm gonna hit him again!" [Romeo eventually ended up at the State Soldiers' Home at Retsil where he passed away.]

I think it was when I was president of the University Lions Club that I went back to New York for a convention, and a couple of us decided to go to Greenwich Village to see what was going on. On Christopher Street we saw this nightclub with a sign saying the featured entertainer was the "Venetian Nightingale."

We decided to stay for the 9:30 show, so we paid the two-dollar cover charge and asked for seats right down front. Well, when the time came, who should we see on the stage but Cliff Newdahl, who wasn't an Italian at all but a singer we knew from the University of Washington glee club.

Cliff spotted us and was momentarily dumbfounded. Then he sort of gave us the high sign not to let anybody know he was really from Wenatchee and not from Venice. He had a beautiful voice and we enjoyed his program. Afterwards he joined us at our table and we heard all about his experiences in the big city. It was another case of just how small the world really is.

Through Ben F. Shearer, who owned movie houses and a theater supply company in Seattle, I got to know Charles Farrell, the movie actor who appeared in films so many times with Janet Gaynor. When his acting career was over, he moved to Palm Springs where he purchased the Racquet Club with Ralph Bellamy, whom I had met when he visited the troops in the South Pacific.

After the war we decided to shift the Rainiers' spring training camp from El Centro to Palm Springs. New stands were erected, and we looked forward to practice games with other teams. If I remember right, we were to open against the Cleveland Indians, and for the pre-game ceremonies I was to pitch to Charlie Farrell, who was mayor of Palm Springs at the time.

Two of Torchy's Palm Springs friends were former movie actors Charles Farrell (left) and William Powell, the latter famous for his "Thin Man" detective role. These photos were taken during their active film-making days.

262

Well, Charlie was a good tennis player, but there was no way he could break 120 on the golf course, and as far as baseball was concerned, he just couldn't hit the ball! We practiced for about a week and then finally decided that he should just make a level swing and I would try to hit his bat.

When the time came, there must have been a paid attendance of about 4,500, and everybody was excited about the affair. Charlie put on his Rainier cap, picked up the bat and went to the plate. I made a couple practice pitches, and when Charlie stepped up just like he knew what he was doing, I managed to put one right down the middle waist high and he drove the ball all the way to the left field fence.

No one was more surprised than Charlie Farrell, but like an actor, he took his bows as if the blow was an every-day occurrence. We became close friends after that and had a lot of fun together in the years that followed. He eventually sold the Racquet Club but stayed on as a celebrity host until he became too ill to continue. The last time I saw him he was bed-ridden and had lost much of his memory. Then I reminded him of that opening day years earlier and he perked up as we recalled many other incidents of our past together.

Mike Janic was a tough little Marine who saved my life on Guadalcanal. He was a boxer who weighed about 135 pounds, and they had to stretch him about half an inch to meet the height requirements.

On that particular occasion I had a small detail out on the lines, trying to recover various kinds of materiel we needed. That's when Mike showed up and told us to get the heck out of there because we were in dangerous territory with Japs all around us. One of the boys with me got hit while we were withdrawing, and Mike covered us until we got out of danger. Later, on Guam, he was awarded the Navy Cross for saving three wounded Marines, dragging them to safety under enemy fire. He gave the medal to me to hold for him until we got home.

After the war Mike developed a hamburger recipe which he tried to copyright and market as Kayo Burgers. Unfortunately, it didn't work out and in time his war wounds and everything else he went through got the better of him and he ended up in a veterans' hospital. He was a great little guy!

When I was working for the March of Dimes, I got into a hassle with the United Fund and the Downtown Rotary which strongly supported the combined effort. On one occasion Mike Dederer of the Seattle Fur Exchange came to me and said if I'd resign as state chairman of the March of Dimes, they'd make me president of the United Fund. I refused, of course.

I had nothing against the United Fund; we just believed it would be to our advantage to keep our own campaign so we could better promote the need for iron lungs and more research. Besides that, the March of Dimes had a unique relationship to President Roosevelt and the facility at Warm Springs, Georgia, which we thought might get lost in a joint program. For a long time Rotary wouldn't let anybody in to speak for our organization until I finally persuaded them to invite Bea Wright to a meeting.

She arrived at the Olympic Hotel's Spanish Ballroom in a wheelchair, a victim of polio herself. She talked for about 40 minutes, and when she finished, I don't think there was a dry eye in the house. She was a marvelous woman and a great help to the March of Dimes all over the country.

A young polio victim promised Torchy good fortune as he began another March of Dimes campaign. During his long tenure the state of Washington invariably ranked among the leaders for contributions nationally. (Special Collections Division, University of Washington Libraries)

Although I was active in the statewide organization for many years, I must admit that I finally resigned my position as president emeritus over a disagreement with the national office. In King County we had an outstanding executive secretary in Mort Bobrow, and we paid him a bonus to keep him. When they changed leadership at the national level, they let Mort go over the bonus issue—and that's when I quit in protest. I never lost my enthusiasm for the March of Dimes cause, however.

Two of my classmates at the University became successful writers. One of them was Max Miller who was best known for his book, I Cover the Waterfront. After working for several newspapers (including one in Australia), he ended up in southern California where, besides books, he wrote scripts for the movie industry before he died in 1967.

When Max was in school, he was gone quite often on the weekends, and when he returned on Monday, he might have a black eye, a bruised cheek or a cut on his nose. It was some time before we learned that he went to various towns around the state for boxing matches for which he got eight or ten dollars a fight. It helped pay his way through school as baseball did for me.

The second writer was Vic Hurley. I lived with his family when I wasn't in the SAE house, so I got to know him especially well. He had been in World War I, and when he returned to the University, he was an outstanding track man. He set a Pacific Coast Conference record of 9.8 in the 100-yard dash, which in the early 1920s was considered almost superhumanly fast.

After college he went first to Chicago where he ran for the Illinois Athletic Club, but he wanted more adventure than that, so he moved to the Philippine Islands where he said he wanted "to wear white suits and grow coconuts." His experiences there became the basis for such books as Southwest of Zamboanga and The Swish of the Kris.

In World War II he served as a Navy intelligence officer in the South Pacific because of his knowledge of the region. When he eventually returned to the United States, he mostly wrote stories for magazines under various pen names. For a short time he and his wife lived in Yakima before he lost her to cancer. He then moved to Panorama City, a retirement complex near Lacey, where he continued to write.

One day in 1978 he called and asked if I could come to Olympia because he had something he wanted to talk over with me. About a week later I did and spent an hour or so visiting with him. Just as I was about to leave, he said this would be the last time I'd see him. Then he told me he was going to commit suicide within the week. "You'll hear about it, but I'm not going to tell you when or how," he said.

I thought he was kidding, of course, because we used to do a lot of that in school. However, true to his word, a few days later he put a .45 pistol to his head and killed himself. It didn't make sense. There was no reason in the world for him to do such a thing, unless, after the exciting life he had led, the inactivity at Panorama City was too much for him.

Another sad story has to do with Herb Fleishhacker, my recruiting counterpart at Stanford. If I could have gotten Ernie Nevers at Washington when we had George Wilson and Elmer Tesreau, we would have had the dream backfield of all time—but Herb had the inside track on him.

I used to see Herb quite often when I'd go to San Francisco, and occasionally we'd go to Tanfaran for a day at the races. One morning when I was staying at the St. Francis Hotel, I got a call from the desk saying there was a man there who wanted to take me to breakfast. It was Herb, and while we were eating, he told me he wanted me to go to Tanfaran with him that day.

I told him I couldn't because I was on my way to Los Angeles and then had to go over to Palm Springs for several days. "When I come back through, I'll be happy to go to the races with you," I said.

"Well, if it's longer than a week, it'll be too late," he answered. "I've got a bad heart condition and my doctor says I'll be dead by next Tuesday."

"That's ridiculous," I argued. "You look great, and I'll see you when I get back."

I caught my train then and went on to Los Angeles and Palm Springs as I had planned. Then, on the following Tuesday I got a long-distance call, and it was Herb, Jr., on the phone. "Dad passed away this afternoon," he said. "I'm sure he would have wanted you to know."

That was another time I should have believed what somebody was trying to tell me. I just wish Herb would have been alive when

I was caught up in the recruiting hassle and the Cherberg affair. He would have torn the papers apart!

I can't take credit for the hiring of Jim Owens as the Husky football coach, but I might have had a little hand in it indirectly. The year before he came to Washington, I was back at the Kentucky Derby and while I was there, Happy Chandler, Adolph Rupp (the great basketball coach) and I went to see the University of Kentucky football team on the last day of spring practice.

Bear Bryant was coaching the Wildcats at the time, and as we stood talking with him, he pointed to one of his assistants and said: "That fellow will make a great coach for somebody some day." The assistant was Jim Owens.

When I returned to Seattle, I mentioned the incident to George Briggs, the athletic director. I don't know if my comments had anything to do with it, but when George hired a replacement for Darrell Royal, it was Jim. He was a tough coach, and he put heavy emphasis on physical conditioning with his so-called "death march." Some of the kids didn't like it and dropped out, but the final result was three Rose Bowl appearances.

On the 50th anniversary of the 1926 Rose Bowl game, the Huskies played Alabama again. Coach Bear Bryant and the university officials there invited the survivors of the '26 team to Tuscaloosa, and because I was involved, I was included. I didn't get there in time for the big banquet the night before the game because the plane I was on missed connections in Houston. However, on Saturday noon they had a luncheon, and as I was sitting there enjoying myself, I heard the master of ceremonies say that Torchy Torrance would deliver the invocation.

Well, it came as a surprise to me, but I had given invocations before at American Legion and Shrine affairs, so I was not totally at a loss. However, I don't know if the Alabama people liked it too well when I asked the Dear Lord for a little extra help for the Huskies. As it turned out, my prayer wasn't too effective because we got beat 50-0.

That night Bear Bryant had a few of us over to his house to console us a bit. It was a nice gesture, but it didn't help much. Bear did give me one of those little checkered hats which became a trademark of his. I wore it occasionally, but Madge didn't like it much so I had to put it with my other souvenirs.

267

I've always been partial to the 101 Club, and in 1988 our president was Kay Chorlton. He was one of the players I signed after World War II out of Roosevelt High School in Seattle. He had lots of speed, a good arm and could hit pretty well. He went to our farm club in Vancouver, British Columbia, first and then was with the Rainiers under Paul Richards. However, when Rogers Hornsby took over, he put him in left field and his first fielding chance was a sinking line drive which hit the heel of his glove and popped out. Hornsby pulled him out right in the middle of the inning which was a real blow to his morale.

After that he was shuttled between Vancouver and the Rainiers under Sweeney and Priddy, but I think what happened with Hornsby stuck with him and really discouraged him. I still think he had what it takes to become a major leaguer, but he became a successful businessman instead and I was proud of him for that. [In his last year with Vancouver, Chorlton had a batting average of .347 with 16 homeruns.]

Through the years I have known literally scores of sportswriters, sports editors and broadcasters. In Seattle, of course, there were Royal Brougham, George Varnell, Alex Schultz, Cliff Harrison, Por-

Torchy and Royal Brougham, the long-time Post-Intelligencer *sports editor, were friends for many years, although they had periodic disagreements and minor feuds. When Royal established a Sports Hall of Fame Museum in the Kingdome, Madge Torrance helped make it a reality as a major donor. (Kingdome photo)*

Torchy had many sportswriter friends and, except for an occasional misunderstanding, he was generally well treated by the press. This was typical of the publicity he was able to generate. As executive vice-president of the Seattle Rainiers, Torchy (who was also vice-chairman of the Community Chest campaign of 1950) accepted a Red Feather Pennant for the ball club after team members turned in 100% of their quota to the Chest. Children from St. Anne's School made the presentation, and Torchy quipped: "After finishing in sixth place in the league, you don't know how good it is to win this pennant." (Seattle Post-Intelligencer photo)

tus Baxter, Leo Lassen, John Owen, Georg Myers, Emmett Watson, Lenny Anderson, Hy Zimmerman and others. Along the way I've crossed paths with such nationally known figures as Damon Runyon, Grantland Rice, Bill Stern, Walter Camp, Clem McCarthy, Arch Ward and Keith Jackson. But there were many more across the country and up and down the coast. Most of them were pretty good to me, except maybe Mark Kelly of the Los Angeles Examiner, but I guess that was more his problem than it was mine or Baggy's because the Huskies survived without him.

Before he became a sportswriter, I remember George Varnell as an athletic official who saved dimes. When we hired him for a game, that's the way we paid him off—maybe $75 all in dimes. He used them to send his daughter Virginia to the University of Washington.

Roscoe Conkling Torrance got his given name from an avid 19th century Republican, Senator Roscoe Conkling of New York. True to his namesake, Torchy himself was a life-long supporter of the Grand Old Party. He and President Gerald R. Ford were fellow members of the Palm Springs Desert Senior Golf Association. (Special Collections Division, University of Washington Libraries)

Chapter 17

And the Memories Linger On

I consider Bob and Dolores Hope to be two of the greatest Americans of our time. What he has done for our boys in the service in three wars can never be truly measured—and Dolores was always behind him in support. You can hardly count the charities they've benefited through the years.

Ruth and I first met the two of them at Bing Crosby's house at Taluga right after the Rose Bowl game in 1936. After that our paths crossed many times. When I first started bringing the Rainiers to Palm Springs for spring training, he used to come out to watch us, and we got better acquainted then. We played golf together every now and then—especially after we started the Desert Seniors—but one of the games I remember best was one we had with Bob Littler and Bing Crosby at the Seattle Golf Club.

Bob (Hope, not Littler) and I were playing to about the same handicap at the time—I believe it was eleven—and we were having quite a duel. Going into the 18th hole, he had me one up. I hit a couple of good shots and then sank a long putt for a birdie, so it looked like I had a good chance to tie or even beat him. Well, he had a chance at a birdie, too, but it took a 25-foot putt—and I'll be doggoned if he didn't sink it. He let out a whoop, and I never saw him jump up and down so much. I had to pay him fifteen dollars! I was glad to give it to him because I knew how much he needed the money.

In Palm Springs I played more with Dolores than with Bob because he was gone so much. John Malatesta and his wife Mildred— Dolores Hope's sister—were often in our foursome. I think the only time I ever beat John was when Dolores and Bob celebrated their 50th wedding anniversary in 1984. John must have had a lousy day

271

Torchy first met Bob Hope at Bing Crosby's house in Taluga, California, in 1936. After that their paths crossed periodically for more than half a century, including occasional golf matches. (Special Collections Division, University of Washington Libraries)

because, at 84, my game wasn't very good. Anyway, the Hopes celebrated the important event alone at home—no friends, no parties, no nothing; just the two of them. Dolores didn't want anything to spoil it. [He married Dolores Reade on February 19, 1934, when he was just becoming known on the Broadway stage.]

Earlier Madge and I had the privilege of sharing another anniversary with the Hopes: Bob's 75th birthday party in Washington, D.C. We stayed at the Madison Hotel where Bob and his family were registered. He had been born, by the way, in Eltham, England, on May 5, 1903, making him about four years younger than I. To attend the affairs with us, I had invited General Louis H. Wilson, Jr., the Marine Corps commandant, and his wife Jane. He picked us up in an official car with his general's insignia on it and we went first to a reception at the White House where we met President Jimmy Carter and his wife. From there we drove to the Kennedy Center for a special performance in Bob's honor. We had a box

272

not far from the Hopes'. Bob was the center of attraction, of course, but Lou Wilson in his formal white uniform with the Medal of Honor around his neck caused quite a bit of excitement, too.

It was an extra bonus for us to attend a dinner the following night at the Marines' headquarters house with the Wilsons. Other guests, as I recall, included an assortment of admirals and generals and Senator John C. Stennis, chairman of the Armed Services Committee from Lou's home state of Mississippi. We also watched a full dress parade of Marines from the Wilsons' house; and if you've never seen that beautiful and inspirational sight, you've never seen a parade! Incidentally, Lou Wilson served with the 9th Marines on Guadalcanal, Bougainville and Guam. As a 24-year-old captain in the latter compaign, he left the aid station to lead his company in an all-night hand-to-hand battle with counterattacking Japanese, even though he had been wounded three times the previous day. He then led a 17-man patrol to capture a critical slope. He was one of four survivors of that mission. For such heroics, he was awarded the Medal of Honor, the nation's highest military decoration.

Getting back to the Hopes, their house in Palm Springs has to be the biggest and most beautiful I ever saw. More than 300 guests can be seated in the main dining room. Parties I have attended there have included celebrities of all kinds—entertainers, golfers and

Once mistaken for Admiral Hyman Rickover, Torchy at least got a taste of Navy high command when he was invited on a seven-week cruise of the USS Kittyhawk around South America enroute to join the Pacific fleet in 1961. Stops included Rio de Janeiro (where there was time for sightseeing, a soccer game and golf) and Valpraiso, Chile, where men of the aircraft carrier engaged in some international public relations by repairing a dilapidated school. Torchy was pictured here with Captain William F. Bringle, skipper of the ship. While her husband was cruising, Ruth Torrance enjoyed a tour of Europe.

political figures. On one occasion various people kept mistaking me for Admiral Hyman Rickover. A lady thanked me for my service to the country, and even Tip O'Neill, then the Speaker of the House, said to me: "You've been in my office several times. If there is anything I can do to help you, just left me know." I wanted to explain that they had me confused with somebody else, but Dolores, with her great sense of humor, told me to go along with the gag and enjoy it.

My memories of Bob also include the 1973 Super Bowl game together. He had invited me to stay over in Los Angeles, so after lunch we drove out to the Coliseum to watch Washington play Miami. I told Bob to bet on the Redskins, but he went the other way and the Dolphins won 14 to 7.

While we were there, we had a chance to visit with George Halas, the "Papa Bear," as they called him. He and I talked about the time in 1940 when I phoned him from Denver after a baseball meeting to ask if I could get a seat at Wrigley Field when his Bears were meeting the Washington Redskins for the league championship three days later. He told me that the game was sold out but to come anyway and he'd get a chair for me by the baseball dugout. Well, that turned out to be one of the historic games in professional football. The Redskins had beaten Chicago 7 to 3 in a disputed regular season game, and when the Bears had claimed interference on the final play of the game, the Redskins called them "cry babies." Well, on December 8 the "cry babies" got even. I watched as they gained 372 yards rushing to Washington's three, intercept eight passes and finally won the game 73-0.

Bob Hope's theme song has always been "Thanks for the Memories," and Torchy could well have borrowed it to express his feelings as he recalled the people and events of a long and ever-exuberant life. Those memories also included another dear friend, Albert B. "Happy" Chandler, twice governor of Kentucky, a U.S. senator and the commissioner of major league baseball.

The two of them didn't know it at the time, but when Torchy was coaching baseball at the University of Washington, Happy was the football coach at Centre College in Danville, Kentucky. Their mutual interest in horseracing, baseball and golf brought them together in a relationship which spanned more than half a century. They adopted a pet expression – "Whoop-de-do" – with which they greeted one another, and it was somehow appropriate to the fun of their various times together – on the golf course,

Happy and Mildred Chandler (at left) hosted Torchy and Barbara Boreson at the 1976 Kentucky Derby. When their picture appeared in a Lexington paper, they were identified as "Mr. and Mrs. Roscoe C. Torrance"—and they promptly sent a clipping to Barbara's husband Stan in Seattle, saying that they were sorry about the way their relationship had developed after he had agreed to let her take the trip. With the two couples was Dr. Eslie Asbury, a friend of the Chandlers. (Special Collections Division, University of Washington Libraries)

at the governor's mansion in Frankfort and especially at the Kentucky Derby.

One of the most memorable Derbies was when Bob and Dolores Hope were there, too. After the race Bob wanted to play golf, so Happy arranged for us to meet at the Bright Leaf Course operated by his friend, Bucky Blankenship. Before we got there, Bucky had put up a sign—"Chandler and Hope Here at 2:00"—so we had a small gallery when we teed off. Bob and Happy rode in one cart, and I was with Dolores in another. The course was quite new and a little rough, but we had a fine time—good friends together. Bob chipped in for a birdie on one hole and the folks got quite a kick out of that.

Afterwards we were invited to Harrodsburg, the first settlement in the state. We were guests of the mayor at what was to be a small dinner party, but about 60 showed up. We all sat at a long table with Bob on one end and Dolores on the other. The mayor made a little speech and we had several songs by a local quartet for entertainment as we enjoyed an evening of southern hospitality. The Hopes then went back to Louisville, and Happy, Mildred and I returned to Versailles where the Chandlers lived when he wasn't in public office.

For the 1976 Kentucky Derby—after I lost Ruth and before I married Madge—I invited Barbara Boreson of Seattle to go with me. (We had her husband Stan's permission, of course.) Barbara had done outstanding work with various organizations such as the Salvation Army, the March of Dimes and the Easter Seal Society; and Stan, who was well known for his accordion playing and Scandinavian dialect songs, was a good friend and member of the 101 Club.

Barbara loved horses and once kiddingly asked me if I'd take her to the Derby some time, so this seemed like a good opportunity. I called Happy to see if it was all right to bring a young married woman back with me, and he said he'd be delighted to have her come. (I don't remember if he said "whoop-de-do" or not.)

We went first to Palm Springs for a brief visit with my son Bill. We caused lots of heads to turn when we went out to dinner. I explained who the pretty lady was to a few friends; the others we just let think whatever they wanted to.

We arrived in Kentucky in time for the usual chicken dinner at Happy's place on Thursday evening. The next day we went to the "Running of the Oaks," which is the second most important race in Kentucky, and finally we watched Bold Forbes win the Derby we'd come to see. Barbara also got to meet Bob Hope who spotted us when we were walking towards the betting ring.

On Sunday we attended a brunch where I introduced Barbara to Mary Rose, a sister of the Crosbys. Then a photographer asked if he could take a picture of us with the Chandlers, and we agreed, of course. We didn't think any more of it until we saw the Lexington paper on Monday with a three-column photo identified as "Mr. and Mrs. Happy Chandler, Dr. Eslie Asbury and Mr. and Mrs. Torchy Torrance of Seattle." We airmailed a clipping to Stan with a note saying we were sorry for the way things had changed after we left him.

I sort of have mixed-emotion memories about the time Happy visited me in Seattle with Clare Goodwin, a pal of his from San Francisco. We were joined by Charlie Adams, my friend who helped us go broke in 1929, and then I borrowed Paul Pigott's yacht and crew for a cruise up to Victoria and Vancouver. We had a delightful trip in spite of the fact that I didn't get much sleep because Happy snored louder than anybody I'd ever heard. We enjoyed golf games *at Shaughnessy and Capilano before we drove back to Seattle by car.*

Previously I had arranged for a breakfast gathering of about 200 guests at the Seattle Golf Club to hear Happy, who was well known as a great story-teller. Unfortunately, he caught a bad cold which turned to pneumonia; and if it hadn't been for Doctor Don Palmer, we might have lost him. Everybody was disappointed at not getting a chance to hear Happy, but we were lucky things turned out as well as they did.

In 1945 Happy, who had been serving as a U.S. senator from Kentucky, was named commissioner of major league baseball to succeed Judge Landis. As a stickler for the rules, he proved too tough for some of the owners, and in time a move was underway to oust him.

It came to a head at a meeting in St. Petersburg, Florida. As one sportswriter put it, the deck was stacked against him

ALBERT BENJAMIN CHANDLER

"HAPPY"

BASEBALL'S SECOND COMMISSIONER,1945-1951. UNITED STATES SENATOR (1939-1945). GOVERNOR OF KENTUCKY (1935-39, 1955-59). IRON-WILLED AND HONEST, HE WAS KNOWN AS A "PLAYERS' COMMISSIONER" BECAUSE OF HIS BROAD CONCERN FOR ALL PHASES OF THE GAME.

When Happy Chandler was ousted as commissioner of baseball in 1951, Torchy accompanied him on a leisurely golf-playing trip back to Happy's home at Versailles, Kentucky. Later Torchy campaigned to get his friend inducted into the National Baseball Hall of Fame at Cooperstown, New York.

277

Torchy's memberships included the Shriners of Seattle's Nile Temple and the Royal Order of Jesters affiliated with it. He was fifth from the right in the front row at the latter organization's annual meeting in 1967. (Special Collections Division, University of Washington Libraries)

going in, and several of the owners who were supposedly on his side found it political to be absent for the critical vote.

Taylor Spink, the publisher of Sporting News, *asked to appear before the group and made a passionate plea for the renewal of Happy's contract. Spink meant well, but some of the owners thought Happy had put him up to it and he didn't know anything about Spink's voluntary move on his behalf. The meeting was controlled by the younger group, primarily the Yankee organization, and I don't know if it would have been any different if Connie Mack and Mrs. Comiskey had been there. They would have been out-voted.*

At any rate, Happy was canned, and I'm glad I was at the meeting to try to help ease the blow. The two of us decided we'd take our time going back to Versailles, stopping to play golf along the way whenever we wanted to. It gave us time to talk, and I think Happy got rid of some of the hurt and anger during our two weeks on the road—sort of like a Hope and Crosby movie. After a little time out, Happy went back into politics and was elected governor again, serving from 1955 to 1959.

Although they were of opposite political parties, Torchy had great respect for Senator Henry "Scoop" Jackson of Washington State. He especially appreciated Scoop's strong stance on national defense. Torchy sponsored Jackson's induction into the Jesters, the "fun" organization of the Shrine. (Special Collections Division, University of Washington Libraries)

279

It wasn't too long after Happy's ouster as commissioner that Torchy, too, was edged out as vice-president of the Seattle Rainiers. Like his friend, though, he quickly moved on to other interests. That has been the story of his life: no time for second-guessing or regrets. There was always something else on the horizon to keep his enthusiasm bubbling.

Another trait he shared with Happy: you always knew what he believed in and where he stood! As one of his friends said: "I have never known him to be wishy-washy about anything. As a matter of fact, he not only called a spade a spade; he called it a damned shovel!"

Politically he remained always the staunch Republican true to the heritage of his middle name, but when national security was involved, party didn't matter.

When we lost Senator Henry "Scoop" Jackson, we lost one of our strongest advocates for military preparedness. I had the pleasure of bringing Scoop into Court 52 of the Jesters (which is sort of the 101 Club of the Shrine), and through the years we exchanged many letters and had numerous phone conversations, especially about national defense.

Although Senator Warren Magnuson and I had our differences, he went to bat for me on several occasions when I needed help. I remember when he was out for football at the University. He never made a letter and took a terrible beating because of his size, but he hung in there as a member of the scrub team, one of the shock troops who helped the varsity prepare for the game each week.

I was King County chairman for Emmett Anderson when we tried to beat Al Rosellini for governor, yet Al became a friend and was very good to Ruth and me during the Seattle World's Fair. Later he took my place in raising funds for the Olympics.

"Torchy has always been an All-American patriot," another friend said. "He proved it by volunteering for the Marines when he could have avoided military service and later when he suffered a heart attack because of his concern about respect for the flag."

We've got the best country in the world. I don't see many people climbing over fences trying to get out, but there are a lot of them trying to get in. I don't understand people like Jane Fonda and Pat Hayden who probably cost the lives of many of our servicemen because of their actions during the Vietnam War. Or athletes like Lou Alcindor. [Kareem Abdul-Jabbar] who wouldn't stand still for the national anthem when he was in college. Or Tommie Smith and John Carlos who raised their fists in protest at the 1968 Olympic Games in Mexico City.

I remember another time when I was upset. It happened at Rotary Club when Dick Everest, the University's faculty athletic adviser, said that there were no football bums at Washington, although the closest to it was probably Roland Kirkby who did not want to go to class and didn't care if he graduated.

I jumped to my feet and told Dick I was sorry he made such a statement because Roland, at that time, was in Korea fighting for his country—and that I felt pretty safe when I knew that men like him were representing us against our enemies.

Well, that caused quite an uproar in Rotary, but afterwards Dick and I had a talk and we developed a close friendship which lasted until his death.

I've been a very lucky man. I'm proud of my family. Bill did a tremendous job as a Marine in Korea, and John, with Herb Mead, has followed me in the recruiting of athletes for the Huskies. Tim Cowan, who ended up playing quarterback for the British Columbia Lions, was one of his prodigies. Shirley, of course, made a courageous recovery from polio. And they probably wouldn't have turned out so well if it hadn't been for their mother who held things together when I was gone so often.

I'm proud of Madge, too, especially for the generosity she has shown to so many important causes. The Madge E. Torrance Endowment of $250,000 has been set up for athletic scholarships at the University of Washington, along with a student loan fund she has established at the University's School of Nursing. Other beneficiaries have included the Children's Orthopedic Hospital, the Salvation Army, the Salk Institute, the Campfire Girls (Madge was a leader in Spokane), the Washington Children's Home, The Northwest Hospital Foundation, the University Congregational Church, the March of Dimes, the Fred Hutchinson Cancer Center and the Marine Corps School in Harlingen, Texas. She also helped pay off the indebtedness of the Washington State University stadium. All in all, her gifts have totaled more than a million dollars.

She deserves all the credit because the money has come from

her and her family. As for me, I guess I have mostly had to give just of myself. Part of my philosophy of life has been not to be jealous of anybody else's accomplishments. I have always enjoyed seeing other people succeed, and I've been happy for them. In my case, what I have tried to build up—like before the stock market crash—I've lost. What I've given away in time and service, I still have. I guess that's what makes life worthwhile.

Torchy Torrance never followed in the footsteps of his youthful idol, Roger Peckinpaugh, but in the game of life, he's been a major leaguer all the way.

The Salvation Army slogan, "Share With Others," aptly describes the personal philosophy of Torchy Torrance: "What you have in material things, you can lose; what you give can never be taken from you." (Salvation Army photo)

Jack Ehrig, one of the creators of the 101 Club's Roscoe C. Torrance 101 Per Cent Award posed with the namesake honoree and the permanent plaque which perpetuates the annual winners. Among the early recipients have been Walter F. Clark, Waldo J. Dahl, Morrie J. Alhadeff, George H. Weber, F. Mort Frayn, Donald K. Weaver, Sr., Conrad Knutson and Frederick E. Baker. (Washington Athletic Club)

Remembering Torchy!

Because Torchy was always doing something for somebody else, his friends in the 101 Club decided that something should be done for him.

Advertising executive Jack Ehrig, who was president of the organization in 1981-82, recalled how a special recognition came about:

"Several of us were talking about the remarkable contributions many of the 101 Club members have made to our community over the years. We decided we ought to honor them

Governor Booth Gardner proclaimed July 6, 1988, as Torchy Torrance Day in the state of Washington. The Downtown Seattle Rotary Club—of which Torchy had been a long-time member—honored him at a special luncheon at which the certificate above was presented.

with some sort of an award. We arrived at the idea of a "101 Per Cent Award"—for people who had given 101 per cent of themselves in inspiration, leadership, service and dedication to the spirit and lifestyle of our community.

"Certainly Torchy Torrance was the first name that came

At age 88, Torchy enjoyed a Rotary Club reunion with two outstanding University of Washington football stars, Luther Carr and Hugh McElhenny. In various ways he had been involved in each of their college careers. (Wallace Ackerman photo)

to mind. We wanted to throw a real recognition dinner for him and thank him for all he had done for Seattle and all of us. We even had plans to fly in Torchy's old buddy, Bob Hope, for the festivities.

"Well, Torchy would have none of it. He didn't want a big bash; and besides that, he said he was going to be in Palm Springs. So we tried again. This time we boiled it down to a luncheon to recognize him, and we were going to have the governor and a few others there for the event. Torchy said he just wouldn't be available.

"Next we suggested we'd have a quiet 101 Club luncheon and just have the 101 Club gang. We'd give him a plaque or something and simply say "thank you." Torchy said, "I don't need any more plaques."

"So, after about two years of exasperation, we still felt it was a nifty idea to recognize some of the 101 Clubbers who had done so much for all of us. Of course, guys like that have already had plenty of accolades, but we wanted to cap it off

In 1988 the Washington Athletic Club honored its long-time member and past-president by naming its remodeled casual dining room "Torchy's." With him for the ribbon-cutting ceremony were advertising executive Donald B. Kraft, WAC president, and Margaret Hagerty. She represented her late husband—F. W. "Pop" Hagerty, a popular athletic official—after whom the club's bar was named. (Washington Athletic Club photo by Karin Holmes)

some way: no big banquet, no big fund-raiser, just a simple expression of appreciation for inspiring us all. And thus was born the Roscoe C. Torrance 101 Per Cent Award."

The club members had finally slipped one over on Torchy. He couldn't stop them from honoring him by honoring others. When they drew up the criteria for the selection of an annual winner, the club's trustees—with obvious tongues in check— added a final proviso:

Due to his stubborness, evasiveness and lack of coopera-tion, Roscoe C. "Torchy" Torrance will never be eligible to receive this award.

There was one further honor Washington Athletic Club members had in store for their past president who had literally and figuratively been "in on the ground floor" of the organization and its landmark building.

Following an extensive remodeling project completed in 1988, the club's president, Donald B. Kraft, revealed the well kept secret: the WAC's casual dining room would hereafter be known as "Torchy's."

For once the feisty redhead from the Palouse Country was virtually speechless!

Acknowledgments

Both Torchy and I are grateful to all who, in one way or another, have helped make this book a reality.

First of all, it was a nostalgic pleasure to work with Torchy again because it sparked so many memories of Seattle for me. Secondly – as I have done in more than two dozen other books – I must express special appreciation to my wife Phyllis (who, for some unknown reason, Torchy has nicknamed "Sweet Pea"). Once again she has been my sounding board, research assistant and ceaseless goader who kept me at the typewriter when golf clubs and fishing poles beckoned. She and I both would be remiss not to thank Bruce and Toy Baker and Jack and Gloria Ehrig for making our fact-gathering visits to Seattle so enjoyable and comfortable.

In the accumulation of illustrations and background information, John Owen of the *Seattle Post-Intelligencer* was especially helpful. So, too, were the various staff members of the Suzzallo Library at the University of Washington, the Seattle Public Library and the Yankton (South Dakota) Community Library, my home-base source of inter-library loan assistance.

Madge Torrance and the immediate members of Torchy's family were extremely cooperative, as were Kirby Torrance, Jr., and Emily M. Wilson who provided valuable genealogical material relating to the Torrance clan.

There were many others who made my task easier or who added to the scope of the book. They include James R. Collier, vice-president for university relations at the U. of W.; Chip Lydum, the University's assistant sports information director; Donald B. Kraft, president of the Washington Athletic Club; Bill Wilmot of Colfax, Washington; Robert Glenn of American Falls, Idaho; and a litany of others: Ed Donohoe, John F. "Jack" Gordon, Hugh McElhenny, Dick Klinge, Ralph Grossman, Dick Beverage, Silja Griffin, Dan McFadden of the March of Dimes, Jack Sullivan, Don E. Douglas, Robert A. Baker, Gary Waddingham, Albert B. "Happy" Chandler and Dick Rockne, the Husky football historian.

As we have collaborated throughout this book in two different type styles, Torchy wants to add his note of gratitude:

It would take another whole book to thank all the people who have helped me during my lifetime. I have mentioned a number of them in the previous chapters but there are many, many more. I'd like to take this opportunity to pay special tribute to Lucy Gagner who worked for me for almost fifty years. She was my secretary, confidante and adviser, so she knew well the ups and downs of my career.

Many of the men I have acknowledged, but there were other women besides Lucy I could turn to for assistance in my various activities. To name several, there were Lulu Fairbanks, the inimitable editor of the Alaska Weekly; *Maude Williams, wife of one of my best friends, L. A. "Bill" Williams of Puget Sound Power & Light Company; Sadie Murphy, whose husband Arthur was president of the Union Pacific Railroad; and Ione Erp, who was especially helpful to me when I was commander of the Seattle American Legion Post No. 1. Needless to say, my wife Ruth was always there when I needed her.*

Now, more specifically in relation to this book, I want to thank Bob and Dolores Hope for saying such nice things about me in the introduction. I am likewise very grateful to Jack Ehrig who was largely responsible for getting the project off dead-center and for making it possible for me to renew my acquaintance with Bob Karolevitz. I want to repeat Bob's mention of Kirby Torrance, Jr., and Emily M. Wilson who taught me things about my heritage I didn't know before. I can't say enough about Madge who was very patient with me throughout this long effort, listening to the reliving of my life and offering suggestions to improve the final product. Shirley, Bill and John were always supportive, for which I am most appreciative; and, because he has been sort of an ex officio member of our family for a long time, I also want to include Herb Mead for his continuing interest in my various endeavors.

Because of his ready wit, Torchy was regularly called upon to be master of ceremonies for various events. Here he engaged in hi-jinks with noted trumpeter Al Hirt at a Seattle Chamber of Commerce meeting. (Special Collections Divisions, University of Washington Libraries)

To form the basis for this book, I dictated a small mountain of memoirs which Connie Nicholson at Craftsman Press and several other young ladies typed for me. In her efficient, friendly manner, Connie also took care of much of my correspondence relating to the book. At the University of Washington I can't forget Athletic Director Mike Lude and Pete Liske who were given the added responsibility of handling the sales of an old alumnus's life story which I hope will be a benefit to a new generation of student athletes.

After all of that, if Torchy and I have somehow overlooked others who deserve our appreciation for services or smiles rendered, we have certainly done so inadvertently. To them, in their anonymity, our gratitude is no less sincere.

—B.K.

TRIBUTE TO TORCHY TORRANC[E]

..... *good citizen* .....

The final day of another successful Seafair celebration seem[s] good time for the following friends of Roscoe C. "Torchy" Torra[nce] sent this tribute to a good citizen. As president of Greater Seattle[,] had much to do with the success of our great summer festival.

However, this was but one of the many jobs he has cheerf[ully] taken for the community, as exemplified by his service in the fol[lowing] tions: Washington State Chairman of the March of Dimes, Past [of] Seattle Post Number One of the American Legion, Past Presid[ent of] Washington Athletic Club, Director and member of the Executive [Committee] of the Seattle Chamber of Commerce, member of the board of th[e Salvation] Army, Boys' Clubs of Seattle, International Trade Fair Associati[on] Arboretum Foundation; Vice-President of the American Legion and Vice-President of the Seattle Rainiers.

This is only a part of the record of his contributions of se[rvice to the] city. Whenever there's a job to be done, Torchy can be relied [on to roll] up his sleeves and go to work with his customary enthusiasm, goo[d will and] know-how. The amount of time he has expended on civic jobs, w[ithout com-] pensation, cannot be measured.

Thanks for your efforts and good work in behalf of our to[wn.] Seattle is fortunate to have you as a citizen.

This full-page tribute to Torchy appeared in the Seattle-Post Intelligencer *on August 7, 1955, following the Seafair celebration that year.*

About the Collaborating Author

Bob Karolevitz first met Torchy Torrance when he was recalled to Army duty during the Korean War. As a public information officer, he was sent first to the Seattle Port of Embarkation to help set up and promote the receptions for returning veterans which came to be known as "Welcome Lane." Torchy was on the civic committee which worked with the military in developing the nationally recognized program. Karolevitz himself then went to Korea to serve in the public information office of the U.S. Eighth Army before he, too, was welcomed home with a confetti parade through downtown Seattle.

As a freelance writer and president of the Seattle Advertising Club, Bob crossed paths periodically with Torchy as a publicist for the Seattle Seafair, the Seattle World's Fair, the Walker Cup matches and a Greater Seattle professional football game between the then-new Dallas Cowboys and the San Francisco 49ers – all projects in which Torchy was involved in one way or another. Among his more than a thousand magazine and newspaper features has been a profile of the then-owner of Western Printing Company for a national printing publication.

After almost two decades in the Seattle area, Bob and his wife Phyllis returned to their native South Dakota where he has continued his writing career.. He has won regional and national awards for several of his 28 books, which include biography, history, nostalgia and humor. Among his titles are *From Quill to Computer*, the history of community journalism in the U.S. from 1690; *Where Your Heart Is*, the biography of famed *Saturday Evening Post* artist-illustrator Harvey Dunn which won a coveted Wrangler Award from the National Cowboy Hall of Fame,

Oklahoma City, as best art book of the year; *Flight of Eagles,* the story of an American squadron flying for the restored republic of Poland in the Polish-Russian War of 1919-20; *Yesterday's Motorcycles; Doctors of the Old West; Tears in My Horseradish* and *Challenge: The South Dakota Story.*

Karolevitz is a graduate of South Dakota State University which has honored him with its Distinguished Alumnus Award. He also holds a master's degree in journalism from the University of Oregon. He is a charter inductee into the South Dakota Hall of Fame and has been recognized by the South Dakota Press Association as its Distinguished Citizen of the Year.

Bob Karolevitz was recalled to duty to promote the receptions for Korean War veterans at the Seattle Port of Embarkation. It was during that time that he first met Torchy Torrance. Karolevitz himself was later sent to Korea as a public information officer for the U. S. Eighth Army, and on his return (above) he and his wife Phyllis rode in the lead convertible of the "Welcome Lane" parade he helped develop. His former desk and a secretary were awaiting him when he came down the gangplank. (U. S. Army photo)

Index

Because of their numerous mentions throughout the book, Torchy, Seattle and the University of Washington have not been included in this index.

297

Colophon

This book was lithographed by Pine Hill Press at Freeman, South Dakota. The text was set in Debonaire roman and italic, with headlines in Compugraphic's Hobo. Carpenter Paper Company provided the paper, Simpson Opaque Vellum Offset. Binding was by Midwest Editions of Minneapolis, Minnesota.